The Meaning of Luxury in Tourism, Hospitality and Events

John Swarbrooke

(G Publishers Ltd

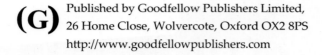 Published by Goodfellow Publishers Limited,
26 Home Close, Wolvercote, Oxford OX2 8PS
http://www.goodfellowpublishers.com

British Library Cataloguing in Publication Data: a catalogue record for this title is available from the British Library.

Library of Congress Catalog Card Number: on file.

ISBN: 978-1-911396-07-9

 Design and typesetting by P.K. McBride, www.macbride.org.uk

Cover design by Cylinder

Printed and bound in Great Britain by Marston Book Services Ltd, Oxfordshire

Contents

Dedication

I dedicate this book to a number of people without whom I would not have been able to enjoy the life I have enjoyed or the 'luxury' of being able to write books, which has given me so much pleasure, not least through the reaction of those who have read them.

My wife Susan, who has stood by me for over twenty-five years and supported me every day. It has also been great that we have had the opportunity to write together which has also given me enormous pleasure.

Our son, John, who is a constant inspiration to me, a great travel companion, and has provided me with more intellectually stimulating conversations than I have ever had in any university!

My mum who made great sacrifices so that I could get where I am today and my dad, who taught me to question everything and who introduced me to the joys of reading and debating.

Acknowledgements

Every book I have written, including this one, have been motivated by a desire to inspire students around the world to find the phenomenon of tourism as fascinating as I do and to encourage them to want to discover more about it for themselves.

During my years in higher education I have had the pleasure of teaching students in many countries from China to the UK, the USA to Switzerland, Brazil to Russia, and Indonesia to Mexico. Teaching has always been my first priority and the success of my students my greatest reward.

As educators we are in a privileged position for what we do helps people transform their lives for the better.

I would like to take this opportunity, therefore, to thank all of my former students who have enriched my working life and whose thoughts and questions have often been the trigger for me to start thinking about a new book project. Indeed it was the excellent young people I taught at César Ritz Colleges in Switzerland between 2008 and 2011 who first put the idea of this book in my head.

I would also like to thank all of those academics and industry professionals who have, over the years, given me the pleasure of their company all around the world.

Sadly, too much of my time in academia has been spent in meaningless meetings and seeing great teachers being pressurised for career reasons into pursuing the 'fool's gold' of journal publication. The research which tourism, hospitality and events academics could do has the potential to make the world a better place if it was focused on influencing government policy-makers and industry leaders. These are largely vocational areas and no less valuable for that. We need the confidence to celebrate the fact that our research could make a difference to people's lives and the future of the planet.

Finally, I would like to thank Goodfellow Publishing, the only publisher I have worked with that is interested in what a book says rather than just what it earns! First, Tim Goodfellow, for commissioning this work, it has been a delight working with a publisher who is committed to disseminating knowledge and stimulating debate. Second to Sally North, who I have worked with over a number of years and has always been supportive even when she was trying desperately to tie me down to a completion date!

Preface

Well this is, I believe, my tenth book and it has been a joy to write.

I have never written a book just for the sake of it. I have only ever written them when there was a subject that interested me and I thought there was something I could contribute to our understanding of the subject.

More important, perhaps, I have always written books with the express aim of encouraging researchers to become interested in these subjects and push the boundaries of our knowledge so we understand them better. I never see what I write as a final output but rather as part of an organic process of knowledge creation and generation.

I also do not want my readership to be limited to academics and researchers; I write primarily for students and also for practitioners. I firmly believe that if we truly wish to disseminate knowledge and engage students and other citizens in intellectual activity then we need to communicate in language which will not alienate or confuse potential readers. Any fool can make the simple seem complex with a poor or pretentious writing style; the skill is in managing to make the complex understandable. While I may not often succeed, that has been my aim in the way I have written this book.

You will also notice that in general there are fewer references in the text than would normally be the case in an academic text, and this is for three main reasons. First, there is a general dearth of recent literature on the evolution and future of luxury in tourism, hospitality and events. Second, much of the literature in tourism, hospitality and events is on a micro-scale, focusing on particular places or a type of hotel or restaurant, for example, whereas I have tried to produce more of an overview, a macro-scale perspective. Finally, I wanted to try to look at the subject with a fresh eye without the pre-conceptions that often come from undertaking a major literature review. Nevertheless, some thoughts about possible further reading are provided at the end of the text.

The idea of luxury is all around us and we are bombarded daily with images of luxury designed to motivate us to spend our money, and often our valuable leisure time too. Luxurious living, it seems, is something that it is believed that we all aspire to enjoy. Certainly when I taught in Switzerland my fantastic students were literally obsessed with luxury in the form of designer label clothing, fast cars, business class air travel and five star hotels. For some of them, even at their age, a luxurious lifestyle was their everyday reality.

Yet when I moved to Manchester some of my students had never even been on an aeroplane or stayed in a hotel. However, they still had an image of luxury, and aspirations of what living a luxury lifestyle might be like and a desire to experience such a lifestyle. Their perceptions of luxury were largely derived from the media and the lives of celebrities, and seemed to be best described by words such as glitz and glamour, and by ostentatious displays of wealth.

At the same time, I saw travel companies charging tourists lots of money – luxury price levels – to stay in a tent in the desert or on a mountainside without even running water. Simultaneously hundreds of people were being packed into concrete box hotels that described themselves as luxury, while online travel agents offered five star hotel rooms at heavily discounted prices. I read of five star hotels in Paris that have been bywords for luxury over decades saying they were losing business to private apartment owners, with no training or experience in hospitality, offering their homes through Airbnb. And on my television I saw Michelin starred chefs extolling the virtues of street food which until now tourists had been advised to avoid for hygiene reasons.

I was thinking about all this one evening at our home in Cornwall in the UK, looking out over the Atlantic Ocean. It is in an area of stunning beauty with thousands of years of history still evident in its landscape, and it attracts hundreds of thousands of tourists every year. Suddenly the sky turned an amazing shade of red as the sun went down, the scents of the garden filled my nose, the freshly caught local sea bass was sizzling on the barbecue and all you could hear was the sound of the waves. At that moment I thought I was experiencing the ultimate in luxury, a stunning moment when everything came together to create perfection. Yet it cost me nothing and did not involve any tourism, hospitality or event organisation.

At that moment I concluded that there was more to this idea of luxury than I had thought and that was when I decided to write this book. My aim was to explore what luxury in tourism, hospitality and events means today, how it is changing and what it may mean tomorrow.

I hope you enjoy reading the book and that it makes you want to find out more about the subject whether you are a student, academic, industry professional or tourist.

John Swarbrooke
Trewellard, Cornwall
August 2017

Part 1 : Setting the Scene

Part 1 consists of three chapters that are designed to set the context for the rest of the book.

In Chapter 1 we seek to explore and define the concept of luxury but I endeavour to suggest that the concept of luxury is going through a period of rapid change. This chapter also identifies the fact that luxury is a subjective idea rather than an absolute and that in many ways it is in the eye of the beholder.

Most of the book focuses on the present and the future, but in Chapter 2 we focus on the evolution of the term 'luxury' in the context of tourism, hospitality and events. This is important because many of today's ideas of luxury have their roots in the past.

In Chapter 3 we look at the individual factors which are influencing the evolution of the idea of luxury today. We will identify and discuss more than a dozen such factors.

1   Introduction

We are bombarded by the terms 'luxury' and 'luxurious' on a daily basis by marketers, who clearly believe that they are powerful words that can encourage us to spend money we may not have, and consume goods and services we may not actually need.

Indeed, luxury has always been associated with the purchase and consumption of products and services human beings do not actually need to survive, from holidays to high-end cars to designer brand fashion. This fact is recognised when we say, as we buy such things, 'yes I know it is a bit of a luxury but …', by way of justifying our actions to ourselves.

Luxury has, therefore, always been associated with disposable income, the money left over when we have bought the essentials of life, such as food, and paid our electricity and water bills.

Yet, today, it seems that the idea of luxury has been extended even to everyday items that we do need or at least feel we need to be part of a civilised society. Unusually soft toilet paper is described as 'luxurious', as are sweet smelling shower gels, and microwaveable convenience foods!

In this book I will ignore the hyperbole of the marketing professionals and focus on luxury in the context of products and services which are not everyday purchases and are not essential to human survival, and are primarily in the tourism, hospitality and events sectors.

Let me also begin by highlighting what the book will not be about. I will not be talking about business tourism for, while it certainly has a luxury dimension, it is a form of tourism where enjoyment is not the aim and where the consumer usually does not make the decisions about what to consume, but is instead told what they may consume by an employer.

I will also not be looking at the large area of the market represented by the phenomenon of 'visiting friends and relatives'. Although luxury may well be present, again here consumption is shaped or even distorted by the coincidence of who your friends and family are and where they have chosen to live.

The rationale for this book

The very fact that someone is prepared to pick up a book and read it could be seen as sufficient justification for a book to be written. However, I would like to outline why I believe that a book such as this is warranted in the context of tourism, hospitality and events.

In the early days of the modern tourism and hospitality sector, virtually everything was luxury as only a small social and economic elite was travelling. This was the era in which much of our modern thinking about luxury and travel originated, from the grand hotels to the cruise ships. Destinations such as the French Riviera were developed in this era, destinations that have remained symbols of luxury ever since.

Yet since that time things have changed dramatically with leisure travel now being much more democratic, with most people in so-called developed countries, at least, being able to participate. At the same time it is my belief that our thinking on luxury has not evolved sufficiently to reflect this change.

Furthermore, the concept of luxury in the modern tourism industry was born in Europe and was based on a European values and tastes. Yet today the rapidly growing markets of Asia are setting the pace in the global market. Interestingly, though, the first generation of Asian global tourists appear to have been heavily influenced by these European concepts of luxury, from designer brands to the grand old hotels of London or Montreux or Nice. However, I believe that we are at a cusp where the Asian tourists, as they become more experienced travellers, will begin to develop their own concepts of luxury that are less dependent on the European tradition.

I am also of the opinion that for all tourists the concept of luxury is being changed by factors that are at play today and are changing the market forever. Mobile devices are allowing tourists to become their own travel agents and concierges; online travel agents are offering luxury hotels at discounted prices; and the 'experience economy' means that all travellers now seek personalised experiences rather than standardised products and services. This is reducing the power of traditional industry suppliers and increasing that of the consumer, which will have a real impact on the luxury sector, as these suppliers themselves have often been the arbiters of what constitutes luxury. For example, the term, 'Ritz' has become a by-word for luxury well beyond the hotel sector.

We are also seeing a breaking down in boundaries between sectors and a growing fusion of industries which is going to impact on the meaning of luxury. The rise of branded 'fashion hotels' is a clear example of this trend.

Terrorism and the global threat of being a victim of terrorism may also lead to a change in the meaning of luxury. Instead of being taken for granted, safety and security has now become a rarer commodity – perhaps it will be seen now as a luxury in its own right.

So, the main justification for this book, I believe, is that changes of many kinds are making a rethink of the idea of luxury essential, particularly at a time when companies and destinations, desperate to succeed in an increasingly competitive market, are using the term 'luxury' in ways which are increasingly meaningless.

This is the intellectual rationale for the book but there is another more mundane one from the point of view of an academic audience.

The fact is that luxury in tourism, hospitality and events has received little attention from researchers previously, despite its importance in terms of the aspirations of individual tourists, the economic impact of luxury travel spending and the efforts of new product developers. I hope this text will stimulate further research that will deepen our understanding of this intriguing subject.

Now let us start at the beginning with some definitions of luxury.

Traditional definitions of luxury

Where better to start than by going back to the first use of the term in the English language. The source for this and the definition that follow is the Oxford English Dictionary

Apparently the nearest term to it in Middle English relates to lechery! In Old French and Latin the terms were 'luxurie' and 'luxeria' respectively with both indicating the idea of 'excess' or perhaps indulgence.

According to the same dictionary, 'From the Middle Ages to the 19th century luxury was lust, lasciviousness' …the Latin source luxuria also implied indulgence as a vice'.

The current definition in the Dictionary is cited as, 'A state of great comfort or elegance, especially when involving great expense'.

The Merriam-Webster Dictionary has three definitions . Luxury is:

'a condition or situation of great comfort, ease and wealth'

'something that is expensive and not necessary'

'something that is helpful or welcome and that is not usually or always available'

All of these definitions define luxury in terms of comfort and price in particular, which as we will see fits well with how the various sectors within tourism, hospitality and events have tended to see luxury. However, as we will see some parts of the industry are beginning to suggest that changes are taking place around the meaning of luxury.

■ Definitions of luxury in tourism, hospitality and events

Interestingly most of what has been written recently about definitions of luxury in these sectors has come from industry insiders rather than academics. It is a little corporatist in tone in places but fascinating, given that I would argue that industry people know more about the sectors and what is happening in them than researchers do, unfortunately.

In 2013 'A Luxury Travel Blog' asked ten industry experts for their definition or view of luxury travel and received some fascinating responses, including the following:

> 'Luxury travel is a privilege truly experienced by a few'. Andrew Carr, Kennedy and Carr Ireland Travel.

> 'Luxury is a much over-used term. One traveller's luxury is another's ordinary'. Steve McAllen, Wexas Tailor-Made Travel.

> 'The definition of luxury travel to me is to undertake a new experience and immerse oneself in a new destination whilst indulging in the very best levels of personal service...lavish accommodation ...unrivalled levels of gastronomy ...'. Gareth Harding, The Cruise line Ltd.

> 'Luxury travel does not just mean opulence, comfort and a range of amazing amenities on offer at the destination; it is the full journey of the traveller from the point they make the first phone call to discuss their needs' . Roy Pilkington, Bailey Robinson.

> 'There has been a dramatic change in how we define the concept of luxury travel over the past few years, largely due to the current economic climate The current climate has deepened the definition, making it more multi-layered than it once was. It has pushed consumers away from conspicuous consumption towards more authentic, simple and genuine experiences that incorporate elements of environmental awareness and social responsibility'. Engi Bally, SilverDoor.

In relation to cruising, the employees of the CruiseWeb Blog offered the following definition in 2013:

> Luxury is hard to define; it is not a tangible thing. It's sometimes seen as extra special care and attention, or a high quality product made with precious materials. It can be defined by some as a feeling of being treated like royalty and knowing you are in good hands. There is no singular definition but it's something you know when you see or experience it.' Cruiseweb.com.

In terms of hotels and airlines I found no definitions that I believed merited inclusion here. But I did notice that most attempts to define luxury in both sectors in recent years have tended to focus on the tangible elements rather than the service, perhaps because the quality of the intangible service is taken as a given. Or perhaps we have learned how hard it is to guarantee the quality of service, when that service is delivered by human beings who have bad days as well as good ones! It may even reflect the fact that the hotel companies in particular have given up the naïve attempts to persuade us that the only thing on the minds of their staff when they wake is how they can please their customers today!

Instead the emphasis now is often on the quality of the hotel bathroom or the seat on the aeroplane. Aesthetics are seen as equal in importance, it seems, to functionality in respect of luxury hotels and the front end of aeroplanes. This may partly reflect that in recent years interior design has been elevated to a new status within consumer society.

In relation to restaurants, luxury seems easier to identify as it has its own terms such as 'fine dining' and 'gastronomy', which recognise places to eat that are out of the ordinary and exceptional. Gastronomy suggests consumers who have a particular body of knowledge and an exceptional palate, which separate them from other diners. Gastronomy can also be defined in terms of the culinary tradition of a region or country, which suggests that it may also be possible to make the authenticity of this tradition part of the concept of luxury in the restaurant sector.

Interestingly, there were no real definitions available specifically relating to luxury destinations. Yet most people seem easily able to name, if asked, places they consider to be luxury destinations. Perhaps this is partly a result of the media portrayal of 'dream destinations' in magazines and on television.

■ The concept of luxury in the wider business world

Discussions about luxury in the business world have tended to revolve around luxury brands rather than worrying about trying to define luxury. It is assumed everyone knows what luxury is, particularly in relation to tangible goods. Luxury is largely about exclusivity, high production values and equally high prices. However, it is also about the status which possession bestows on the owner of the product and how this possession makes the owner look in the eyes of their peers.

However, the purchasers of luxury brands are also expected to buy brands for the same reasons as those who buy cans of fizzy drink for a dollar or a hamburger for 60 cents, namely consistency, reliability, a recognisable logo and a certain set of brand values.

Many luxury brands are, interestingly, produced in quite large numbers, which somewhat undermines the idea of exclusivity. Efforts are constantly made to try to convince the customer of the uniqueness of their purchase through personalisation, because why would one pay thousands of dollars for a product that is exactly like that owned by many other people?

■ Less traditional definitions of luxury

Lindsey Saletta contributing on the 'theeverygirl' website offers a really interesting perspective on how the concept of luxury may be changing, particularly from the perspective of the younger generation. She begins by stating that luxury can be a divisive concept which distinguishes between those who can have something and those who cannot. She goes on to suggest that younger consumers may be rejecting the idea of using money to acquire things that are perceived by society to be luxury goods. Instead, she argues, the younger generation see luxury as having exceptional experiences, albeit in mundane locations or everyday situations, such as a great sunset or a perfect cup of coffee. Such experiences can be enjoyed by anyone regardless of wealth.

If she is right, this may be the result of two very important factors. First, that in many developed economies younger people have been disproportionately hit by the recent economic crisis and globalisation, so jobs are harder to find and homes harder to buy. But second, it may also reflect the fact that the Internet and mobile devices now allow these experiences to be shared globally, which may bring the young person the status and recognition that their parents sought from their purchase of an upscale home or a top of the range car.

If true, this has major implications for the future of the youth travel market and raises the interesting question of whether, as they grow older, these young people will change their idea of luxury to that of their parents or not.

Heinz Ramseier, with Sam Tinson, on Zai Blog in 2015 made some interesting points about luxury including the following quotes:

'The fact is that luxury can mean countless different things to different people …Often it is just used as a convenient prefix in order to justify a higher price tag. However as society changes the concept of luxury changes too. [We are increasingly exposed through the media to the] luxury lifestyles of the rich and famous. Advertisers would like us to aspire to these lifestyles. For the most part it is a tactic that works. There is a flip side to that record however…. Over-exposure to the lifestyle dream has desensitised us to the idea of luxury as a purely material concept …It is possible to see the green shoots of a new luxury paradigm. Discerning buyers are beginning to favour products that offer a deeper; more lasting emotional capital…Real luxury is becoming less about status and more about state-of-mind'

Ramseier goes on to talk about the importance to the new wave of luxury consumers of corporate social responsibility, environmentalism, and the switch from materialism towards the experiential.

Key words and ideas in luxury today

Let us now try to draw out from everything above some key words and ideas in relation to luxury today.

The first word should perhaps be *change*, for it seems clear that there is growing acknowledgement that ideas of luxury which have been pretty standard for so long are starting to change due to social, economic, and technological change. This is not to say that the old familiar words associated with luxury such as *expensive, exclusive, rarity, status, prestigious, indulgence* and so on are not still relevant because they are. However they are being joined by more recent words such as *experiences, authenticity, ethics* and *sustainability*.

I would now like to explore some general ideas around luxury that I think are particularly relevant to tourism, hospitality and events.

Traditionally luxury has been defined often as things you do not need to but want to buy. As these sectors do not offer products which are essential to everyday life, it could be said that any vacation or trip to an event or hotel stay or meal out is 'a luxury', by definition. However it seems to me that leisure has ceased to be seen as an 'unnecessary luxury' by many families, in more affluent countries at least, and is now seen as an essential part of life. This has implications for the meaning of luxury in tourism, hospitality and events.

Travel requires both disposable income and disposable *time*, for if one does not have free time one cannot travel. In today's world working people appear to feel more and more stressed and whether true or not, they seem to believe they have less and less free or spare time. This means that, to quote the musician David Mead and the title of his 1999 debut album, we should be thinking about 'the luxury of time'! It is my belief that time availability will be one of the elements of the concept of luxury in the future. This idea links very nicely to the emerging idea of 'slow tourism' which requires consumers who are 'time rich' but may not be 'cash rich'.

If the concept of luxury continues to include the idea of *rarity*, then sustainability will have a direct relationship with it. The reality is that our environment continues to be damaged by human activity and this is, in some places, leading to the gradual destruction of some tourist attractions, whether they are a coral reef, a particular animal or an archaeological site. The same is true of cultural events, where social change is altering the nature of many traditional events or even leading to their ending. Tourists desperate for what they perceive to be authentic, 'luxury experiences' may therefore be prepared to pay more and more to experience these finite and increasingly rare attractions.

Authenticity appears to be emerging as an important element in modern definitions of luxury. This is a field which has been well dug over in tourism research.

1

However, it is very interesting that future luxury travel could involve doing things which are not expensive, nor rare nor comfortable, but which are authentic. So is it a luxury travel experience if you stay with a family in a South African township or go out fishing with local fishermen in Sri Lanka? And what does this mean for all those artificial tourism products set up in recent years that bear no relation to their location or local culture, such as a ski slope and luxury hotels in Dubai or the plethora of music festivals in beach destinations all over the world?

One aspect of luxury that is likely to remain constant is the idea that luxury will *cost* more than non-luxury and this is true in many industries but maybe not in tourism, hospitality and events, where customers travel to consume the product, rather than having it available near where they live. So medium income Europeans travelling to poorer parts of south-east Asia, may be able to enjoy a seven night stay in a five star hotel for less than the cost of a seven night stay in a budget hotel in a neighbouring country. Indeed the chance for such middle income Europeans to enjoy to 'live the high life' on the cheap has been a major factor behind the growth of tourism in many Asian countries.

The brief examples highlighted above should serve to illustrate that the question of luxury in tourism, hospitality and events is a particularly complex one.

Conclusions

I hope that this chapter has convinced you that this subject of 'luxury' is one which merits attention. One of the main reasons for thinking that now is the right time to write this book, is the belief that the concept of 'luxury' is currently undergoing perhaps its greatest change yet, in response to a number of factors that are all occurring simultaneously.

The rest of the book will focus specifically on tourism, hospitality and events but you should always bear in mind that whatever happens in these areas will be a reflection, somehow, of whatever is happening in the wider society. In terms of the limitations of what follows throughout the rest of the book, it is for you to decide. However, even at this early stage, I would like to acknowledge that there is a geographical bias to this book, in that it has been written by a European, resident in the UK, who can only read literature in English and French. This needs to be borne in mind when reading the book. In my defence, on the other hand, I would like to say that I will be going out of my way to ensure that the examples and case studies are drawn from as many countries as possible.

In the next chapter we will look back into history to see how the concept of luxury developed over time in tourism, hospitality and events.

2 The History of Luxury in Tourism and Hospitality

In this chapter I will present a short and necessarily superficial history of tourism, focusing on how the idea of luxury has developed and changed. Before attempting this, it is important to recognise that our knowledge of this history is sketchy at best in relation to the earliest days of travel and tourism. We certainly cannot state any dates and claim them to be the beginning of travel.

While most of this chapter will focus on Europe it is important to recognise that tourism is a global phenomenon with many regions of the world having their own historical story to tell of its development.

The Euro-centric focus is less a function of where I live than of the fact that the most documentary evidence, such as it is, exists for Europe and it is fair to say that modern mass market tourism was born in Europe. Readers looking for more detail on the historical development of tourism in the different regions of the world are advised to turn to the third edition of *Consumer Behaviour in Tourism*, by Horner and Swarbrooke, published in 2016.

The earliest days of travel

The earliest travellers in the world, several thousand years ago, were likely to have been of at least five distinct types, namely:

- Business travellers whose motivation was the desire to sell their goods and services for gain.
- Pilgrims, travelling as part of the practice of their religion whatever it may have been, visiting shrines and holy places or participating in religious festivals.
- Military travellers who travelled to conquer and occupy new lands.
- Explorers and adventurers, seeking new places and new routes.
- Sightseers, people of leisure, whose motivation was to see new places and no doubt go back and tell their friends all about their experiences.

2

We certainly know that all five activities have a history of at least two millennia, and much longer for at least the first three. In one way there is a distinction between the first three and the other two in that the former involved 'involuntary journeys' that were required because of one's occupation or religion, whereas the latter were 'voluntary journeys' that a traveller chose to make.

However, in terms of luxury, one suspects that the idea meant nothing to the business traveller crossing a desert on a camel, a pilgrim sleeping in the open, or a soldier marching for mile after mile, or an explorer sailing the seas in a tiny open-decked boat. For these people any improvement in their situation might seem like a 'luxury' whether it be a new cloak to keep out the cold or some fresh fruit picked from a tree on the journey. Already though there would have been a distinction between rich and poor, high and low, for some soldiers marched while others rode and some pilgrims walked while others were carried. To the poor, having a horse or being carried, would have seemed like a luxury.

The 'sightseeing traveller' however is a different case, in that this option would always only have been open to those who had both disposable income and 'free time', a very rare commodity in ancient times. Travel was so slow that any sightseeing trip would probably have been measured in weeks rather than days or hours. The lack of infrastructure would have ensured that even the affluent leisured sightseer would have had precious little by way of luxury on their trip.

However, as we can see from the Roman Empire, for example, people did make sightseeing trips, sometimes over long distances. And there were fine villas to stay in en route and wine to drink if the traveller had wealthy friends, and the towns offered a few of what we might today call attractions, such as theatres. It is likely that the quality of life for the traveller would be at best similar to that enjoyed by them at home, but is unlikely to have been better than their home environment. It could therefore still not be seen as luxury, although it would have bestowed status through the tales the traveller could tell on his or her return. And we do know that both the Romans and the Greeks did travel as tourists, albeit in small numbers, for a century or so ago, in 1916, J. Gilford-Milne published a paper on this very subject!

Over the centuries things changed a little though. The transport infrastructure was still rudimentary, so any journey was a chore at best, a nightmare to be endured at worst. Yet things were improving a little in terms of accommodation, such as the caravanserai on the Silk Routes or the hostels for pilgrims. Some of the caravanserai in countries such as Azerbaijan, Iran and Turkey have been renovated and are again performing their original function as accommodation and providers of food and drink for travellers. For business travellers hundreds of years ago these must have seemed truly luxurious compared to the alternative of sleeping in the open.

However, the idea of luxury transportation would have to wait, in reality, until the arrival of the railway in the mid 19th century.

The Grand Tour

This very European, or rather more accurately British, phenomenon is perhaps one of the first embodiments of the idea of luxury travel in history. It was also a forerunner of what today might be called educational tourism.

The Grand Tour was, in short, an extended vacation designed to be part of the 'coming of age' of young aristocrats, in much the same way as a 'gap year' might be seen today. It was designed to broaden the experience and horizons of the young gentleman – for the vast majority of those taking the Grand Tour were men. These were cultural trips, but no doubt with some hedonistic pleasures also being enjoyed by the traveller. The favoured destination was Italy where Renaissance art and the remains of the Roman Empire were favourite attractions; but France, Germany, the Netherlands, Switzerland and Greece also featured on many of the trips.

This was travel for those with the luxury of disposable income and disposable time, for they often took up to two or three years and involved lots of travel and the best accommodation , meals and entertainment available in the destination. These 'classic' very Grand Tours were at their peak in the 17th and 18th centuries.

However later in the 18th century something began to happen that has been mirrored countless times since in the world of luxury travel. People with less spare time and disposable income wanted to enjoy the same kinds experiences as the aristocracy but on a smaller scale. So there started a new type of Grand Tour, where it was older people who travelled for hedonism and sightseeing, rather than education, and travelled for weeks rather than months and years.

It has been estimated that at times there could have been as many as 20,000 young British people taking the Grand Tour in Europe at any one time (Sharpley, 1994).

Those on the Grand Tour really set the parameters for modern tourism, and tourists today in Italy still tend to do a greatly pared down version of what these people did two hundred or so years earlier. However, in the context of a discussion about luxury, it is illuminating to note that whereas the tourist of today may bring home postcards of Renaissance masterpieces, those on the Grand Tour bought home original works of art by Renaissance and later masters, which now cover the walls of the stately homes of the UK! We will see later in the chapter that the link between luxury travel and art did not die with the end of the Grand Tour.

Health and luxury

Luxurious living is one thing, but staying alive and healthy was recognised as a challenge for everyone long before Maslow talked about his 'hierarchy of needs'. Across the world, centuries ago, living conditions were poor for all classes and diseases such as the plague or Black Death affected all classes. The fear of disease motivated the rise of a form of tourism which is now almost synonymous with luxury, namely health tourism. Yet when people began to visit spas and take the medicinal waters, the motivation was survival rather than leisure. However, if one was going to spend weeks recovering from, or avoiding, illness one needed distractions and good hospitality facilities. Thus were born the spa resorts.

Yet the European spa resorts do not represent the first link between travel and health, for in Japan and Korea spas have been used for hundreds if not thousands of years, although these spa waters also had a religious significance that was not generally the case in Europe.

The great European spas such as Vichy in France, Bath in the UK, Baden Baden in Germany and, of course, Spa in Belgium were famous as places where the rich and famous went to play, and they continued to have this reputation well into the 20th century.

The railways and luxury

As we noted earlier, one impediment to the rise of luxury travel was the poor transport networks that existed all over the world. Roads were often little more than mud tracks, while sailing ships were at the mercy of the winds.

The invention that changed this situation and began the transformation of the tourism phenomenon was the railway. In the UK where it was invented, its first impact was not to generate what we would call luxury travel, but instead to put a modest opportunity for leisure travel within reach of the less affluent. Over the second half of the 19th century, railways opened up coastal resorts for vacations for the burgeoning middle classes in Europe and North America, while even factory workers might now be able to enjoy a day trip to the seaside thanks to the railway. For these people twxravel was a new luxury but it was one which would quickly start to be seen as a necessity of modern life.

However, the development of the railways also created some of the most iconic tourism experiences ever seen, in terms of the luxury train, most notably the world renowned *Orient Express*, a byword for glamour and indulgence. Of course, today, many destination countries have such luxury trains, still expensive but perhaps less exclusive.

In terms of the rise of luxury travel the railway was also the catalyst for the emergence of Mr Thomas Cook, who quickly went from organising day trips for urban dwellers to luxury trips around the world, and in doing so became a symbol of the rise of modern tourism.

Playgrounds for the rich

The later 19th century, in Europe and North America at least, saw many developments which set the standards by which luxury travel would be judged for the next century or more.

Perhaps the most significant development at this time was the 'creation' of the French Riviera, a place largely created by foreigners to meet the desires of the aristocracy and mega-rich of Europe and North America. This formerly little known area of coast rapidly became a world famous playground for the rich, with beautiful scenery, the casino at Monte Carlo, moorings for luxury yachts, top end hotels, famous restaurants and promenades such as the Promenade des Anglais in Nice, whose very name alone tells you who the biggest market segment were in the early days. Furthermore whereas most European vacations occurred in the summer, the Riviera became popular with those from northern and eastern Europe seeking to escape for harsh winters at home. Ironically, these 'winter sun' holidays had by the late 20th century become low cost and mass market products across much of the Mediterranean.

The rich did not just find luxury at the coast, they also found it in big cities, most notably Paris. In something like a later version of the Grand Tour, young aristocrats and the sons of rich industrialists visited 'Belle Epoque' Paris to 'complete their education' in art, culture…sex and drinking. This was not the classic luxury of high end hotels and expensive dinners, but rather the 'luxury' of having to do absolutely nothing except experience Paris with its risqué cabaret shows, absinthe bars and Impressionist painters. Their activities in Paris created an image of romance and/or hedonism for the city that has survived until now, while their befriending of the artists is a major reason why Impressionist art is so popular across the world.

At the same time wealthy, well educated people were discovering another part of Europe and doing things that were new and exciting. They discovered the Alps and the joys of rock climbing, mountaineering and skiing. By day these travellers endured bad weather and physical exertions in the mountains, but over time they found themselves spending their nights in a new generation of luxury hotels in Swiss resorts such as Zermatt. The Swiss hospitality sector also benefitted from the rise of the more sedate leisure activity of sightseeing based primarily around the lakes. Here again luxury hotels were created in places such as Montreux, to meet their desire for luxury.

One result of the popularity of Switzerland with the rich was the creation of the famous hotel school in Laussanne, since which Switzerland has had a reputation as *the* place to learn about managing luxurious hotels. This reputation continues today when the country is home to a number of schools. I had the privilege for three years of being Academic Director of the world famous César Ritz Colleges hotel school, named after the man who became known as the 'king of hoteliers and hotelier to kings'.

Europe therefore, at this time, was a veritable playground for the rich, where the 'old money' of the aristocracy and the 'new money' of industrialists was spent lavishly on a leisure lifestyle that was beyond the wildest dreams of the vast majority of the population. What happened in this period created concepts of luxury that have endured over time, but have also been taken up by the new markets in Russia and Asia, who still see Europe as a destination for a certain kind of luxury travel.

Empires and luxury travel

Throughout history, empires have always created demand for travel, particularly amongst soldiers, traders and administrators. However, until the 19th century luxury had rarely played much part in such travel. In the late 19th century the infrastructure of empires began to include provision for luxury travel and high end leisure, partly thanks to the invention of the railway.

The first manifestation of this, perhaps, was the opening up of so-called 'hill stations'. In hot countries there had always been a tradition of monarchs and aristocrats escaping from the lowlands or cities in the hottest season to travel to cooler upland areas. However, the British colonists in India and Malaysia raised this to a new level with the development of resorts such as Shimla and the Cameron Highlands in these respective countries. Railways were developed to serve these new destinations and these railways themselves are now major attractions for tourists in their own right, particularly in India and Sri Lanka.

The development and management of empires also required hotels at staging posts around the world, for passengers arriving in colonies by ships or travelling around them by rail. This led to the opening of a generation of hotels that became a byword for luxury and had reputations that are still strong today. Many have survived long after the empires that gave birth to them have died and now attract today's luxury leisure traveller. In Singapore there is the *Raffles* hotel where the 'Singapore Sling' cocktail was invented. Interestingly, in recent years the *Raffles* brand has been used for a chain of hotels in various parts of the world in an attempt to capitalise on the reputation of the name, 'Raffles'. Another fine example of this hotel genre that has survived is the Eastern and Oriental in Penang, Malaysia.

However, many of the luxury hotels and railways have not survived or are now a picture of faded glory, a shadow of their former selves for they were the product of an era which has, in many ways fortunately, gone for ever.

As we will see in the next section, the pioneering inter-continental air routes that were developed in the early days of flying, largely to meet the needs of empire administrators, military people and business travellers, were to have a perhaps more enduring legacy.

Before looking at that we need to recognise that the 'empire era' also created so-called luxury activities that have continued in modified versions ever since. An interesting but controversial example relates to wildlife. The colonialists used some of their leisure time in their adopted countries to irresponsibly shoot native wildlife, to extinction in some cases. The rich of the 1920s and 1930s continued this practice, by travelling between continents to take part in organised big game safaris. Fortunately, we no longer shoot the wildlife except with cameras, but safaris are now part of the mainstream mass market tourism industry.

1920s and 1930s – the Golden Age of luxury travel

Many would argue that the period between the two World Wars was the era when the process of travelling itself reached its zenith in terms of luxury, for this was the time of the ocean liners and airliners with few passengers but luxurious passenger cabins and personalised service.

We are all aware from movies such as *Titanic* about the opulence that existed on liners in the early 1900s and this was certainly still the case in the 1920s and 1930s. However such movies also showed the huge disparity in the quality of the on-board experience between first class and third class, so it was not all luxury by any means.

However, when it came to international air travel there was only a luxury option, due to the small size of the craft and the high operating costs. The reality of air travel at this time though was a mixture of luxury and risk, as accidents were frequent and long distance journeys were measured in days rather than hours. Imperial Airways, a pioneer of early civil aviation, therefore felt it was a major selling point to be able to claim in a 1937 issue of *Flight* magazine that it was possible to travel ' by air [from London] to South Africa or India in under a week!'. (paleofuture.gizmodo.com, 2016)

And the cost was certainly luxury too. The eight day trip from London to Singapore in 1934 cost £180 or about £10,900 when adjusted for inflation. But this included hotel stopovers en route and food, but not alcohol! (paleofuture. gizmodo.com, 2016). By comparison the same journey today could cost as little as £500 return and would take less than twelve hours.

However the level of service was something air passengers today can only dream about! Passengers could check in at city centre terminals rather than the airport and were then transported by road to the airport. On the aircraft seats were large and comfortable with lots of leg room. Food was individually prepared and served on china. Aircraft flying overnight had full beds which could restrict capacity to twenty or fewer passengers.

However, no matter how luxurious the interior, it could not disguise the fact that air journeys were plagued by turbulence and air sickness, as well as frequent mechanical delays. Despite this, there is no denying the glamour of air travel at this time. But perhaps we need to recognise that the main 'luxury' of air travel in this era was the luxury of time, as the journey time to Australia was reduced from months to days.

Some would argue that the age of luxury air travel continued beyond the 1940s and even in to the 1960s. Certainly the Pan American Stratocruisers that crossed the Atlantic in the 1950s were both luxurious and glamorous. However by this time slow luxury airliners were being overtaken by a new invention, the jet airliner, where success was measured by how many passengers you could fit on the plane, and flights were so fast that there was no longer any need for overnight stays in hotels or full beds on aeroplanes. Ironically the latter would enjoy a revival of interest decades, later as airlines fought each other for the lucrative business class market.

However there was still glamour in the air at this time with roomier seats even in economy class, unlimited alcohol being available, high quality meals prepared on board and cabin crew wearing designer fashions. And of course no need to show ID to get on an aircraft.

As far as liners were concerned, they entered a period of massive decline after World War Two as more and more wanted to travel but could not afford the time required for sea travel. The rejuvenation of cruise tourism had to wait until the 1980s and 1990s when new types of cruises were developed. But if these still include luxury cruises, it is a different type of luxury suited to a modern, more democratic world.

It is now time for us to look at how the market changed after World War Two and how this signalled the end of what might be termed 'old-style luxury'.

The birth of the modern tourism industry and the death of true luxury?

By 1950 , there can be little doubt that across the world international leisure travel was still an activity only open to a tiny fraction of the global population. Over the next twenty years this situation was to change dramatically for reasons which are well known and much rehearsed in tourism text books. However, before we go on to explore what happened in more detail we need to recognise that in many parts of the world international leisure travel is still something only available to a tiny minority of the population.

Table 2.1 illustrates how international tourism grew between 1950 and 2000 notwithstanding what was said in the last paragraph.

Table 2.1: International tourist arrivals 1950-2000 (in millions). *Source:* statista.com. 2016

1950	25	
1960	69	Nearly triple the figure for 1950
1970	166	More than double the 1960 figure
1980	286	Less than double the 1970 figure
1990	435	Less than double the 1980 figure
2000	674	Less than double the 1990 figure

Between 1950 and 1970 the number increases by a factor of almost seven compared to a figure of four for the period from 1970 to 2000.

The rapid growth from 1950 to 1970 was caused by a number of factors, including the reduction in the real cost of travel due to the economies of scale created by jet airliners and the rise of a competitive tour operation market driving prices down. There were also factors such as longer paid holidays, rising wages and political stability, at least in Europe and North America, which between them representing the overwhelming majority of international travellers in the 1950s and 1960s.

The growth of truly mass market tourism over those two decades should rightly be celebrated as a triumph for democracy as travel slowly began to be available to a larger and larger number of people. However, this trend meant that the proportion of international leisure travel that might be seen as 'luxury' probably fell within twenty years from near one hundred per cent to a figure that may have been as low as ten per cent although no clear data exists to prove this.

However, at the same time we need to remember that, by 1970, the practice of taking any kind of foreign holiday was a minority activity even in the economically developed countries of northern Europe, let alone less wealthy parts of the world.

The other impact of this change in the volume and nature of international travel was in the behaviour of the richest tourists, those whose tastes and behaviour were honed during the luxury era of tourism. They seemed to have little desire to mix with the new mass market tourists and so often moved on from their former haunts leaving them to the 'new tourists'. They seem to have despised these 'new tourists' who were more interested in beaches than culture, wanted to eat food from their own country rather than the host country and so on. This rather snobbish attitude was even encapsulated in the idea that 'I am a traveller but you are a tourist', and it is an idea that is alive still today!

It is no exaggeration to say this transformation of the tourism market was a major challenge for the established tourism industry, which for so long had made profits by meeting the needs of upscale clients.

At the same time it was also a shock for many destinations as the small number of artists who painted picturesque scenes around Benidorm while drinking local wine were replaced by large numbers of people who had never left their own countries before and wanted to know where they could get Bratwurst or a cooked English breakfast. Yet these destinations were quick to realise that a large crowd of mass market tourists could bring far more economic benefits than a few luxury lifestyle visitors, so they rushed to provide what these new visitors wanted.

Virtually everything we have discussed in the past few pages has focused largely on Europe and for good reason. Even today Europe generates and is the destination for over half of all international trips taken in the world, and in terms of the tourism product it has been very influential in creating perceptions of what constitutes luxury in travel – as well as in fashion, food and most consumer goods. This has not really been changed by the rise of the USA in the 20th century, because the USA has been more about the democratisation of luxury and leisure rather than focusing on the privileged few. The luxury end of the US market still seems to look to Europe in many ways; top end art, for example, is still represented by the French Impressionists in the American market. But as we will see shortly, things are now changing.

New geographies of demand and of luxury

Let us begin this section by saying that virtually every country today has luxury market travellers within its population and in most cases always has had. However, until recent decades these people tended to be royalty, aristocrats, senior politicians, and those who inherited wealth and privilege. This picture of the luxury market was particularly common in countries lower down the GDP table and also in countries that were under the control of a colonial power.

In recent years, though, we have seen countries in Asia, such as China and India, enjoy high rates of economic growth and development, which have in turn created an affluent middle class. Ironically, as the middle classes in Europe and North America have felt themselves to be losing buying power, the middle classes in these emerging economies have become exceptionally affluent in comparison to the majority of their fellow citizens. This has occurred alongside the rise of a class of super-rich business people in these same countries. Given the populations of China and India, their affluent middle classes are measured in tens of millions, meaning in size they are actually almost mass markets although they represent a minority of their national populations. At the same time we have seen great political change in Russia in the past twenty years which has created a tiny class of 'oligarchs' with levels of personal wealth rarely seen since Tsarist times.

Given that in all three countries, and in others on a smaller scale, affluent consumers are a relatively new phenomenon, it is not surprising, perhaps, that they often seem to have wanted to indulge in ostentatious displays of wealth, including high profile luxury travel. This is simply repeating what happened in earlier times with the *nouveau riche* in Europe and the USA.

It is equally unsurprising that much of their consumption has been taking place in Europe and the USA, where luxury demand for travel has a long history and where much of the luxury supply is located, whether it be high end retailing, Michelin starred restaurants, and five star hotels with global reputations for elegance and style. So the luxury travellers from the emerging economies have begun to visit Europe and North America in large numbers in recent years, much to the delight of these destinations whose tourism sectors have been transformed by these new high spending visitors. And they have been arriving at a time when many of the traditional luxury clients from Europe and North America have been moving further afield in search of luxury experiences. For the tourists from China, India and Russia, for example, travel to Europe, in particular, gives them the opportunity to enjoy experiences previously only accessible to Europeans and North Americans, along with very limited numbers of people who generally inherited privilege in other countries and regions. Thus their choice of destination bestows status upon the traveller in their home country as well as giving them the opportunity to enjoy some of the iconic hotels, restaurants and destinations that have become bywords for luxury globally, encompassed by words such as 'Ritz' or 'Riviera', for example.

Sometimes the behaviour of these markets is fascinating. When living in Switzerland, I have seen Chinese and Indian visitors in places like Zermatt coming to experience what are perceived as the icons of luxury tourism, namely the ski resorts of the Swiss Alps. They stay in the most prestigious of the 19th century hotels, buy multi thousand dollar watches in the shops but never go skiing, the *raison d'être* for the existence of the whole destination! Another aspect of demand from the new luxury travellers has been the purchase of second homes or holiday homes in their favourite destinations. These may cost millions of dollars but only be used for a few days every year. In fact one does not have to even go to a destination to see evidence of the behaviour of many of the new luxury travellers. A visit to any airport duty free retailing area will reveal a disproportionate number of people from the emerging markets spending large amounts of money on everything from designer handbags to rare whiskies.

I am very conscious that this is a generalised and rather stereotypical picture but I believe there is enough evidence available to suggest it has some truth within it. However, markets are changing all the time and there is already a view that in the Chinese market, consumers have become more experienced and confident travellers.

The changes outlined above have certainly transformed the luxury travel market but they have also changed the geography of supply too. While old traditional luxury destinations have sought to exploit these new markets which are described euphemistically as 'quality tourists', governments and entrepreneurs around the world have invested heavily to create new luxury destinations, most notably in the Gulf States. Here the aim has been to attract both the old money of western Europe and the new money of Asia and the Gulf states themselves. At the same time we have seen a massive growth in luxury hotels, restaurants, retail outlets and casinos across Asia, designed to attract both the regional emerging luxury market and high spending travellers from other parts of the world including Europe and North America.

This competition is eating away at Europe's reputation as a market leader in luxury in tourism and hospitality. High labour costs and the problems of recruiting and retaining staff are giving Europe a competitive disadvantage, and are leading to a situation where in Asia staff to guest ratios are higher and service is perceived to be friendlier and more attentive. Furthermore, the reality is that in the Gulf States and much of Asia, workers generally have fewer rights than their European counterparts, which can make them easier to exploit. Sometimes luxury consumption does seem to be based on the exploitation of staff.

Ironically, therefore, it is often the poorer countries with the lowest costs which are becoming more and more attractive for many luxury segment travellers, because they get better value for money. Even luxury travellers appear to like value for money but they are also attracted by the fact that such countries have invested heavily in everything from hotels to airports, visitor attractions to roads.

The airlines of Asia and the Gulf States have also changed the geography of luxury transport because their airlines – some of them state owned and subsidised, others benefitting from economic development in their home region – have been setting new standards of 'luxury' even in their economy cabins. It could also be argued that the growth of Dubai as a destination owes much to the reputation of Emirates airlines and the airport in Dubai. Many can remember that Dubai started as a popular stopover between Europe and Asia or Australasia before it developed into a fully fledged destination in its own right, because of the quality of its airline and the amazing duty free shopping in its airport.

Conclusions

I believe I have just provided, in a few thousand words and admittedly rather simplistically, an overview of the historical evolution of the concept of luxury in tourism, hospitality and events. The next twelve chapters will explore that concept today and how it is changing, before we look to the future in Chapter 15.

Let us begin this summary with the obvious statement that luxury has a long history but let us note that in travel the term has only become meaningful in the last century or so. Only over that period has transport developed to the point where the journey to a destination has become comfortable to the point where it can truly be described as luxurious. Before that a destination could be luxurious but the gloss would be well and truly taken off the experience by having to arrive there by horse, horse and carriage, dirty steam train or sailing ship dependent wholly on nature for its speed.

It is important to re-state that the history of luxury in our sector has really been dominated by Europe but that now it is Asia and the Gulf States which are setting the pace in defining modern luxury.

The point also needs to be made that the rise of modern mass tourism has challenged and undermined traditional views of luxury travel. Luxury travel is no longer just about being able to travel while most of your fellow citizens are unable to for time or financial reasons, so that by definition any travel could be seen as luxury travel. Instead it is more about how and where you travel, as more and more people can afford vacations and can aspire to visit different parts of the world.

I would argue that we are currently in a transition phase between a time when vacations of any kind were seen as a luxury, to a time where they are seen by many almost as a necessity. From a time when luxury was just an extension of one's everyday lifestyle, to a time when it can also be something one experiences just occasionally by saving up or using the credit card. Or between a time when luxury travel meant conspicuous consumption, high spending, and hedonism and self-indulgence to a time when it may be as much about responsible tourism, authenticity and values. It could even start to mean *time* as well as just *money* as increasingly stressed people feel they have less and less 'spare time' to spend on leisure away from their homes.

Yet I believe that the older traditional meanings of luxury will cease to apply in future but I do believe that the meaning will actually be *meanings* and will become more diverse and heterogeneous. This will be discussed throughout the rest of the book in much more detail.

3 The Evolution of the Concept of Luxury in Tourism and Hospitality

Introduction

Throughout this text I will be arguing that the nature of luxury is changing rapidly in response to a wide range of complex and disparate factors, many of them not even barely understood yet. These factors are influencing the idea of luxury in their own right, but it is the results of the interactions between the factors which are perhaps of most interest. It is my opinion that the evidence of this change is clearly visible around us, but the process by which it is happening and the pace of change is much harder to detect.

In this chapter we will seek to explore the myriad factors which are shaping the evolution of the idea of luxury in tourism, hospitality and events, and will try to explore some of the relationships between them. Clearly, whatever can be said in a few pages will be a simplification of reality because what is happening varies from place to place as do the factors driving the change.

Figure 3.1 sets out to illustrate, in diagramatic form the factors which I believe are changing the concept of luxury.Before we go on to look in detail at how these factors affect the concept of luxury let us simply note that the relationship is not purely one way, for the idea of luxury itself certainly influences some of these factors in return. For example:

- The luxury sector makes a major contribution to many national economies.
- The aspiration for luxury and how it is manifested lays behind many consumer fashions and trends.
- The idea of luxury is a powerful one in the world of politics; for some politicians it is a carrot to dangle in front of electors to help secure their vote while to politicians on the left the existence of luxury lifestyles for the few are evidence of the inequities and unfairness of a society.

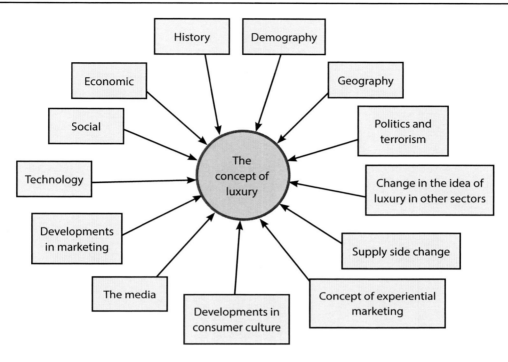

Figure 3.1: Factors which are influencing the evolution of the concept of luxury in tourism, hospitality and events

- The luxury market is one which is highly attractive to industry players who will invest heavily in new product development to attract luxury consumers.

- The desire to experience so-called luxury has been a prime motivator for people to buy the increasing number of 'lifestyle' magazines that have proved such lucrative ventures for publishers in recent years.

- Technological innovation has been driven often by the desire to create products aimed at the luxury market with high disposable income and a desire for new experiences.

However the main focus of this chapter is in how all these factors are affecting the evolution of the idea of luxury and so we will now return to that subject

Historical factors

This point has been alluded to in the first two chapters but it needs to be said again here. The ideas about luxury that have been dominant until now have clear roots in history, dating back perhaps two or three hundred years, although some would argue they have a much longer history. For me, our construct of luxury has been driven by three main historical factors as follows:

- The tastes and activities of European royalty and aristocracy which have influenced attitudes towards everything from interior design to food, architecture to fashion. While the influence of such people has waned dramatically it is always there in the background. Take a look at many luxury hotels in Paris, for example, which reflect the tastes of the 17th and 18th centuries.

- The tastes and activities of the wealthy class that emerged from the grime and suffering of the industrial revolution in Europe and the USA. This group of people, who did not inherit wealth but instead gained it through their own efforts, became increasingly powerful throughout the 19th and early 20th centuries. The rise of this class coincided with the railway and steamship age. Alongside the aristocracy, but in ever larger numbers, these people were at the heart of what has been called the 'Golden Age of Travel', a nostalgic term for the time when travel was the preserve of a fortunate small minority within societies. Conspicuous consumption was important, whether it be through travelling first class on ocean liners, buying art, or gambling at the casino.

- The tastes and activities of colonialists, who tended to be from Europe and found themselves spending prolonged periods of time or even the rest of their lives in far-flung places. For them 'luxury' often appeared to mean creating things that would remind them of 'home' in their new home, such as the English country-house style buildings of the hill country in Sri Lanka or hill stations of India or Malaysia. They also exported to their new homes things from their birthplace, from sports to social institutions. This travelling class was also the origin of some of the most famous hotels in the world, such as *Raffles* in Singapore or the *Eastern and Oriental* in Penang, Malaysia.

In recent years though we have seen changes taking place that have had an impact on the concept of luxury. We will now examine a few of these changes.

What all three groups had in common was they came from or formed a very privileged class in societies where most people could barely earn a living and mere survival was sometimes a struggle. In their age, any travel for pleasure was a luxury by definition, because only a few could afford it. While great discrepancies still exist, the gap in most countries has declined and there are larger groups in most societies forming a buffer between the mega rich and the ultra poor.

The other thing that the three factors highlighted above had in common was that they were largely European phenomena. That is not to say that such elites were purely European, although the second group largely was until the rise of the USA as an industrial power. However, only in Europe did these three elite groups define luxury on a global scale, due to the forces of industrial development and colonialism. Also, it was in Europe where we saw the rise of leisure travel, whereby those with wealth used their privileged position to indulge in leisure travel, starting perhaps with 'The Grand Tour'.

Traditionally too, all three groups had another great advantage and that is the availability of time. Most of them either enjoyed inherited wealth and had no need to work or were rich enough to pay others to manage their businesses. So for them travel could be a leisurely affair, so they could have 'the luxury' of relaxing over a prolonged period of time. So, luxury became associated with a slow pace of life, giving one the chance to savour experiences.

However, from the early 20th century onwards the position has been changing and will continue to change. First, as we will see when we look at the economic and geographical factors, the distribution of wealth changed first from Europe to the USA and then from these two to Asia. While many ideas of luxury from Europe were taken on board, first in the USA and then in Asia, they have somewhat different perspectives on the meaning of luxury.

While our own era has also seen the growth of economic elites based on 'earned wealth', it seems now that even the rich no longer have the luxury of time. Making money seems to offer little chance for lengthy vacations and the much faster pace of life has reduced the opportunities to simply 'stand and stare', no matter how rich you are. Even if you are lucky enough to fly in a private jet, a seven hour flight from London to New York will never be as relaxing as a seven day sail from Southampton to New York on an ocean liner. If luxury is about rarity value, then time is now a luxury for almost everyone.

As we will see in Chapter 7, history has also had an influence on where luxury travel takes place and what constitutes a luxury destination. Before air travel, all places thousands of kilometres from Europe were *de facto* luxury destinations for the European travellers, because the journey would take days if not weeks and cost enormous amounts of money. Today a German tourist can get up and fly to India for a few hundred Euro and arrive in time for a late dinner that evening!

At the same time, places change and the rise of mass market tourism has changed some formerly exclusive destinations into mass market honeypots, not least because of their inherited reputation as upscale places to be and be seen. The French Riviera is a good example of this phenomenon but few recall that in the 1950s, Benidorm, the icon of modern mass market tourism, was a place for famous artists but few other tourists

These historical factors are continuing to influence the evolution of the concept of tourism, hospitality and events, not least because when tomorrow dawns even today becomes history!

Economic factors

In this book I have been arguing that the traditional definitions of luxury are evolving and luxury is no longer always just about spending large amounts of money. However, in most cases luxury does involve spending on products, services and experiences, and at levels above the norm. To do that consumers need to have the ability and the willingness to pay premium prices. That is why economic factors are important to an understanding of the changing nature of luxury in tourism, hospitality and events.

The first factor relates to the level of economic development of a country and its living standards. The higher the level of economic development the more of its citizens should at least be able, if they wish, to purchase high end products and services. However, as we will see shortly it is not as simple as that. In terms of straightforward household income, Gallup in 2013 estimated that the median household income across the world was some US$9,733 with median per capita income at $2,920 (Gallup 2013). However, these figures masked a huge variation between countries, as we can see from Table 3.1 below

Table 3.1 : Worldwide median household income 2006-2012 (US Dollars)

Country	Median household Income	Median per-capita income
Norway	51,489	19,308
USA	43,585	15,480
China	6,180	1,786
Liberia	781	118

Source: Gallup, 2013, based on averaged data from 2006 to 2012

This data is a few years out of date but the picture is clear and the gap between the top and the bottom is unlikely to have changed much, although the figures for China would probably have grown rather faster than most countries.

Let us now focus on household wealth, which includes the wealth families have in terms of things such as stocks and shares and bank accounts. Here OECD data from 2016 shows big differences even between OECD members. Mean household wealth in Switzerland, reported in 2016 but possibly from older data, gives a figure of $120,265 compared to $16,937 for South Africa. The average for all OECD countries was $85,547 (OECD, 2016).

However, as all tourism students should know, it is disposable income which is important to the market for tourism, hospitality and events, because these sectors represent products and services that are not essential to our lives in the way that food and shelter are. To that extent all expenditure on leisure and travel in these sectors could be viewed as a luxury!

Disposable income is a complex matter and reflects a range of factors, from salary levels to family size, taxation policies to the cost of living. The OECD was reporting in 2016 mean household disposable income of $8,712 in South Africa compared to $35,952 in Switzerland. And we must remember that this data is only for OECD members and excludes the poorest countries.

The other dimension of economic development that affects the luxury market is how wealth is distributed throughout society. This, again, is the result of many factors from history and government policies, to corruption and ownership of raw materials, resources, and recently privatised former state enterprises. In some countries in Northern Europe, such as Scandinavia and the Netherlands, the wealth 'pyramid' is relatively flat while in emerging economies, such as Russia and China, we see a large gulf between those who are very rich and those who are poor. In the poorest countries of the world there is still wealth, but it is the hands of a tiny minority whose level of individual wealth will be extremely high. It is the 'mega rich' of such countries as these, Russia and China which have fuelled the ultra-luxury market in recent years.

In recent years there has been some criticism of some of the segments of the luxury market based on the source of their wealth, with allegations that it has been derived from corruption, tax avoidance and involvement in criminal activities. It is also linked to the rather 'snobbish' distinction between 'new money' and 'old money' and the idea of a class of *nouveau riche* consumers, in particular countries who, it is claimed, have wealth but no taste and simply want to show off their wealth to the world through ostentatious consumption. This may be a mixture of fact or envy, but I will leave you to decide.

One important consideration when looking at how the concept of luxury is changing, is how much economies are growing, because over time that should have an impact on the number of people able to buy premium priced products and services. So let us end this section by looking at national economic growth rates for 2015 as identified by The World Bank; Table 3.2 presents the annual growth rate of selected countries.

Table 3.2: Economic growth rates of selected countries in 2015 (in percentages)

Country	Growth rate of economy
Venezuela	-5.7
Brazil	-3.8
Greece	-0.2
Australia	+2.3
India	+7.6
China	+6.9

Source: The World Bank, 2016

We need to be careful when interpreting this data because the global economy is highly volatile and these rates can change significantly from year to year.

So far we have focused on the economic factors that affect the demand side, the consumer. However, the changing nature of luxury in tourism, hospitality and events is also partly due to economic factors within the supply side, most notably in terms of the cost of being a tourist in different destinations.

In recent years we have seen more and more tourists making long haul trips to so-called developing countries as the cost of air travel has fallen in real terms. The real growth in inbound tourism has been seen in poor countries where wages are so low that luxury hotels can charge rates that seem modest by European standards. This means that even middle class, middle income consumers can stay at hotels, eat in restaurants and buy souvenirs that would be priced out of their reach in their own country. This is a relatively new dimension to luxury in the international tourism market, where teachers and administrators can live like kings and queens, at least during their annual vacation.

It will be interesting to see what happens, for tourism usually helps a destination economy develop, so that costs and thus prices rise. This means that over time the gap between costs in the home country of the tourist and those in a destination will narrow so that they can only afford to buy luxury experiences if they are willing and able to pay significantly more. Experience suggests that to date, where this occurs, tourists simply move on to the next slightly poorer country where they can still afford true luxury at a bargain price. Surely, though, this process cannot go on for ever as at some point we must run out of poorer countries!

Demographic factors

I believe that, traditionally, the stereotype of a luxury consumer would be of a middle-aged or elderly white man, possibly with a younger glamorous wife. Let's say a Donald Trump type person, although this is clearly something of a cliché of course. However, I am suggesting that demographic change is taking place which is leading to much more diversity in the luxury segment.

First, in terms of age, we have seen the rise of a group of wealthy people who are millionaires before their first grey hair appears and may even have 'retired' before they reach middle age. This has been particularly true in the newer industries where youth is a positive advantage, because the young are better able to identify and exploit opportunities. This has been very evident in IT, the field of social media and the creative arts for example, exemplified by people like Mark Zuckerberg, co-founder of Facebook.

The rise of a younger group of high end consumers has really redefined luxury in some ways. They tend to eschew the 'bourgeois' tastes of the older generation and instead embrace a lifestyle with more emphasis on informality. They are also more interested in active rather than passive experiences, not least because they are young enough to have the energy to indulge in them. However, at the same time, they are likely to be time-poor compared to the older segment that may well be retired or semi-retired. This is fuelling the growth of short duration mini vacations where a lot is packed into a short time, with little room left over for conventional 'relaxation'.

Amongst the younger generation we seem to be seeing a growing polarisation between the rich and the very poor, as young people seem to have borne much of the brunt of the recent global economic crisis particularly in terms of unemployment and cuts in welfare spending. However, suggestions are being made that for both ends of the spectrum the notion of luxury is moving from material possessions to values and experiences.

In most countries, until recently, women tended to have children early in their adult life. If they worked, they usually gave up work while the child grew up. Money then became tighter and disposable income even tighter. However in so-called developed countries in recent years we have seen more women choosing to have careers and delaying child birth until they are in their 30s or even later. Child care provision has also allowed a larger number of women in higher paid jobs to continue to work after the birth of children. This means they and their partners have often made up double high-income households well into their forties and maybe even all the way to retirement. This has given them extra years of high disposable income before the birth of children and still a decent level of disposable income afterwards. This effect has been reinforced by the tendency of families to have fewer children, which also results in them having more disposable income to spend on tourism, hospitality and events. Interestingly, the 'One Child Policy' in China may well be one of the reasons why we have seen the growth of a luxury segment amongst the younger generation of upper class families in the cities of eastern China in recent years.

We also need to recognise that more and more couples in the more affluent countries are choosing not to have children, so they should not experience any drop in their disposable income during their working life.

I do not want to give the impression that women can only become luxury consumers as part of a couple, with a partner. A growing number of women are becoming rich in their own right through their own work, either as senior managers or as entrepreneurs or as artists of various kinds. At the same time we should not ignore the discrimination that women still experience in terms of employment and salary levels in most countries.

This raises the interesting question about supposed differences in how men and women differ as luxury consumers. The conventional wisdom is that women prefer shopping, spa pampering, and fashion while luxury male consumers like fast cars and boats, expensive liquor and belonging to exclusive clubs, while both genders enjoy travel and fine dining. Yet we are clearly seeing this view becoming less and less realistic as more women buy fast cars and more men indulge in fashion.

In many socio-economic classifications around the world, people who are better educated are supposed to get better jobs and thus be more likely to enter the luxury segment after a number of years. However, many rich and successful entrepreneurs appear to have had only limited education and a number of young millionaires are rich before they even reach the age to go to university.

It is clear that the populations of most countries are now more diverse and cosmopolitan than they were a generation ago. In such countries the luxury market has also become more diverse, although it often takes time for immigrants to reach the higher socio-economic levels because of the discrimination they may face in their new home country. But in many countries today a growing proportion of those in the luxury segment will come from ethnic minority communities, unless institutional racism makes that almost impossible. For these consumers their view of luxury may or may not be different to that of the indigenous population, based on their background and experiences.

Geographical factors

A number of times so far we have noted that one of the main reasons for the changing nature of the idea of luxury is the continuing evolution of the geography of wealth with the rising economic power of India and China, the oligarchs of Russia and oil-fuelled growth in the Gulf States and Kazakhstan. However, there are other interesting geographical factors at play in relation to luxury in tourism, hospitality and events.

Traditionally, luxury was often associated with places that were aspirational which usually meant a long way away and difficult to get to, which also meant visited by few tourists. That partly explains the luxury label often attached to islands, particularly those in the Indian Ocean, Pacific Ocean and the Caribbean.

However, today, with low cost air travel being readily available in many countries, inaccessibility is becoming rarer and rarer. Perhaps that is why the super-rich are showing such interest in space travel, where access is still very difficult and the price very high, meaning the numbers able to take part in such travel are minute at the moment.

At the same time, where you live is also a factor in the changing idea of luxury. Most luxury consumers in the travel market until recently resided in the Northern Hemishpere in cooler climates, by and large, so for them luxury was being in the sun, particularly in their winter. Now as countries such as India experience rapid economic wealth and develop a large luxury segment, their citizens will not be influenced in their destination choice by the search for sun. Instead in the hot and dry summer months they may seek out cool, and even rainy, places to vacation.

On the other hand not all luxury travel today is about travelling long distances or even internationally at all. Many countries have developed their own domestic luxury offers to tempt domestic as well as inbound international tourists. Indeed India's luxury tourism sector could survive very well on the basis of the domestic market with no need for international visitors.

In the past most luxury destinations were places that had unique existing attractions that were much admired by luxury travellers. This could encompass everything from a fantastic beach to amazing views, rich wildlife to stunning historic buildings, a great micro-climate to unique museums or art galleries. All of these attributes are rooted in the idea of place, reflecting the geographical and historical realities of the specific location. Over time they develop the infrastructure of luxury, such as high end hotels, upscale restaurants and expensive shops. However, in recent decades we have seen destinations developed that are totally at odds with the realities of the location. Dubai is an excellent example of this phenomenon, a desert city with golf courses, a city with temperatures regularly above 40°C which has a ski slope with real snow! And a place with bold new architecture that attracts visitors, but has no great views, very little wildlife and virtually no historic buildings. Furthermore these destinations have, from the beginning, been targeted at the luxury segment, and have been created in a few years rather than decades or centuries. And what Dubai has done yesterday and today, other places will try to do tomorrow but with no guarantee of success.

Social factors

In my mind, this means social trends in terms of what is popular or fashionable and what are the issues that are of concern to society.

Traditionally luxury in tourism, hospitality and events usually meant travelling long distances in great style, staying in high end resorts or villas fenced off from the outside world, often only mixing with local people when they served your drink or meals, and taking part in truly out-of-the-ordinary and very expensive activities. The aim was to indulge yourself with excesses of fine food and wine as part of a hedonistic experience. And the food and drink had to be the finest even if that meant transporting foie gras, caviar and champagne to remote

Indian Ocean islands or Pacific resorts. The whole experience was meant to be an escape from reality, almost a fairy story existence, usually summed up in the term 'dream vacation' and the idea that on vacation you did not have to think about anything but your own pleasure.

Yet evidence is emerging, I believe, that indicates that change is underway, at least amongst some segments of the luxury market. I am not suggesting that all luxury travellers have developed stronger social consciences and ethical approaches to vacationing, although some undoubtedly have. Instead I think that some things that would formerly have been seen as down-market have now become trendy and bestow status on consumers.

So, today's 'cool' luxury tourists, particularly the younger ones discussed earlier, may well be found today renting a luxury apartment from a local person in a less fashionable and less visited neighbourhood, through an organisation such as Airbnb. They do not need the hotel concierge, as they can arrange everything they want to do through their various mobile devices, providing wifi is available in the apartment. There are no staff looking after them but the owner is on hand to tell them the best local 'secret' places to go to discover the 'real' city or resort. The owner may even take them on an impromptu guided tour of the neighbourhood. They may eat out in everyday restaurants frequented by locals and indulge in 'street food' which is, ironically, becoming something of an obsession with high end tourists who could afford to use fine dining restaurants every day. Having eaten carefully to ensure they did not take in too many calories, they will go for a run just as they would if they were at home. I recognise that both of the above cases are rather stereotypical, bordering on caricatures. However, I believe that there is enough truth in them to show that change is underway.

As we will see in a later chapter about sustainability, there is also evidence that some luxury end tourists are trying to be ethical in their behaviour, whether that means trying to minimise damage to the environment or ensuring that the economic benefits of tourism reach the poorest in the community. The success of the tour operator Responsible Travel, clearly demonstrates that this segment is large enough to sustain a successful business.

Technological factors

In recent years technology has been transforming our lives in many areas so it is not surprising that it has had, and is continuing to have, an impact on the idea of luxury in tourism, events and hospitality. It is widely acknowledged that the Internet has revolutionised the way in which tourism and leisure products and services are purchased and consumed. However, the impact of the Internet has been increased dramatically through the use of hand-held devices. These have enabled consumers to not only purchase in advance online, wherever and whenever they want, but have also given them access to a wide variety of digital services during the journey and in destination. And they have allowed travellers to share their experiences in real time with people across the world. This sharing has had a real impact through social media sites and organisations such as TripAdvisor. If consumers sharing experiences use the word 'luxury' to describe a destination or airline product or hotel room, their views will, over time, influence the perceptions in the market as a whole.

These new communication technologies have given virtually all consumers access to more choice and information, which could in itself be seen as a luxury. Previously the luxury segment would have had more access to choice and information than other consumers through their use of paid professionals to arrange their itineraries. It could be argued that ICT has 'levelled the playing field' in the tourism market because now everyone, by and large, has access to the same choice and information through the Internet. Indeed, as noted earlier in the section on demographic factors it may positively have shifted the balance of power in favour of the younger generation of travellers for whom the use of a wide range of devices is almost second nature.

Technological innovation has also benefited all consumers through giving them greater convenience, through online check-in for example. With time at a premium, it seems these days that convenience, which means saving time on mundane tasks, could again be seen as 'luxury' in its own right. Of course, this move towards self-service, which we will explore in more detail in a later chapter is very appealing to industry as it tends to help reduce their costs.

Another area of change in relation to luxury is around how technology is creating opportunities to enhance the experience of consumers on vacation through Virtual Reality (VR) and Augmented Reality (AR). A few years ago VR was being put forward as a solution to sustainability challenges, with the idea that it could be used as a substitute for the actual trip; if you could have a virtual experience why bother visiting the real thing? As we know this did not happen but in the past year or two VR has come back into vogue in tourism and has been joined by AR. Now the focus is on enriching the travel experience of the consumer and providing opportunities for them to spend more money.

Developments in marketing

With the rise of the Internet, traditional marketing has lost some of its power in the relationship between consumers and suppliers, particularly in tourism, hospitality and events. I think it is fair to say that marketers are still struggling to come to terms with the implications of this change. However, it seems apparent that in their reactions to this new world marketers have done some things that have real implications for the concept of luxury in tourism, hospitality and events.

First, in an attempt to attract and retain aspirational customers they have latched on to the word 'luxury' because they know it is a term which has positive connotations to many consumers. In doing this perhaps they have debased the term to the point where it is rapidly becoming meaningless. I do not wish to be rude about any form of tourism and leisure, but is sleeping in a tent ever a 'luxurious' experience? Some tents may have more facilities than others of course, but luxurious? Marketers, realising that camping was not seen positively by many people, chose to stop talking about camping and instead talk about 'glamping' – glamorous camping. It is still a tent!

Second, the Internet has had another impact on the luxury sector through the rise of OTAs, or online travel agents. These have become incredibly popular in recent years and have captured a large share of the hotel booking market worldwide. People use such websites because of the choice, but mainly because they believe that is where they will find the best prices, the most attractive deals. Lluxury is not supposed to be about low prices but rather the quality of the product, yet because the OTAs sell hotel rooms at all levels of the market and deliver incredibly high numbers of bednights for hotels, even luxury brands cannot afford to ignore them. The result of this is that luxury is now being discounted and hotels being marketed on the basis of price. For example, on 1 December 2016, booking.com was offering discounted rooms at luxury hotels carrying brands such as Four Seasons, Dorchester, Intercontinental, Hyatt and Marriott. The prices were obviously still high but they were advertising reductions in price, sometimes of hundreds of pounds. If the price of luxury is now to be heavily discounted, using reduced price as a major attraction, because of the impact of the OTAs, we are certainly living through a time of change in the luxury market.

■ The concept of experiential marketing

Traditionally, since the dawn of modern mass market package tourism, it was a product-led sector where providers put products and services into the market and tried to persuade consumers to buy them. This was also true of hotels, restaurants and events, as all three areas experienced rapid growth from the mid-20th century. The expectation was that the consumer was a recipient rather than a participant in the service delivery process, passively accepting what they were given.

Throughout the 1980s and 1990s, the industry focused on standardising the offer and growing volume. Then, after Pine and Gilmore published *The Experience Economy: Work is Theatre, Every Business a Stage* in 1999, corporate thinking started to change. Now the emphasis seemed to move to talking about experiences rather than products and services, and the focus was on how the experience could be customised and personalised. This is challenging in a hotel with 600 rooms, an A380 with more than 500 seats in economy class alone, or a concert venue with many thousands of seats. Practice may not have matched rhetoric, but the idea of experiences appears to have become embedded in corporate thinking in tourism, hospitality and events. And as this has happened, the consumer has changed from being a passive receiver in the service to an active partner in the process. This has underpinned the concept of co-creation, which has become fashionable in recent years. In this way every experience is truly unique and should, in theory at least, be driven by the desires of the consumer rather than the convenience of the service deliverer.

3

What is really interesting is how all this relates to the idea of luxury. In the days before mass market tourism, when pretty well all international travellers were in the luxury category, we had both experiential marketing and co-creation in many ways. Itineraries were usually designed individually and all aspects of the experience were developed around the preferences of the individual traveller.

So what we are seeing today is an approach that was born in the early days of travel, largely forgotten in the transition to mass market tourism and leisure, and which is now back. However, industry is trying to persuade consumers that everyone can now enjoy personalised experiences, not just the luxury segment. In a later chapter we will explore these ideas in more detail.

Developments in consumer culture

Let us now move on to look at developments in consumer behaviour that are having an impact on the idea of luxury in tourism, hospitality and events.

First, across much of the world, tourists are becoming more and more experienced travellers and as a result their expectations are rising based on their experiences. This means that what was seen as luxury yesterday will be seen as the normal standard today and sub-standard tomorrow.

Second, traditionally luxury was about paying a high price for a top end product or service and perhaps as importantly, being seen to pay a high price by others because this said something about your status in society. We see this very much in the behaviour of tourists from emerging, or recently emerged, markets, such as China, Russia and India visiting Europe where the focus is on buying famous expensive brands and staying in hotels with famous reputations. It is about making statements that "I can afford this and I have the taste to appreciate it" and it is perhaps due to the fact that these markets are from counties where the opportunities for international travel have been limited until recent years. As these markets mature this behaviour pattern may well change; we are already seeing signs of this in the Chinese market.

However in the longer established international tourism markets we are seeing a different phenomenon, whereby status is gained by spending the least not the most. This is particularly true of airline seats and hotel beds on city breaks trips. Even people who could afford to fly business class and stay in a five star hotel may prefer to fly economy or even use budget airlines and may stay in mid-priced accommodation booked through Air BnB. However, in the destinations these people may still spend heavily, using the money saved on the utilitarian parts of the trip (the flight and the bed) to enjoy the hedonistic pleasures of fabulous restaurants, exclusive events, nightlife, expensive sight-seeing experiences and so on. In other words they are separating the destination experience from the functional requirements of the trip, and are deciding that the 'luxury' comes from what they do in the destination not how they get there or where they sleep.

Third, we may also be seeing the rise of another source of personal status in tourism which differentiates the traveller from other tourists, and that is the idea of the 'ethical traveller'. This means the tourist who goes out of their way to ensure local people, and particularly poor people, benefit directly from their spending while seeking to minimise the impact of their trip on the environment. They may take part in volunteering tourism where they pay money to take a vacation where they work on a project to benefit the local community or wildlife. They may even set up a local charity project to benefit the destination over a longer period of time. This can bring recognition and status in the home country of the traveller and distinguish them from the market as a whole; this in itself may be a new form of 'luxury' behaviour. Indeed it is somewhat reminiscent of the philanthropy of rich people seen for many years in countries such as the USA, where the luxury segment 'do good' as a way of giving back something to society. Perhaps the ethical tourist is similar, giving something back to destinations because they are able to and it makes them feel good about themselves.

■ The media

The media plays a huge role in communicating ideas and images of luxury although first we need to distinguish between the different kinds of media such as namely traditional or new, travel and non-travel, professionally produced or consumer generated content. The idea of luxury in tourism, hospitality and events is being increasingly influenced by four factors in relation to the media.

First, the news media is increasingly globalised thanks to satellite broadcasting and online content, so any portrayal of luxury in the home country of a television network will now reach a global rather than a national audience, thus increasing its impact dramatically in the mind of consumers

Second, as more and more people have enjoyed greater amounts of leisure time and growing levels of disposable income, we have seen an explosion of what we might term 'lifestyle media' in terms of television programmes, magazines and online content. This has been seen in every aspect of lifestyle from interior design to cooking, leisure activities to vacations. Magazines such as *Condé Nast Traveller*, for example, provide seductive images and text, with frequent use of the word 'luxury' which creates aspirations for tourists who may not always have seen themselves as 'luxury end' consumers. So these powerful lifestyle media are also influencing the concept of luxury in tourism, hospitality and events.

Third, the media in recent years appear to have become increasingly obsessed with the idea of celebrity, while the rise of so-called reality television shows have created a class of celebrities who are famous for being famous, though they may have no obvious talent as such. Nevertheless, many people now seem to aspire to emulate how these 'celebrities' live their lives, which extends to where and how they take their vacations. As celebrity and the idea of luxury have always gone hand in hand, if a celebrity makes it known in the media that they will vacation in a destination, its reputation is instantly enhanced and uplifted.

Fourth, and perhaps most important, we have the rise of social media which is affecting the idea of what constitutes luxury in two main ways. In the first instance, the real-time sharing of experiences by travellers on social media both promotes luxury and helps defines it for other users of social media. This may lead to differences in attitudes towards luxury between social media users and those who do not use social media. The next agent of change is the rise of the social media based 'influencers' in society, the travel bloggers who can attract huge numbers of followers until they become celebrities in their own right. Their endorsement of, or criticism of, places, organisations and services can have a great influence on their 'followers'. Companies and destinations have realised this and may now offer free vacations to these bloggers in the hope of receiving positive recommendations, just like they have done for travel writers for many years. However, the bloggers have more power than the travel writers because they reach mass audiences and people actively 'follow' them and interact with them rather than just reading what they say, passively. So what the bloggers say about luxury will have a big impact on how social media users perceive luxury!

Supply side change

The industry has also been evolving in a number of ways in recent years which have had an impact on the meaning of luxury.

First, the sheer growth in capacity of supply has intensified competition but has also made the idea of luxury more complex. Given much of this growth in supply has taken place outside the so-called developed world, in countries with lower labour costs, it has meant that these new countries can offer higher levels of personal service and staff to guest ratios that are more in keeping with the ideas of luxury on which Europe built its original reputation for luxury in the hotel sector

Second, in addition to the growth in the number of suppliers we have also seen an increase in the size of companies as acquisitions have created mega tour operators such as the TUI Group and new openings, franchises and management contracting have meant hotel chains have been able to add more and more hotels to their portfolios over just a few years. The challenge of this at the top end is how can large corporations and hotels with hundreds of rooms and airliners with more than five hundred seats per plane offer customers the personalised, customised 'experiences' they want and which the companies appear to promise at the high end. This challenge may explain why those seeking to operate at the luxury end can receive such negative customer feedback on consumer-generated media sites. Maybe they are promising – because of growing competition – more than can actually be delivered and thus disappointing customers who have been led to have unrealistic expectations.

Third, we have the phenomenon of 'upgrade luxury'. Until a decade or two ago luxury products were for those who could afford luxury prices. However, the growth then was in the mass market and companies found themselves increasingly competing on price rather than quality. Then two things occurred which changed this situation – upselling and loyalty programmes. Hotels, keen to grow revenue, started offering more upgrade deals so you could pay a few dollars more to enjoy a better room. This way a consumer could enjoy a high quality room for much less than the rack rate. At the same time airlines introduced loyalty programmes which gave frequent travellers the opportunity to use their loyalty points or 'miles' to upgrade an economy ticket to business or even first. Some airlines now even have online auctions for these seats or allow passengers to upgrade for a relatively low cost to fill empty capacity in the premium price cabins. This can lead to irritation on the part of those who paid full price for a top end hotel room or a seat in first class on the airliner. This is undoubtedly making high end air travel, for example, much less exclusive than it was previously. In terms of the democratisation this is a great development, but in the long term it may damage the whole ethos of luxury in tourism, hospitality and events.

Fourth, as noted earlier we have seen a growth of non-professionals entering the hospitality market, most notably through the rise of Airbnb whereby 'amateurs' open part of their home or a second home to tourists. In 2015-16 several five star hotels were complaining that they were losing business as people chose to stay in luxury apartments with private owners being marketed through Airbnb! This is changing the idea of luxury, in that luxury accommodation does not always now mean accommodation run by professionals. Furthermore, the idea that Airbnb hosts give their guests a chance to "experience the place as locals do" and offer a truly personalised service, could be seen as a 'luxury' market product even when it is a medium price rooftop apartment in the suburbs of a city.

Finally, in the destinations sector we are seeing more and more mass market destinations stating that they want to re-position to attract 'better quality tourists' which translates usually as higher spenders. This means these places will be hoping to compete with established destinations that have a reputation for luxury, thus adding to competition in the market.

3

Changes in the concept of luxury in other sectors

It is important for us not to believe that tourism, hospitality and events exists in a bubble. In many ways what is happening in our sector is mirroring developments in the concept of luxury in other sectors of the economy.

In fashion, for instance, consumers are seeing status not just in buying expensive garments but also in buying garments that have a back story around who made them, where they were made, who grew the raw material and so on. This has great similarities with what has happened in fine dining, with its focus on the back story relating to the ingredients. Both are examples of the idea of authenticity which has become such an important part of how products and experiences are communicated to markets today. There is also a growing interest in fashion and much retailing, around the issue of ethical consumption and sustainability. This very much mirrors what has been happening in tourism in recent years.

At the same time we have been seeing the rise of what might be termed 'fusion luxury', where companies with a reputation in luxury move into other sectors to capitalise on their brand reputation. A great example of this phenomenon is the rise of fashion hotels, where fashion brands develop their own hotels such as Karl Lagerfeld's Odyssey in Monaco and the Palazzo Versace in Dubai. Brands such as Lacroix and Bulgari have also developed luxury hotels in recent years. This is an interesting phenomenon which is blurring the lines between different sectors and between the meaning of luxury in these different sectors.

Terrorism

I contend that the growing global threat from terrorism may well be something of a 'game-changer' in respect of luxury in tourism, hospitality and events. We have seen, sadly, in recent years that terrorists have increasingly targeted tourists and the infrastructure that facilitates travel and leisure. Until recently tourists usually felt themselves to be in a safe environment, particularly once their flight to their

vacation paradise landed. Not now. It seems to be much riskier to be in a destination, in a hotel, bar or restaurant these days in many parts of the world. I believe
that this will affect the luxury concept, in that safety and security may become a
new way of defining luxury. The luxury destinations of the future may be those
where consumers perceive themselves to be safest. This may mean particular
countries or remote rural areas rather than busy city centres, beaches or mega-
events. Perhaps events such as the atrocity committed on the Promenade des
Anglais in Nice in July 2016 will affect the reputation of Nice as an aspirational
high end resort for a long time to come.

At the same time the growth of global terrorism may also mean hotels, in particular, being forced by events to become more like airports in terms of security to
ensure the safety of their guests. This may affect the idea of a 'luxury' experience
by imposing certain security controls on guests that will run counter to the idea
of a luxury vacation being about relaxation and escaping from the everyday cares
of life. Terrorism is bringing these cares to the doorsteps of vacation hotels and
bars and the industry is having to respond, if only to maintain its duty of care to
its guests.

The inter-relationships between these factors

This chapter has identified and discussed a number of factors that are changing
the meaning of luxury in tourism, hospitality and events. However, it is important
to recognise that these factors do not operate in isolation. Many of them interact
with each other in a variety of ways. Sometimes they combine to push change in
a single direction while at other times they may almost cancel each other out as
they drive change in opposite directions. At times two factors will interact while
at others many of the factors may be linked together. Let us just look at a few
examples to illustrate this point.

Demographically, across the world we are seeing the growth of a generation
of young travellers who have the confidence with technology that allows them to
purchase and consume tourism products and experiences in ways that are totally
different to the older generation. They may not be rich but they have access to
knowledge and experiences that are denied to older generations by their lack of
confidence using new communication technologies. Here knowledge is the new
concept of luxury in that it creates an element of exclusivity to experiences but
it is not based on wealth. Industry marketers are recognising this through their
attempts to get the 'influencers of consumer behaviour' to endorse their products.
Yet these influencers today are more likely to be young bloggers than elderly travel
journalists or guide book writers. This phenomenon is creating a new meaning of
luxury travel and luxury traveller.

Economic factors and geography are also clearly inter-related in that economic development in a particular country generally increases the number of luxury consumers in the national market. However this will also be dependent on how wealth is distributed within a society. Rapid changes in economic development in countries such as India and China have, in recent years, transformed what we might term the 'geography of luxury demand'. However there is an interesting paradox in terms of economic development, for as economies grow and the number of domestic luxury travellers rises, labour costs rise too. This in turn makes it difficult for a labour intensive industry such as hospitality to continue to have the staff to guest ratios to make it an attractive luxury travel destination.

There is obvious link too between consumer culture change and changes in the supply side, although this is not always one way. There is no doubt that growing consumer concerns around issues such as sustainability, health and the desire for authenticity is affecting what industry offers. Industry also influences consumers and sometimes either pre-empts changes in consumer culture or even leads changes in it. I would argue, for instance, that many tour operators, including at the luxury end, have taken the lead on sustainability and then tried to take their consumers with them. However, the link between consumers and industry is becoming more complicated than this, for consumers are now becoming part of the industry with the rise of couch-surfing, Airbnb and so on. Some areas of tourism, hospitality and events have low barriers to entry and technological innovation is further lowering those boundaries. This is affecting the luxury concept perhaps more than other areas of the market.

As a final example of the inter-relationship of factors let us look at the rise of the concept of experiential marketing. This has been driven partly by history and changes in consumer culture in particular countries where international travel has been an established activity for many years. Here the most affluent, and most frequent travellers are apparently becoming bored with the standardised products and services offered by the mainstream industry. There is a desire for personalisation and customisation at a time when across all sectors of the economy mass production and standardisation appears to be the norm. Experiential marketing endeavours to suggest that everyone seeks and can enjoy a personalised experience that is not dependent on how much they earn. For the industry, experiences seem an ideal way of increasing yield because by giving personalisation they bestow status on the consumer and reinforce the idea of exclusivity which has traditionally been at the heart of the concept of luxury. Interestingly many 'experiences' are built around social concerns such as health or the desire for authenticity.

Hopefully these few examples illustrate that none of the factors identified in Figure 3.1 exist in isolation and that how the luxury concept evolves will be dependent on how they all interact.

Conclusions

Well, this has been a broad chapter looking at how a range of individually complex factors are changing the meaning of luxury in tourism, hospitality and events, so what conclusions can be drawn, apart from it being incredibly complex! I believe that there are two.

First, I think it is clear that the meaning of luxury is changing so rapidly at the moment because we have a number of powerful factors at play. And their influence is being magnified because of the inter-relationships between them and the fact that often one is reinforcing another.

Second, the impact of these factors appears to be challenging traditional ideas of luxury and generating new meanings in luxury, whether that be time availability, authenticity, or safety and security. In some ways the new meanings of luxury can seem counter-intuitive, such as the idea that one definition of 'luxury' may be paying less than anyone else for a flight so you have either the maximum to spend on leisure and pleasure when you reach the destination and/or enough money to allow you to make more trips. Perhaps the key word in the last sentence was '*meanings*' rather than 'meaning' for it is my contention that we are moving from a simpler concept of luxury based on a few key words to a more fragmented set of concepts of luxury with distinctive sets of key words!

Five of the issues discussed in this chapter are so important, in my opinion, that each will be the subject of a separate chapter later in the book

---

Conclusions to Part 1

So what have we learned from the first three chapters overall?

☐ First, there is no commonly agreed definition of what luxury means, but much of our understanding of the term and even the 'language of luxury' has its roots in history, particularly in Europe.

☐ Second, it is clear that luxury is a highly subjective concept and that people view it differently based on their personality, experiences and personal circumstances.

☐ Third, the whole idea of what constitutes luxury is going through a period of rapid change due to a range of factors, including everything from economic development to the role of the media, technological innovation to geographical factors. We also saw that the impact of these various factors is being magnified because many are inter-related and are reinforcing each other.

In Part 2 we will approach luxury from the demand side, looking both at markets and the behaviour of individual consumers.

Part 2: The Demand Side of Luxury

We are now going to examine the demand side of luxury both in terms of markets and the behaviour patterns of individual consumers in tourism, hospitality and events.

In Chapter 4 we will look at what is termed the luxury market and try to come up with an answer to the question: "How large is this market worldwide?" We will also explore the geographical differences in luxury demand and will look at some interesting perspectives on the demographics of luxury.

Chapter 5 focuses on the behaviour of individual consumers in relation to luxury. The approach is a conventional one, starting with a discussion of motivators and determinants and seeing how these combine in the decision-making process. An attempt will then be made to produce a typology or typologies of luxury consumers and we will try to see how traditional approaches to market segmentation work in relation to luxury consumers.

4 The Luxury Market in Tourism, Hospitality and Events

Introduction

This is a fascinating chapter to try to write because we are about to discuss the size and characteristics of a market for which there is no agreed definition! Let us spend a few moments considering what this statement actually means in reality.

In general, there are no common specifications for what constitutes a luxury hotel except outdated systems of stars that vary between countries in terms of the criteria. Most stop at five stars but we have seen hotels claiming to be six or even seven star! This concept is now meaningless.

On an airline many see business class as a clearly defined luxury market but if the aircraft also has a first class cabin, is business class really still luxury?

Michelin star dining is often taken as a touchstone for luxury eating, but many one star restaurants now offer more modestly priced menus. Furthermore, while Michelin starred restaurants may serve say 60 twice a day, perhaps 300 days a year making 36,000 diners a year, a pop up restaurant in someone's apartment may have service for only five days, a capacity of ten per service, and thus only 50 people will ever enjoy the experience.

Some would say luxury simply means a higher price. However, this concept of price is not a simple one in these industries. There may be no direct price charged for the use of some products such as a beautiful beach. Price paid usually involves a journey and time spent at a destination, so is a budget airline flight to Nice to stay in a five star hotel a luxury trip? In a city centre full of luxury hotels, a night in a five star hotel may cost less than a homestay in the same city or an ecolodge with no air-conditioning in a nearby national park. And of course, because of differences in levels of economic development and labour costs, a five star hotel in Cambodia may cost less than a two star hotel in France.

And this is a market most people aspire to be seen as part of, because it carries positive connotations, so it is in the interests of industry to use the term loosely and broadly. People want to be seen as luxury travellers and will pay more for the privilege. Instead of particular activities being seen as luxury activities, the industry has tried to suggest that a luxury level product is available in every area of tourism, hospitality and events. Hence the concept of 'glamping' or glamorous camping with its 'luxurious tents' which despite their 'luxury' are still tents!

I do not want to overplay this point about how can we measure a market that is based on such subjective definitions and interpretations, but I think it is worth bearing in mind when reading the data in this chapter.

4

The market for luxury in general

In 2015, EuroMonitor International produced a report for ILTM which contained some fascinating insights on the development of the global market for luxury goods. According to this report the luxury goods market worldwide grew from just over $250 billion dollars in 2010 to some $317 billion in 2015 (EuroMonitor International, 2015) despite global challenges, including political instability, terrorist threats, and ongoing economic issues. Furthermore they went on to predict that spending would continue to rise steadily to some $370 billion by 2020.

However, as if to reinforce the point made earlier about the lack of clear definitions of luxury, a report by Bain and Company in 2014 suggested that the global luxury market in 2014 was worth some $850 billion, which they said represented a 7% rise compared to 2013. It went on to suggest that this growth had been particularly driven by an increase in spending on luxury cars and hospitality. However, they suggested that accessories and apparel remained the major parts of the luxury good market (Bains and Company, 2014).

According to EuroMonitor International, in 2015 Western Europe remained the major market, but they predicted that by 2020 Asia-Pacific would be neck and neck with Western Europe, given its faster growth rate. Interestingly, they believed that Latin America would see the greatest growth of any region in the luxury goods market between 2015 and 2020. Between 2014 and 2015 rapid growth was seen in the luxury goods markets in India, Malaysia Indonesia and Thailand, while reductions in market size were seen in Ukraine, Russia and Hong Kong, and even China achieved only a 1% rise (EuroMonitor International, 2015)

Luxury travel demand

Measuring and commenting on the volume and characteristics of the luxury travel market is no easier than analysing the luxury good market. If anything, it is even more complicated by the fact that there are fewer mega-brands in travel, and sales do not tend to be through physical high street retail units.

The conventional wisdom is that luxury markets are affected by economic recession, although there is a counter view that the rich are less affected by recession than the poor or even the middle classes. As far as travel is concerned there appears little clear empirical evidence that the luxury travel market was seriously affected by the recession which began in 2008.

However, a paper delivered to the 2010 International Luxury Travel Market (ILTM) Leaders Forum in Cannes had some interesting observations on the relationship between luxury travel and recession. It stated, "During the recession in 2008-09, the idea of luxury was seen as taboo. High-end consumers began developing a 'deals' mentality, and they didn't want to be perceived as flaunting their wealth and extravagance. The word 'luxury' became a diluted, meaningless, commodity that needed to be re-defined. In the course of recovery in 2010, travel companies have been faced with more savvy consumers – many of whom have questioned if the rate they had been paying for high-end travel was really worth it". (ILTM, 2010)

Some other commentators have also suggested that the recession had a significant impact on the luxury travel market. A report by Jeri Clausing on *Travel Weekly* online stated of luxury travel that: "It fell the hardest but also bounced back the fastest, and as the world's most affluent consumers continue to gain confidence in the global economy, industry observers see nothing but increasingly good times ahead for the luxury travel market." (www.travelweekly.com, 2013)

Today, while the world continues to experience economic uncertainty, most industry commentators remain optimistic about the prospects for market growth, despite concerns about reduced demand from Russia and the possibility of dark clouds gathering in the market in China.

A 2015 report by Mimi Knet in www.travelmarketreport stated that, "In a new report from Zicasso, nearly 90% of specialist travel agents … said the number of luxury travellers has grown over the past two years" (www.travelmarketreport.com, 2015). The source went on to say it had conducted its own survey and found the same results.

Clearly the luxury travel market is made up of two types of consumer: namely the rich who are regular consumers in this market, and the less affluent who make 'once-in-a- lifetime' luxury purchases to celebrate special occasions in their lives. However, it is the former group who are the bedrock of the luxury travel market. The popular term for these people today is 'high net worth individuals', or HNWIs! EuroMonitor International estimated that in 2014 there were some 33 million such individuals across the world. The distribution of the majority of these individuals is illustrated in Table 4.1

Table 4.1: The geographical distribution of high net worth individuals (HNWIs), 2014

Country	Number of HNWIs in the national population	Proportion of national population represented by HNWIs
USA	16,000,000	7%
Japan	2,300,000	2%
France	2,200,000	4%
Uk	2,000,000	4%
Germany	1,800,000	4%
Italy	1,400,000	3%
Canada	1,100,000	3%
China	1,000,000	0.1%
Australia	900,000	2%
Switzerland	600,000	9%

Source: EuroMonitor International, 2015

The most striking figures in this table are perhaps:

■ The USA, with 16 million HNWIs has seven times more of them than any other country. Yet it is a country with a relatively low propensity to participate in outbound travel, so its impact on the luxury travel market may be less than expected, and less than on the market for luxury cars or art, for example.

■ In China, which we read so much about in terms of the luxury market, less than one person in a thousand is a HNWI. This makes us realise that this market has the potential to grow enormously in the future. If the proportion of HNWIs simply rose to the level of Japan, China would have well over 20 million of them, far more than the USA

■ One in eleven citizens in Switzerland is a HNWI. This makes it a prime market for the luxury travel sector despite the small size of the population.

■ The absence of India given its economic growth and the size of its population

The position in the global tourist market as a whole appears to be a picture of slow but steady growth in numbers, and consumers seeking to spend less on each trip. Travel has moved from being seen as a 'luxury' to a necessity by most citizens in so-called developed countries but for the luxury segment it always has been!

In its 2015 report for ILTM, EuroMonitor International noted an interesting fact that despite their pace of economic development, developing countries are not yet generating the volumes of outbound travel one might expect. It identified

Mexico, Indonesia, Nigeria and Turkey as such countries, suggesting this was a result of "incomes remaining too low for many citizens to travel" (EuroMonitor International, 2015) However, even in such countries, and in the poorest ones too, there is always a segment of luxury travellers who are usually politicians, civil servants or leading industrialists. Even the poorest country will have luxury travellers.

The geography of demand

Let us explore the geography of demand in terms of both source markets and destinations, although reliable hard data is in short supply.

The traditional geography of luxury travel demand was originally concentrated in Western Europe, based on a combination of aristocratic wealth and later wealth earned and inherited thanks to industry and commerce. The latter in particular also fuelled the rise of the luxury travel segment in the USA from the late 19th century. This geography began to decline as the end of European colonialism led to a reduction in the economic power of Europe and created opportunities for the development of a wealthy industrial capitalist class in the former colonies.

In the past twenty years or so the process of globalisation and political change has altered the geography of luxury travel further. Low cost manufacturing in Asia, with the products being exported to the rest of the world, has driven impressive economic growth rates in these countries, which has in turn provided opportunities for people from less affluent classes to become rich through commerce. At the same time, the fall of communism, particularly in Russia, created opportunities for individuals to become fabulously rich 'oligarchs'. These so-called 'new Russians' have become a globally recognised stereotype in the luxury travel market.

In both markets, and in others which have seen a recent growth in the number of 'super-rich', the phenomenon has led to a rise in luxury travel which has also led directly to an increase in the purchase of luxury second homes in other countries. London provides an excellent illustration of this trend.

No discussion of the global outbound luxury travel market would be complete without mention of the Gulf States, where oil wealth has also stimulated both outbound luxury travel and international property acquisition.

However, the outbound luxury travel market varies dramatically between countries and regions of the world. In 2015, the report by EuroMonitor International, referred to above, made the following observations about the outbound market in China:

- While global outbound tourists spend on average 24% of their in-destination budget on accommodation, the figure for the Chinese market is only 10%!

- The average global tourist spends a little over 20% of their in-destination budget on shopping, compared to around a third in the Chinese market.

- Nearly 30% of Chinese in-destination spending is on things other than lodging – food, shopping, travel in the destination and activities – twice the global average. A significant proportion of this spend is on gambling

- Chinese tourists spend less on food than the global average.

Source: EuroMonitor International, 2015

While this data relates to the Chinese outbound market as a whole, there is no reason to believe that these points are not also accurate in relation to the luxury segment. By contrast the luxury travel 'tradition' in Western Europe and North America accords a higher priority to top end hotels and fine dining.

So far we have focused on outbound travel, but of course top end travellers also indulge in domestic tourism. However, in countries where status is a particularly strong motivator of the luxury traveller, domestic travel may earn far less kudos than an ostentatious international trip. This is probably a stronger phenomenon in recently developed countries, where travelling internationally is a sign that you have 'arrived' as part of the international elite.

In Western Europe, domestic travel can be as high status as an international trip. A weekend 'gastronomy' trip to eat in a three star Michelin restaurant in Paris or a stay in an Italian castle or play on a world famous golf course in Scotland, certainly represent luxury travel domestic tourism products for the French, Italian and UK residents respectively. However given the traditional domination of the world travel market by Europe, each of these experiences is also well established and a luxury vacation opportunity for inbound international luxury tourists.

However, in parts of Western Europe, wealthy tourists do not always seek ostentatious displays of wealth even in domestic travel. I remember that when I lived in Switzerland, people who by any global definition were rich, would still use a bus or a train to get to their preferred ski destination for a weekend break. And in Scandinavia even those who are HNWIs may choose to spend large parts of their vacations relaxing with family in a relatively simple country cottage that they own. And finally, we do need to note that even in those countries where travelling abroad is seen as the true definition of luxury travel, there are domestic trips that will be seen as luxurious, such as to spas in China.

■ Destinations

Now let us turn our attention to where the luxury travellers choose to visit. Again data on this is not easy to find and we are left making some general observations.

First, I would strongly suggest, despite the paucity of hard evidence, that perhaps the most favoured destinations for luxury travellers are the major cities of the world. High on any such list would be London, Paris, New York, Hong Kong, and Geneva. The appeal of such places for high end travellers is easy to understand. They are where most luxury hotels and fine dining restaurants are to be found, together with the greatest range of shopping and the best choice of designer brands. Furthermore, they are the most likely destinations to be serviced by airlines offering business class and first class flights.

For much the same reasons as they travel to such cities, many luxury travellers will also choose to live, at least for part of each year, in such places. Indeed for the richest people, the dividing line between living and visiting is a very blurred one. They may have several homes which they move between, places where in truth they are neither resident or tourist.

In terms of luxury travel destinations this may be a good time to discuss seasonality and luxury. In the days when only a minority travelled in Europe, and by definition every leisure traveller was a luxury traveller, there were clearly established seasons for the rich to visit particular places. Spa resorts such as Baden-Baden, Bath or Vichy had their 'seasons', while the aristocracy visited the French Riviera in winter to escape the winter at home, and in the colonies the high end colonial administrators in India left the hot plains for the cooler hill stations at the warmest times of year.

The same seasonality is still seen today albeit but with subtle differences. While the French Riviera has become a more mass market destination than a hundred years ago it still attracts its share of high end tourists. But now they come in the summer, and if they are looking for 'winter sun' these travellers are more likely to be found in the Caribbean. Or they will be enjoying winter sports and après-ski in the fashionable resorts of the Alps or North America.

Another aspect of the relationship between luxury travel – indeed any travel and seasonality – relates to the destinations where world famous events take place at particular times of the year. The luxury travel dimension comes from the nature of the events themselves, with high end travellers being attracted to those events based on activities which are pitched at an affluent clientele, whether that be polo or opera.

Finally, though, there is one type of geographical feature that seems to be over-represented in any list of luxury destinations and that is islands. For many the dream luxury destination is the 'desert' island bathed in sunshine, lapped by blue seas and fringed by golden sand. And importantly, empty of people, apart from the tourist and their family. For the richest tourists this can be a reality rather than just a dream. But it seems that islands themselves hold an appeal for luxury travellers, reinforced by the fact that their geographical isolation often makes them expensive to travel to and stay on. This statement is equally true of islands from the Caribbean, to the Seychelles, to the resort islands of Australia. However, it is equally true of the Isles of Scilly off the coast of Cornwall in the UK, where a 10 minute return flight costs over £100 and accommodation is in short supply and expensive.

The demographics of demand

Yet again, here we are struggling to find empirical data but it is an important subject that needs to be addressed in such a book, so here goes.

One would expect that most luxury travellers would be middle aged to older people, as these are likely to be the ones who have created successful businesses or risen to the higher ends of the career ladder. And you would be right, to a large extent, in many parts of the world. Their dominance of the luxury market should also be reinforced by the fact that once they retire they will have time as well as money, and for many this is the case.

However, in some parts of the world this picture is becoming a little more complicated in several ways. First, we have a growing number of young entrepreneurs, particularly in the field of ICT, who may be rich while still in their teens or certainly their early twenties. They may have huge amounts of disposable income, if not always the time to enjoy it. Although technically luxury travellers, this group seems often to be rejecting the trappings of luxury travel beloved of older generations. They may dress down rather than dress up to travel, and stay in simple accommodation rather than luxury hotels. It will be interesting to see if their behaviour changes as they become older, particularly as some of them should be able to retire before they are thirty years old!

We are also witnessing an interesting phenomenon, particularly in certain Asian countries, notably China. Here parents have worked hard to become affluent and are able to give their children a much more privileged upbringing than they themselves had. Part of this often includes giving the child the opportunity to travel abroad. This experience broadens the outlook of the child and makes them, probably, more confident to travel than their parents. The parent subsidises the continuing travels of their child, which may be within the family or with friends or a tour group or an educational group. This phenomenon of the young luxury traveller is also a feature of the Gulf States and again may sometimes be linked to overseas study in the case of young men.

At the same time, young people in the Anglo-Saxon speaking world are able to indulge in a different form of luxury travel, the gap year, where the luxury is not about money. Here, the luxury is time and having the opportunity for perhaps the only time in your life to travel for months. Traditionally this has become something that middle and higher income students do between high school and university, or between graduation and employment. In some countries it has taken on the role of a rite of passage. In recent years, in the UK and North America, for example, we have seen a new type of gap year travel emerging amongst middle age people who take a career break so that they can travel. Unlike young persons' gap years, which are about travelling as an individual or group, the gap years of those of mature years are usually about travelling in a couple.

There is nothing significant to be said about gender and luxury travel but there certainly is about education. It often appears that highly educated people are heavily represented in the luxury travel market, but that may be because either their education gets them higher paid employment, or because those from more affluent families are the ones most likely to be able to pursue their education to a high level.

Let us now look at the market from another point of view, namely by sector and the nature of the luxury market in each sector. In Chapter 6 we will look at the following from the supply side point of view, but here we are looking at them in terms of demand side characteristics.

Tour operators and travel agencies

One might imagine that in a world where we talk disparagingly about mass market tourists and make distinctions between travellers and tourists, that the luxury market would be concerned with those who see themselves definitely as travellers rather than tourists. This might imply a focus on independent travel, unpackaged and wholly personalised to meet the desires of the individual consumer. One might think, therefore, that there would be no place in such a market for tour operators and travel agents, two types of organisations that have been at the very heart of the rise of mass tourism over the past fifty years. But if you thought this you would be wrong.

Alongside the 'mainstream' mass market operators and agents there are parallel organisations designing personalised experiences for luxury travellers or just providing more exclusive and expensive package holidays.

Luxury travellers may be experienced travellers, but that does not mean they are so confident that they want to always undertake independent travel, organised by themselves. Indeed they may feel their time is so valuable that they simply want to have someone else make all the arrangements for them rather than spending countless hours researching and booking online.

Specialist travel agents are particularly sought out when people not used to luxury travel make 'once-in-a-lifetime' purchases, such as organising a wedding or a world cruise to celebrate a fiftieth wedding anniversary.

One would assume that the main reason why luxury travellers use specialist operators and agents would be less about trying to get the best price and more about minimising the risk of disappointment and guaranteeing the quality of the vacation experience.

Transport

4

In the airline sector, in the early days of commercial aviation, all travel was at the luxury end because aircraft were small and running costs high, hence fares were at the top end. However, this all changed with the democratisation of air travel and the economies of scale achieved by the introduction of 'jumbo jets'.

Concorde, a truly luxury airliner is terms of both time and price, was a commercial failure, perhaps indicating that the era of luxury air travel was over for ever. Yet some airlines have re-introduced their first class cabins, particularly if they serve routes to those parts of Asia and the Gulf States where there are mega-rich travellers able to afford these levels of fare.

Luxury is a relative term in civil aviation. If you are cramped in a tiny economy seat, premium economy may feel like luxury. The regular business class traveller will enviously eye the first class cabin while those in economy class look with equal envy at the business class cabin dwellers!

The numbers tell their own story if one considers exclusivity to be a measure of luxury. According to the website SeatGuru, in a four class configured Cathay Pacific Boeing 777-300 in November 2016 there would be just six seats in first class, 53 in business, 34 in premium economy and 182 in economy. Economy people are supposed to aspire to premium economy and business class passengers to first class, hence both have the smallest number of seats. In the same month SeatGuru reported that a three class configured Emirates A380 would have 14 first class self-contained cabins, plus 76 business class seats and 399 seats in economy class.

Many passengers in business class are business people, not paying their own fares, whose contracts may even make business class travel part of their package of terms and conditions of employment.

However, the luxury of business class and even first class is not just open to those on high incomes or those whose employment contracts give them business class travel as part of their jobs. Airline frequent flyer programmes give regular air travellers the chance to collect miles or points that they can use to buy business class or first class air tickets or upgrade an economy ticket to business class or even first class. This can be a source of irritation to those passengers who have paid the full scheduled fare for their tickets in business or first class.

The ultimate in luxury air travel has always been the private jet, but these days we are also seeing a growth in the private aircraft charter market, where people charter an aircraft for a particular journey. This can sometimes work out less expensive than buying several business class fares for a business trip. In November 2016 Stratajet, a UK charter company was quoting £100,000 for a fourteen seat aircraft to fly a return from London to Miami, which works out at approximately £7,140 per seat if they were all used. British Airways business class at the same time for this journey was quoted from £7,700 to in excess of £8000. And with the private charter the travellers can choose when they fly and where they fly from!

Interestingly, we are also seeing the rise of private luxury air tours where specially converted jets are being used to take groups of tourists on itineraries where the aircraft is the means of transport and the tourists do not have to rely on scheduled flights.

Of course there are luxury markets in all forms of transport, with most rail systems having at least two classes with one having a higher price and elevated level of service. Likewise in road transport, one can take a bus or coach for a trip or hire a taxi or even a chauffeur driven limousine.

However, in recent years we have seen the rise in the tourism market of the luxury train, not so much as a form of transport but more as a combination of a luxury hotel and almost a destination in its own right! We see these trains on all continents now, with examples such as the *Belmond Royal Scotsman* (UK), *Rovos Rail*, *Pride of Africa*, *Eastern and Oriental Express* (south-east asia) and the *Rocky Mountaineer* (Canada).

Hospitality

Discussing hospitality is always difficult as the sector is so diverse, but if one defines luxury in terms of high price, ambiance and outstanding service quality there are many similarities across the various sectors that comprise hospitality, including:

■ The traditional luxury hotels of European resorts where the walls could tell stories of many years of use and the service is formal and highly attentive. These hotels seem particularly attractive to travellers from the countries where large-scale wealth, generated by one's own efforts, is a relatively recent phenomenon, such as China, India, and Russia.

- The modern luxury hotels of Asian cities where low labour costs ensure a high staff to guest ratio and those staying can enjoy the widest possible range of high quality facilities.

- The Michelin starred fine dining restaurants where diners enjoy exquisite cuisine in awed silence, in a dining room designed to be memorable and provide a suitable backdrop to the meal experience.

The market for all of these tends to comprise of two elements, namely:

- Those for whom such hotels and restaurants are a normal part of their life, people of wealth, experienced consumers of such luxury offers.

- Those for whom using such hotels or restaurants are one-off special occasions or even 'once-in-a-lifetime' experiences.

Interestingly the expectations of both groups are very different and this has a direct influence on their subsequent level of satisfaction

However, luxury is also said to be about the concept of exclusivity and uniqueness which implies rarity, and this may not just be about high prices and unusually high levels of personal service in the context of hospitality. It may also be seen in terms of:

- Hotels or restaurants which are located in exceptional locations whether that be a cultural site or a beautiful beach or a natural wonder such as a waterfall and where there are no other accommodation units in the same location.

- Hotels which are exclusive because they are largely inaccessible so perhaps they can only be visited after a long trek.

- 'Pop-up' restaurants that are exclusive because they have only a few covers and may last for only one or two nights. These types of eating places have become increasingly popular in recent years.

- Private homestays where the tourist stays as the guest of a family and in doing so gets to experience a different side of the destination that that normally seen by a visitor. Such accommodation has become very popular in recent years particularly through the rise of Airbnb. Such accommodation is particularly attractive for those who wish to be seen as 'travellers' rather than tourists and want to feel they have gained insights about the destination not normally experienced by visitors

- Hotels with designs which are unique or certainly very different to the norm, whether it be an underwater chamber in Sweden, an igloo hotel in Switzerland, or a converted aeroplane fuselage in Costa Rica. The desire of some tourists for out-of-the-ordinary accommodation has grown to the point where there are now guide books and websites specifically to make tourists aware of unusual types of accommodation

In most or all of the above cases, the price may not be high and there may be little or no high level personal service. It is the fact that the experience is not mainstream and may even be unique that appears to be the main attraction for consumers. This may point to a certain boredom with the existing mainstream accommodation and restaurant offers amongst experienced travellers. It may also reflect the idea of the 'experience economy' where travel is increasingly seen as an experience rather than the consumption of products.

Events

The idea of luxury and events is a very interesting one that has a number of aspects as follows:

- Events where participation is by invitation only and there are no tickets on sale. Attendance at a Royal Garden Party in the UK would be an example of this. It is free to attend, but only those considered worthy of the honour receive an invitation.

- Events where ticket prices are so high as to render attendance something of a luxury. Given the finite capacity of event venues, an illegal market in ticket sales may exist which may inflate prices still further.

- Events which give participants chance to see or do something not normally possible for most people. This could include a 'meet and greet' with the artist at a rock gig or an open day at a military base.

- Events have a rarity value because they only occur very infrequently, such as the Passion Plays in Oberammergau which are only performed once every ten years.

- Events which give tourists a chance to see something that is normally only seen by local people. A good example of this is when tourists visit funeral ceremonies in the Tana Toraja area of Sulawesi in Indonesia.

Just as is the case with airlines, there is always an opportunity to create a more luxurious experience through upgrading. At a play in a theatre, for instance, the consumer can pay more for a seat with a better view and order a bottle of champagne for during the interval.

Cruises

Cruises have an interesting history, for in the era before air travel what we now call cruise ships were a means of transport rather than a leisure experience; then the ships were called 'liners'. For many people the term 'cruise' used to be synonymous with luxury, as they were very expensive and one also needed the luxury of lots of time as the ships were very slow! However, in recent years the cruise sector has gone through a rapid period of change and growth. The sector has sought to attract new consumers by offering short cruises, fly-cruises, and party cruises as well as by focusing on value-for-money. The emphasis has been on trying to broaden the market beyond the 55 plus age group and reduce the formality which was thought to be dissuading many from joining the market.

Nevertheless, there continues to be a luxury cruise segment where the focus is on formality and tradition. This is particularly seen in the large ship cruise market, with companies such as Cunard and Crystal. On the other hand in the mid-size and small ship categories, the leading players are companies such as Paul Gauguin Cruises and Ponant's where the emphasis is on understated, more informal luxury, designed to appeal to a younger affluent clientele.

Destinations

As we noted earlier in the text some destinations are perceived as luxury destinations based largely on their long history and traditional reputation, for example the French Riviera. Others have developed a reputation as luxury destinations since the growth of mass tourism, as the luxury segment looked for new places away from the tourist hordes. The islands of the Caribbean and the Indian Ocean have played a major role in fulfilling this ambition. However mass tourism is always snapping at the heels of the luxury segment. When that happens the luxury travellers often seek to maintain the quality of their experience behind the walls of exclusive hotels and villas.

However, destinations do not always need to be expensive or full of high end accommodation to be seen as luxury destinations. Based on the idea of luxury as rarity, high levels of service, exceptional physical environment, unique facilities and so on several other types of destination could be viewed as 'luxury' namely:

- Destinations which are 'off-the-beaten-track' with few tourists where status is gained from having been somewhere that few others have visited.

- Destinations that have developed a global reputation for being a leader in a particular type of tourism, such as Belize with so-called 'ecotourism', or San Sebastien in the Basque country of Spain for gastronomic tourism.

- Destinations that are perceived to offer an 'authentic' experience and which are thought to be 'unspoilt' by the impacts of tourism.

In all three of the above cases, fashion plays a large role. Tourist destinations are very prone to fashion cycles and somewhere that is 'in' this year can be 'out' in a couple of years time. Celebrity endorsement can also play a powerful role in creating a luxury reputation for a destination, particularly as we are living in an era of 'celebrity culture' where people seek to emulate the behaviour of their celebrity 'heroes' and 'heroines'.

Perhaps the next development will be the idea that a 'luxury destination' is one which goes out of its way to develop responsible tourism, where the luxury experience of the guest does not depend on over-exploitation of either the environment or the workforce. Given such tourism will be more expensive than most, it will have an element of luxury to it, but it remains to be seen if the luxury market will find such destinations particularly attractive. Personally, I believe at least a segment will find them so, because of the 'feelgood factor' they will bestow on the visitor and the enhancement of their image such visits will bring in the minds of their friends and families.

Conclusions

As we draw to the end of this chapter, the first point to be made is that it is very difficult to find empirical data to support any points an author may wish to make about this subject. Of course, this is largely a function of how poor most data in tourism is anyway, together with the fact that luxury travel is something that is very difficult to define and thus measure.

It is also made more complex by the subjectivity of the concept of luxury and the fact that everyone will see it differently. Luxury certainly is 'in the eye of the beholder' and what is more it is constantly changing as expectations rise and people become more experienced as travellers.

The geography of luxury demand in tourism is clearly changing, with the rise of Asia and the Gulf States overtaking demand from what is now the 'old world', in tourism terms, of Europe and North America. Furthermore, it appears that the view of luxury of the emerging luxury markets is different to that of the traditional markets in some interesting ways. It remains to be seen how these emerging markets will evolve as they mature.

5 The Luxury Consumer in Tourism, Hospitality and Events

Introduction

Having looked at the luxury travel market let us now focus on the building blocks of the market, namely the individual consumers, for any market is simply the product of the actions of many individual consumers.

In this chapter we will explore the idea of a luxury consumer in tourism, hospitality and events by using the conventional idea of motivators and determinants. We will also endeavour to put forward ideas about a typology or typologies of luxury consumers. At the same time I will suggest that not everyone is interested in luxury travel, even if they can afford it.

Motivators

Motivators are a vital part of consumer behaviour in the luxury market as in any other market. They represent the desires which stimulate travellers want to:

- Take a vacation in the first place
- Take a particular type of vacation.

In the context of luxury we will not focus on the first of these as it will be taken as a given. Instead we will concentrate on the second issue, the type of trip taken.

The tourism literature contains a number of models about motivators which differ a little from each other. Figure 5.1 sets out one such model (from Horner and Swarbrooke, 2016) which is not atypical. It is important to remember that such models are concerned with the tourism market in general not the luxury sector alone. We will look here at how it applies to the luxury sector.

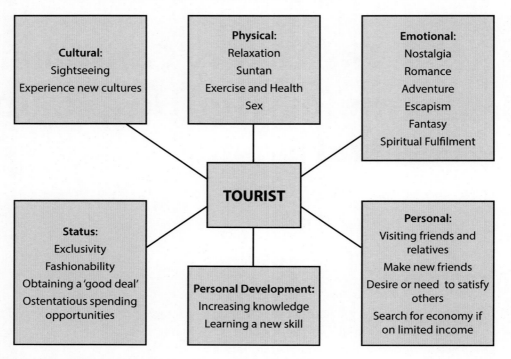

Figure 5.1: Conventional general motivators of tourist behaviour

Source: Horner and Swarbrooke, 2016

I would like to suggest that the most of these motivators are as applicable to luxury travel and leisure purchase decisions as they are to decisions in the rest of the tourism, hospitality and events market. I also contend that the desire for 'status' is perhaps the single most important motivator, particularly in terms of ideas such as 'exclusivity' and 'ostentatious spending opportunities' and even 'fashionability'.

Some may well simply consume luxury experiences for their own private pleasure. However, given that most tourism, hospitality and event consumption takes place in public or at least publicly accessible spaces, it seems likely that luxury consumers also seek to gain status within various communities through their consumption activities. The business class passengers may well enjoy the envious glances of economy class passengers when they take their place at the front of the aeroplane; or the high end hotel guest who is whisked up to the executive floor for a private check-in while the rest of the guests queue for the standard ground floor check-in. The luxury consumer may admire the immediate status they receive at such times from strangers, but the status is probably enhanced if the people in their social circle or neighbourhood find out about their luxury experience even if the traveller has to tell them themselves. And better still if they can post text and images of their experience on social media for the world to see.

We can make a further observation about the nature of motivators in luxury consumption. Luxury status can be gained as a result of buying experiences in response to factors other than those identified in Figure 5.1 as 'status'. This could mean the person who gains a fantastic natural sun tan in the winter in the UK, thanks to a holiday on a Caribbean island. Alternatively, status may be gained from seeing a world-renowned but isolated and little visited cultural site, or doing a cookery course in Thailand, or getting the autograph of a music star during a gig. Indeed most of the factors in Figure 5.1 have potential elements of status attached to them which could suggest luxury.

However, it is worth noting, as we have earlier in the text, that status is not only about spending lots of money or experiencing something exceptional. In this age it may also be gained when one finds a deal that means your flight ticket costs less than everyone else on the aircraft.

If one is interested in ideas of luxury, one needs to be aware that there are both 'expressed motivators' and 'real motivators'. People may answer the questionnaire of a researcher with a list of motivations, but these may or may not be 'true'. This may be because they wish to conceal the truth or because they do not fully understand their own motivations! Another complicating factor is that most travellers and leisure consumers do not consume alone. They are usually with partners, families or friends, so then the issue is the extent to which motivators are shared or not between those travelling and consuming together.

Finally in this section I would like to raise a point about the relationship between motivators, luxury and status; and that is what might be termed 'lifestyle'. I believe that those consuming tourism, hospitality and events experiences purchase products and services that they believe either:

- Are an extension of their normal lifestyle, or
- Represent an aspirational lifestyle they wish they lived, or
- Represent a lifestyle they hope other people will think they lead, or
- Perhaps a bit of all three.

The second and third cases are both based around the interaction between the consumer and the world outside themselves. The aspirations will be based on a comparison between the true lifestyle of the consumer and that of others which the consumer sees as superior. The third point it is about the consumer seeking approval from, and acceptance by, other people, whoever they may be.

Furthermore, the rich person who travels in luxury all the time, is likely to see luxury as an example of the first point. However, for the person who buys luxury priced experiences that are a 'once-in-a-lifetime' or 'special occasion' purchase, their consumption is likely to be much more about either the second point or the third or a mixture of both.

Determinants

Determinants are those factors that determine whether or not you can take a trip and if so, what trip you are able to take. In this chapter we will ignore the former and instead focus on those which influence the type of trip you are able to take. The purchase decision usually represents some kind of compromise between the motivations of the tourist and the determinants that are personal to them.

A number of authors have looked at the issue of determinants and here we will present the ideas of Horner and Swarbrooke, 2016. These authors identified two sets of determinants, personal and external, illustrated in Figures 5.2 and 5.3.

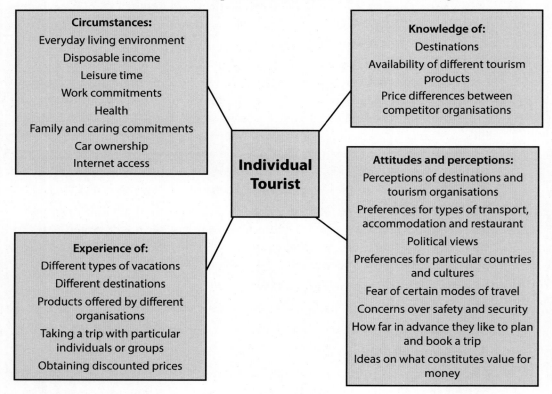

Figure 5.2: Personal determinants of tourist behaviour

Source: Adapted from Horner and Swarbrooke, 2016

In the context of a discussion about luxury it is likely that determinants are a crucial issue. I imagine that the vast majority of people would like to experience luxury if they had the opportunity. Otherwise why would lotteries be so popular? But it is the determinants that decide for whom this will be a reality or an impossible dream.

The model in Figure 5.2 is not comprehensive, but it represents what I believe to be the four main types of personal determinants; so let us look at their role in the luxury market in a little more detail.

In terms of the luxury market, personal determinants are of crucial importance because consuming luxury is about one's personal circumstances, particularly in terms of disposable income. Traditionally it would have also included the need for leisure time, and that requirement is still met for retired people or those who inherit wealth. But for the growing global class of rich entrepreneurs, leisure time is often a commodity in short supply, so their luxury experiences have to be intense as they often want multiple experiences over a short period, rather than simply to relax. Indeed as they often remain connected to their business constantly through mobile devices, the idea of relaxation becomes even more remote for these people and their travel companions.

5

However, there are other interesting points that can be made about personal determinants in relation to luxury.

First, health has traditionally been seen as a constraining factor on vacation choices, as illness or disability limited the options available to the would-be traveller. In the luxury market these constraints can be mitigated by wealth, as those with money can buy the services that allow them to travel despite their medical conditions. But it goes further, in that now it seems that a desire to protect or enhance one's health is a major motivator for the growth of the 'wellness' market, while for those with money health tourism offers the prospect of being able to resolve health issues through travelling to other countries for medical treatment.

Second, in those countries where the luxury segment is long established, the luxury consumers have lots of personal experience of destinations on which they can draw when making vacation decisions. In the emerging markets of Asia this is not always the case, and here the role of intermediaries becomes important in helping the consumer make decisions.

Third, for wealthy travellers the issue of safety and security is perhaps even more important than it is for travellers as a whole, because their wealth may make them feel they will be specifically targeted by criminals. At the same time, wealth can have an even more direct impact on travel decisions. Many wealthy people keep at least some of their wealth in 'offshore accounts' or in banks in other countries. Sometimes they will combine leisure travel with trips to manage their financial affairs. These 'visiting their money vacations' are a feature of a number of destinations including, In Europe, Switzerland and London.

Finally, while the actual price is likely to be less of an issue for luxury segment consumers, there is evidence that they still look for value for money, and have particularly high expectations.

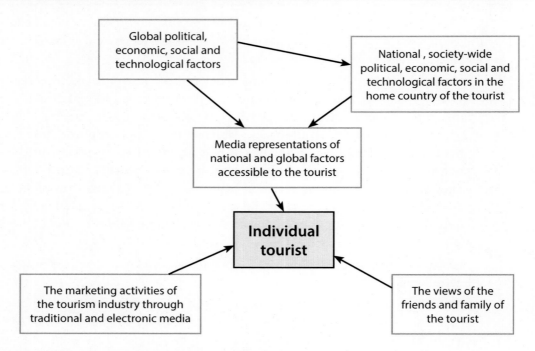

Figure 5.3: External determinants of tourist behaviour
Source: Adapted from Horner and Swarbrooke, 2016

Having developed this diagram, I am conscious of the fact that it might be better expressed in terms of a series of concentric circles, starting with family and friends as the innermost circle, being closest and most frequently connected to the traveller. Then perhaps we have the industry which is constantly seeking to communicate with consumers and persuade them to make particular purchasing decisions. We then come to the media, both the travel and the non-travel media, most notably the news media. The latter is particularly influential but normally has a negative impact on behaviour, indirectly dissuading consumers from choosing a destination as they depict civil unrest, extreme weather, natural disasters, and crime in the places that are trying to attract tourists.

The news media is also important in that it acts as an intermediary between national and global political, economic, social, and technological factors and the individual consumer. The opinions people have on such factors are often the result of what they see and hear in the media they use and take notice of. What is interesting here is that we do not all use the same media in the same way. We read different newspapers or no newspaper at all. We watch different television news programmes and so on. Then we filter what we see and hear through our own prejudices, attitudes and perceptions, as well as our experience and knowledge. The outcome of this process may or may not then be modified when we discuss the events of the day with friends and family.

This last paragraph illustrates a very important point about determinants, and that is the fact that external and personal determinants are linked, although they are different. This is the same in any segment of the tourism market not just the luxury sector, though it is likely to be even more complicated in the luxury market simply because these consumers, by dint of wealth, tend to have more options and opportunities than most travellers.

I would like to conclude this section by repeating a constant theme of this book, which is that luxury is a relative concept rather than an absolute. And money is not the only 'currency of luxury', as we have already noted when thinking about time and luxury. So let us consider a carer who spends every day looking after an ill or elderly relative. For them, the opportunity to have respite care for the person they look after for a week, so that they can have a few days at a caravan at the seaside thirty kilometres away, is as big a luxury for them as the week-long stay in a five star resort on another continent would be for the wealthy luxury traveller.

The purchase decision process

For those with a love of mathematics one can see the purchase decision process in tourism as some kind of simple equation as follows:

$$\text{Motivators} + \text{Determinants} = \text{Purchase Decision}$$

However, the reality is somewhat more complex as you would expect in a number of ways which are relevant to the luxury market.

In the first place, we need to be careful not to believe too strongly in the idea of 'rational decision-making', where decisions are taken on the basis of a systematic and objective evaluation of a range of carefully weighted factors. In luxury travel, perception, aspirations and subjectivity play an enormous role. Furthermore, some people on modest incomes choose to go into credit card debt to take a luxurious trip that they cannot really afford, because the lure of luxury travel and the status it brings is simply too strong to resist.

Second, there is often a 'time lapse challenge' in travel purchase decisions, where people make choices based on their past experience of places and types of vacation experience. Unfortunately for those making such decisions, things change. Destinations evolve and become more developed or go into decline. We ourselves change in terms of our circumstances, if not our personalities, as we have children, get divorced or just get older. If we make decisions based on how a destination was and how we were when we last visited, we may be heading for disappointment. This is particularly true in the luxury segment in relation to destinations, in that a place that was exclusive and 'undiscovered' twenty years ago may well now be a standardised mass market resort with none of the caché or kudos it once had.

At the same time vacation choices are often the result of unforeseen circumstances and opportunism rather than planning. For example, you are planning a camping trip in France when a friend offers you the use of their luxury holiday apartment in Barbados or Tuscany or Mauritius free of charge, an apartment you could never have afforded to rent. Now all you need to find is the price of the flights.

I believe that many of the conventional models of the purchase decision process in tourism, such as they are, do not really accurately identify the process and certainly not in relation to the luxury segment. First, they do not seem to take account of the three points made above. Some models are out-dated and do not take account of key changes such as the rise of budget airlines and the impact of hand-held devices on accessing tourism products and services. The latter in particular has made global purchasing directly by the consumer 24 hours a day possible for the first time. Furthermore most are based on little or no empirical evidence and the majority emanate from Europe and North America, which as we saw earlier are no longer setting the trends as far as luxury travel is concerned.

However, it may be that the process of making decisions is simply so individual and subjective that any attempt at modelling is doomed to failure

Let us now try to see, if it is possible, how these individual behaviours may be aggregated to create meaningful typologies for the luxury sector. We will then go on to look at market segmentation and luxury. These two subjects are clearly closely related, but I see typologies more as an academic construct based on the characteristics of individual consumers, whereas segmentation is an attempt to place individual consumers into types, with the express aim of increasing the effectiveness of marketing activities. This is obviously a personal view rather than a fact, but it is the basis on which the rest of this chapter will be written.

Towards a typology of luxury consumers

In the first instance we have a number of typologies of tourists from the tourism literature dating back at least to the 1970s. Horner and Swarbrooke in 2016 identified no fewer than fourteen different typologies, and this was by no means a comprehensive list. However the most recent of these was nearly ten years old and the most influential ones were still those from the last century! This may be partly a result of recent trends in tourism research, where 'big picture' thinking has been replaced by 'micro picture' thinking, as academics endeavour to place their outputs in journals but can only afford to undertake tiny scale pieces of empirical research. Or it may mean tourism research has started to mature, as we have seen the rise of typologies related to sectors of tourism demand, from ecotourism to dark tourism. However, despite its monetary importance to the tourism industry, few academics seem to have devoted time to the luxury consumer specifically. Perhaps it is not fashionable to be interested in luxury consumers or perhaps it is because those typologies looking at sectors of tourism such as ecotourism have simply encompassed luxury as part of their area of interest.

At this point we also need to recognise that what is being said here relates largely to literature available in the English language, and it may well be that work is being published in other languages. With that said, let us now start to look at what the 'traditional' models of tourist typologies say that is relevant to the luxury sector.

Cohen in 1972 sought to distinguish between what he termed 'institutionalised' and 'non-institutionalised' tourists. The first category included organised and individual mass tourists – people who chose established destinations with a well developed infrastructure. The second category encompasses 'drifters' and 'explorers' – people wanting to 'get off the beaten track' and travel independently. He saw the latter as 'pioneers' who explore new places and are then followed over time by the first category of tourists as the destination develops.

In terms of the modern luxury market this typology does not really work, perhaps not surprisingly as it is nearly fifty years old! It is true that most traditional definitions of luxury tourists would have placed them firmly in the 'institutionalised' category, relying heavily on developed destination infrastructure. Yet they would be horrified to be called 'mass tourists', for luxury is all about personalisation and individualised experiences. Furthermore the 'desert island' of luxury tourism, where it is about exclusivity and being away from the tourist hordes, almost places these tourists in the 'non-institutionalised' category. This may be reinforced by the growing fashion for 'authenticity' and the kudos which comes from meeting 'real' local people, who are not simply tourism industry employees.

In 1977, Plog published his influential work that divided tourists into 'allocentrics' and 'psychocentrics', on a continuum that had sub-categories between these two extremes. This approach distinguishes between those who are adventurous and seek new experiences and those who prefer to stick to the things and places they know. He went on to suggest that the different types would choose different destinations to each other, a suggestion that was criticised by later authors such as Sharpley in 1994. I believe that luxury consumers can fit into either of these categories and all the sub-categories between the two, but I also contend that as people have became more experienced travellers it is possible that on some occasions they can behave as 'allocentrics' and as 'psychocentrics' at others. What can be categorised are types of behaviour, rather than the tourists themselves.

Cohen came back in 1979 with a five part typology of tourists, based on the type of experience they were seeking. One of these categories, in a phrase which appears to have anticipated the later work of Pine and Gilmore, is the 'experiential tourist'. By this Cohen means a tourist in search of authentic experiences. In terms of the luxury market this seems inappropriate, as most luxury products traditionally have been man-made with the sole intention of making money, whether it be an upscale resort on a tropical island, a casino, a high end cruise ship or the first class cabin of an airliner. Yet as we have noted several times, we may be seeing a change in that authentic experiences are becoming fashionable in the luxury travel market. If so this may be a reaction against materialism or even to the excesses of the tourism industry, such as the creation of a ski slope in a desert in Dubai.

Dalen in 1989 published a study from Norway which amongst four types identified 'modern materialists' who sought, amongst other things, to impress people back home with their sun tan. While not specifically concerned with luxury travellers by any means, this typology showed the importance of acquired status through travel which can be gained in many ways. This status acquisition appears to be a key motivator for many luxury travellers.

In the same year Gallup and American Express published a five category typology of tourists, based on research in four countries, and this included a group termed the 'indulgers' – people for whom a vacation was an opportunity to be pampered. This idea of pampering is a powerful one in luxury travel, and is used widely in marketing materials by the industry.

Also in 1989 Smith published a seven part typology that included the category of 'elite tourists' – those people who liked to go on tailor-made expensive tours. He saw these people as likely to be experienced frequent travellers and there are certainly many specialist upscale tour operators around the world for whom this type of tourist is their raison d'être.

In the early days of debates about sustainable tourism, Wood and House talked about the '*Good Tourist*' in a book of the same title. This encouraged people to be good by behaving responsibly, being concerned with the welfare of local people and protecting the environment. At the time this would have seemed the antithesis of luxury travel, which was about comfort rather than sacrifice, hedonistic pleasure rather than responsibility. However I would like to suggest that things are changing, and that soon responsibility and ethical consumerism may be the new hedonistic pleasure for some luxury travellers! Status may come from being seen to behave well, just as rich American philanthropists gain status from their charitable donations.

Pearce in 2008 sought to produce a typology based on how people purchased their vacations, identifying 'package', 'independent', and 'customised' categories, with the latter clearly being relevant to the luxury market with its emphasis on buying tailor-made products not normally included in standard packages.

The existing typologies are open to criticism, not just for their lack of focus on the luxury segment, but also because they tend to be out-dated, based on modest levels of empirical research and geographically rooted in Europe and North America. In Figure 5.4 I will endeavour to offer some simple new typologies of the luxury traveller, albeit based on no empirical research. The point of Figure 5.4 is not to offer a comprehensive set of typologies that answer all our questions about who is the luxury tourist. Instead it is simplistically designed to help you recognise the complexity of the phenomenon of the luxury tourist and demonstrate that luxury tourism has a number of different dimensions.

Perhaps, though, it is worth trying to pick out a few key points from the four typologies.

- In the first one a distinction is made between those for whom luxury is a way of life and those for whom it is an aspiration or even a dream. It also looks as the relationship between everyday life and the vacation experience.

- The second typology focuses on money and time, and the idea of being cash rich or poor and time rich or poor, and suggests that envy may play some part in the luxury market.

- In the third typology we address the question of the compromises people sometimes have to make when they desire luxury travel experiences but cannot afford a complete door-to-door luxury experience.

- The final typology looks at the criteria different consumers use to decide what are the most important requirements for a luxury experience for them.

Obviously in all four typologies we recognise a segment that has to make no real compromises and can have the luxury experience they desire any time. However I would suggest that the majority of the luxury market is probably made up of those who have to make some choices and compromises, because they have personal determinants which do not allow every vacation to be a dream luxury vacation.

As we move towards the end of this discussion about typologies I would like to put on the table a fifth typology which, again, will be a 'broad brush' generalisation. This is a typology based on no empirical research, but I do believe that it reflects commonly held opinions by those involved in the luxury market. However, it has a large element of snobbery to it too. We are talking about the difference between 'old money' and 'new money'.

The stereotype is that those consumers from 'old money' are confident in their social position and tend to avoid ostentatious displays of their wealth They are seen as sophisticated and experienced travellers with refined taste. By contrast, 'new money' consumers are seen to be insecure in their social position and use ostentatious displays of their wealth to impress and enhance their social reputation. They are seen as less experienced travellers who buy designer brands to gain status and show little taste in what they buy. As I said this is a very 'snobbish' view. It is also a typology that tends to be rooted in culture and nationality.

(a): Luxury v. daily life

Luxury is a way of life of which luxury travel is just a part. Daily life is also luxurious.	Daily life is not generally luxurious but vacations are seen as very important and sacrifices are made in everyday life so that vacations can be luxurious experiences.	Luxury generally plays no part in daily life but on rare special occasions or even once in a lifetime major sacrifices will be made for a luxurious vacation.

(b): Cash rich v. time rich

Cash rich and time rich, e.g. wealthy retired. Few constraints on the cost or duration of their vacations. They can take relaxing vacations if they choose. They envy no one.	**Cash rich but time poor**, e.g. successful entrepreneurs. Few contraints on costs but a vacation needs to be short and will probably be intense and not relaxing as thoughts of work are ever present. They may envy those who are time rich and have time to relax.	**Cash poor but time rich**, e.g. students. They can enjoy the luxury of long vacations particularly if they are subsidised by affluent parents. They may benefit from being invited on 'free' vacations with their parents They may envy the cash rich because of their independence.	**Cash poor and time poor**, e.g. workers on lower salaries. They can only take short vacations because of their jobs and can only take a luxury vacation occasionally, if at all, by saving up over a number of years or going into debt. They will probably envy the other three who all have advantages over them.

(c): Destinations and activities

Those who choose luxury destinations, fly in business or first class, stay in high end hotels, eat out at fine dining restaurants and participate in exclusive and expensive activities	Those who choose luxury destinations, travel in business class, stay in moderate hotels, eat at fine dining restaurants occasionally and participate in one expensive activity during their vacation	Those who visit ordinary destinations, book premium economy class air tickets but try to get an upgrade, stay in a moderate hotel but pay for an upgraded room, eat out at moderate restaurants but have one fine dining meal during their vacation, and participate in one up-market activity if they can get a discounted deal

(d): Most important requirements

Every aspect of a luxury vacation is of equal importance including:
Travel to and from the destination
The image and reputation of the destination
The quality of the physical environment of the destination
The quality of the destination infrastructure including transport
The level of tourist numbers and the profile of tourists in the destination
The quality of accommodation and visitor attractions
The level and quality of personal service in hotels and restaurants

Personal service: A high staff to guest ratio and a deferential attitude towards service delivery plus a high level of experience and technical competence.	**The quality of the physical environment of the destination:** including cleanliness, scenery, beaches, and townscapes.	**The image and reputation of the destination:** This also includes the number and profile of fellow tourists and the impact of both on the ambiance of the destination.	**The variety of high quality experiences available within the destination region:** from fine dining to sports, high end retailing to unique visitor attractions.	**The quality of their accommodation** whether five star hotel, all-inclusive resort or a luxury villa. They may spend all or most of their vacation within the accommodation.

Figure 5.4: Some possible typologies of luxury tourists

'Old money' is associated with Europe and North America while 'new money' is often linked with Asia, Russia and the Gulf States, for example. If this distinction is a real one, it is probably a natural part of the evolution of a market, for what is 'old money' today in the USA, for example, was 'new money' a century ago and the comments made about 'new money' tourists today were made about rich Americans one hundred years ago. There is also evidence, from China for instance, that as the recently rich become more experienced travellers their behaviour starts to become more like the stereotypical behaviour of the 'old money' consumer.

I could, perhaps mischievously, have added a sixth typology of satisfied luxury tourists and dissatisfied luxury tourists. When one buys luxury, expectations are often sky high, either because it is a rare experience or because the traveller is used to luxury and therefore has many other experiences with which to make a comparison. Either way there is a good chance that even paying a luxury price can end in disappointment, particularly in tourism when so many uncontrollable factors affect the experience, such as the weather or when service depends on human beings who have moods and bad days.

Having discussed typologies let us now look at the twin topic of segmentation.

Segmentation

As everyone knows segmentation is about dividing a population up into smaller groups based on criteria which it is believed influence their behaviour as consumers. It is, therefore, not an academic activity but a business activity with the aim of improving the effectiveness of an organisation's marketing activities. Segmentation lies at the heart of marketing. As noted by Dibb *et al.* in 2005, market segmentation:

> "is the process of dividing a total market into groups of people with relatively similar product needs, for the purpose of designing a marketing mix that precisely matches the needs of individuals in a segment."

At this point in the book we are going to look at the traditional approaches to segmentation and see how relevant they are to the luxury market. We will also look at some emerging approaches which I believe may become important in the tourism market in the future. In Chapter 15 we will look at some ideas relating to the segmentation of the luxury market in the future. Before we go any further I would like to make a point about segmentation, based on observation rather than any empirical research. I believe that the idea that people can be put into 'boxes', based on certain criteria, is becoming less valid. It is my contention that consumer behaviour is now so volatile that it is virtually impossible for traditional segmentation to place individuals in 'boxes' that accurately reflect their behaviour as consumers; instead, we need to think in terms of segmenting behaviour patterns rather than people. It is hoped that you will bear this thought in mind when reading the rest of this section. Let us now look at the four traditional approaches to segmentation and their relevance to the concept of a luxury consumer.

Geographical segmentation

Geographical segmentation is based on the idea that behaviour is influenced by geographical factors, primarily where a consumer lives. Given what was said above about 'old money' and 'new money' luxury consumers, there is clearly a belief that luxury markets are influenced by geography. Most attention in recent years has focused on China, India and Russia, where the luxury market has been growing fastest, and as such these were the markets that have been of most interest to the tourism industry marketers. The tourism industry has always made great use of geographical segmentation, but there is the risk of stereotyping, suggesting that the behaviour of whole national populations will be similar because they live in the same country. Obviously luxury markets are much smaller than the whole population, but again it is hard to believe that all rich people in China, for instance, have similar behaviour patterns to each other, because they are from China. Surely the logic of globalisation suggests that such geographical differences in behaviour will diminish over time.

Demographic segmentation

Our industry has also used demographic segmentation heavily up to now, seeing age and gender, for example, as major influences on consumer behaviour. But again this has been open to stereotyping, seeing young people as active and adventurous, and older people as passive and cautious. Likewise the idea that women shop while men play golf, which has underpinned the social programmes of so many conferences. Both views are gross generalisations that become less and less accurate as each year goes by, with more women playing golf, more men enjoying shopping and so on.

It is true that much luxury travel advertising seems to be based on age, with consumers frequently seen as more mature although still looking youngish thanks to exercise, a healthy diet and perhaps cosmetic surgery! Yet as we noted earlier, we are seeing the rise of a class of young, wealthy, successful entrepreneurs who have different ideas about what being a luxury consumer means. This is a generation whose business may well be in ICT, but whose leisure is also based largely around their hand-held devices that allow them to manage their own travel experiences with less need for traditional intermediaries.

We have also seen a change in the role of women in society in many countries in recent decades, so that more and more women are entering the luxury market in their own right rather than as the partners of rich men, which was how they were often portrayed by marketers in the past.

One element of demographics, and of geography, that is important in the luxury market is the issue of religion, which is tied up with migration and the increasing diversity of the population in many countries. Immigrants may become successful in business in their new country and become rich, but their behaviour may not be the same as that of the indigenous population because of their religious beliefs. For example, a rich Muslim in the UK may spend their money on making more pilgrimages rather than taking beach holidays in the Caribbean.

Behaviouristic segmentation

Behaviouristic segmentation revolves around the relationship between the consumer and the product. This is illustrated in Figure 5.5

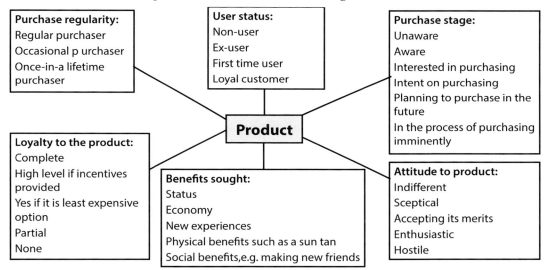

Figure 5.5: Types of behaviouristic segmentation.
Source: Adapted from Horner and Swarbrooke, 2016

While this is a mechanistic and rather fragmented, fragmented approach to segmentation, its relevance to the luxury market is hopefully clear. The *benefits sought* category is particularly appropriate in terms of the issue of status.

Psychographic segmentation

Now let us turn to the final approach to segmentation. Psychographic segmentation is a rather broad concept that basically says that the behaviour of consumers is based on their personal characteristics in terms of lifestyle, personality and attitudes. Its influence can be seen easily in modern advertising for everything from cars to clothing, drinks to perfume. However, while this concept of segmentation seems eminently logical, its problem is how to put it into practice in comparison to other techniques. Adventurous people are harder to identify and target than women, and those who emulate the behaviour of celebrities are harder to identify and target than people who live in China!

At the same time it is clear that lifestyle and personality overlap enormously with the idea of luxury consumerism. It is the only one of the four segmentation methods which has no real basis in concrete fact. It is inherently subjective and soft edged and open to interpretation. So it seems ideally suited to an idea – luxury – which is also not clearly defined, objective or hard edged.

Luxury is for many a lifestyle, either a real lifestyle or one they aspire to, while for others it is a lifestyle they hope other people will think they live. For those in the luxury segment, vacations will normally be an extension of their everyday life although a few may instead seek a contrast in a simple, no-frills vacation experience, based on the idea that we travel to experience the opposite of daily life. Ironically perhaps, for those with a non-luxurious everyday existence their aspiration, based on the same principle, may be to be able to experience elements of luxury during their annual vacation which they are unable to enjoy in their everyday life back home.

Personality is also tied closely to the concept of luxury. Those with money may have a personality that means they want to flaunt it and their insecurity may mean they need the status which they believe comes with ostentatious consumption. Others may view such spending as rather vulgar and feel no need to show off their material possessions because they are self-confident and self-assured. Others may almost feel guilty about their wealth and seek to downplay it or even feel the need to contribute something to a society that has given them a privileged position. All of these personality types are easy to spot in a tourism setting, with the shopaholic buying designer clothes and famous brand watches as if the factories were about to go out of business, the chilled out person relaxing on a beach at a secluded private villa, and the young affluent traveller volunteering at a school for under-privileged children in a foreign land.

For those without wealth, their personalities also influence their behaviour. Some will accept their situation and be perfectly content with a low to moderately priced mass market vacation. Others will do that but be dissatisfied with it and dreaming of being able to enjoy more luxurious experiences feeling. Others will spend money they do not really have to indulge themselves with elements of a luxury experience, such as paying for a room upgrade in the hotel or a seat in business class. For many such people it is important that lots of people see them consuming this luxury, for it is status they seek as well as or instead of more comfort. I could go on but I believe the point is made.

The vacation is also for many a crucial antidote to the ills of the modern lifestyle, whether that be stress and time pressures, feeling you have little influence on the big events in life, or worrying about the future. We want to be treated as individuals and listened to, we want our experience to be unique and we want to be made to feel important. Wealthy people take these things for granted but now most people seem to want these things too, whatever price they are paying for their vacation. So the industry is having to try to meet this somewhat unrealistic demand and treat all customers in this respect, as if they were high spending luxury consumers. In doing so perhaps they are diluting some of the elements that truly differentiate luxury travel from more utilitarian forms of travel.

Whether this is true or not, these ideas of customisation and the importance of the individual underpin the whole concept of the 'experience economy' as set out by Pine and Gilmore nearly twenty years ago. But now every tourist expects to be given the opportunity to create unique experiences for themselves, not just those paying the higher price. And because of their need to make money, companies are pandering to this idea and using the terminology of experiences rather than products. Perhaps we are seeing the dilution or the democratisation of the old world, where luxury travellers enjoyed experiences and everyone else consumed products and services? Perhaps these changes mean we need a total rethink of the concept of luxury, which is actually what I am arguing for throughout this book.

We have just been looking at the four main segmentation methods used today and seeing how relevant they are to the luxury market. I would like to suggest that we should not think in terms of choosing one or other technique, but rather see them as a series of layers placed one on top of the other to create a clearer picture, as all contain an element of truth but none gives us a complete picture.

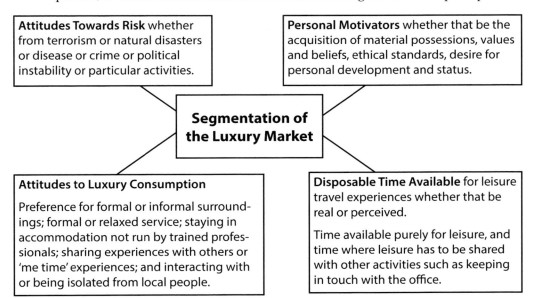

Attitudes Towards Risk whether from terrorism or natural disasters or disease or crime or political instability or particular activities.

Personal Motivators whether that be the acquisition of material possessions, values and beliefs, ethical standards, desire for personal development and status.

Segmentation of the Luxury Market

Attitudes to Luxury Consumption

Preference for formal or informal surroundings; formal or relaxed service; staying in accommodation not run by trained professionals; sharing experiences with others or 'me time' experiences; and interacting with or being isolated from local people.

Disposable Time Available for leisure travel experiences whether that be real or perceived.

Time available purely for leisure, and time where leisure has to be shared with other activities such as keeping in touch with the office.

Figure 5.6: Potential approaches to the segmentation of the luxury market

It is now time to put forward some ideas about other possible segmentation criteria that might have relevance for the luxury market and these are set out in Figure 5.6. The approaches outlined here are by no means comprehensive, but they do have relevance in a luxury market which is changing rapidly and fundamentally. I believe that these approaches highlight a number of important new ways of seeing luxury as follows:

1   In a world with apparently unprecedented levels of threat from terrorism, as well as frequent natural disasters and health scares, attitudes to risk are becoming crucial especially in the luxury market, as the rich may see themselves at particular risk because they travel more frequently than most. This may mean that feeling safe and secure goes from being the expected norm to something which is at a premium and has to be sought out rather than taken for granted. Feeling safe may be a touchstone of luxury in the future, and marketers will need to take this into account

2   As we have noted several times already, time appears to be becoming increasingly an increasingly rare commodity as everyone feels it is in short supply. So, time availability and how time is used may become another touchstone of luxury in the future luxury travel market. If people cannot find more leisure time, the luxury sector may need to find ways of ensuring short breaks can be used to pack in as many experiences as possible in a short period or provide more innovative ways of offering the opportunity for complete relaxation and de-stressing, again over a short period. Perhaps these are the industry offers that will attract the highest prices in future

3   There seems to be growing evidence that the old idea that luxury is about acquiring possessions or doing things others are unable to do because they lack wealth, is beginning to break down and that luxury can be seen in less tangible ways or less in terms of exclusivity. This may be due to the situation of younger generations, who may be reacting against their parents' generation, or they may not believe they can achieve material wealth in an era of economic uncertainty and so they search out alternatives, whether that be embracing new less materialistic values, looking for authenticity or sharing experiences through technology. This trend, if it continues, could redefine or even eliminate the concept of luxury.

4   Subtle changes are taking place in how people choose to consume luxury travel. It is now possible to have a luxurious service experience delivered by staff who are informally dressed, and indeed business class travellers no longer feel the need to dress up to sit in the front cabin of the aeroplane. After years when the only contact with local people tended to be with waiters or guides or drivers, some luxury travellers are now seeking out contact with 'ordinary' local people not employed in the tourism industry. And instead of

staying in a swanky city centre hotel, there is as much status to be gained these days from staying in an apartment in a suburb owned by a local person who shows you the sites away from the tourist hot spots.

As Bob Dylan sang some fifty years ago, 'the times they are a-changing'!

Conclusions

How does one go about drawing conclusions from such a long, some would say rambling, chapter? Let's try!

We have seen that the luxury consumer in tourism is a complex phenomenon who is not easy to understand. The conventional idea in consumer behaviour of motivators and determinants do apply to these consumers, but in terms of determinants they perhaps face less constraints than other tourists, so they are more likely than most to be able to take the kind of vacation they want to without having to make the compromises that other tourists do, between their wishes and the reality of their situation.

It has been noted that academics have not yet produced meaningful typologies relating specifically to the luxury market, although some typologies have categories that are relevant to the luxury traveller.

The traditional segmentation methods have elements which are appropriate to the luxury travel market which is perhaps not surprising given the financial importance of this market to the sustainability of the industry worldwide.

In relation to both typologies and segmentation techniques I have, perhaps foolishly, sought to offer some thoughts about new or modified approaches that relate more directly to the changing luxury travel market. And it is that word 'changing' which is the key one here, for that has clearly emerged now as the central theme of this book.

This chapter, as previous ones have and future ones will, has demonstrated that the concept of luxury travel and the nature of the luxury market in tourism is changing rapidly and quite dramatically as a result of a myriad of inter-related factors.

Having focused on the demand side we will now look at the supply side of luxury in tourism, hospitality and events.

Conclusions to Part 2

Perhaps the main conclusion from this section was the sheer complexity of both market measurement and the behaviour of individual consumers. However, a number of points did appear to be clear including the following.

☐ First, while it is extremely difficult to measure something that is not clearly defined, the luxury market appears to be growing rapidly notwithstanding any temporary slow-downs caused by periodic economic recessions or crises.

☐ Second, while the number of so-called luxury consumers can be counted in millions in some countries, the big differences are in the proportion of the population that is thought to fit into this category in each. It can vary from several per cent down to fractions of one per cent.

☐ Third, in terms of both market size and consumer behaviour, there is an issue of markets being at different levels of maturity which in turn affects both the volume and behaviour of those seen to be in the luxury market. This phenomenon also has a clear geographical dimension, although we have to be careful about stereotyping.

☐ Fourth, status still lies at the heart of luxury but the attributes that bestow status on the individual tourist are changing; it is no longer just about ostentatious displays of wealth.

☐ Fifth, for some tourists luxury is a way of life while for others it is a once-in-a-lifetime experience. These two consumers will view luxury in very different ways.

Part 3 : The Supply Side of Luxury

The two chapters in this section focus on the two sides of supply in tourism, hospitality and events, namely the suppliers and the destinations.

In Chapter 6 we start by looking at the traditional attributes of luxury products and how they are changing, before going on to look at the role of marketing and the messages that are communicated to consumers. I suggest that we are beginning to see signs of a process of 'de-luxurification' taking place in the supply side. The chapter then goes on to explore what luxury means in different sectors, from airlines to tour operations, events to restaurants.

Chapter 7 focuses on the destination, the place where luxury consumption takes place in tourism, hospitality and events. We will look at destinations that have luxury reputations and try to explain where these reputations come from. We will also look at the matter of how a destination image changes over time.

6 The Supply Side of Luxury

Introduction

This chapter is important because past and present industry marketing has largely shaped what the idea of luxury travel today. However, the changes in the idea of luxury that are being discussed in this book are taking place largely outside the control of the industry, and that is starting to pose a challenge for supply side providers.

At the beginning we will look at the traditional attributes of what would be seen as luxury products, but I will suggest that these are changing over time.

Before entering into the main body of the chapter there will be a brief discussion of the role of the marketing, which has helped create many consumer perceptions of luxury. However, it will be suggested that by over-using and inappropriately using the term 'industry', marketing may have served to cheapen or dilute the idea of luxury which may have long term implications for luxury travel.

In the early sections of the chapter I will seek to distinguish between different types of luxury including 'intrinsic luxury', 'single dimensional luxury', and luxury options on basic products including the issue of 'upgrading'. I will then go on to identify a phenomenon I believe is underway and I term rather clumsily 'de-luxurification'.This will be linked to issues of pricing and the rise of 'mass luxury' – two words that until now would have been seen as mutually exclusive.

After that we will explore the supply side in terms of issues such as new product development, quality and customer satisfaction.

More conventionally perhaps, the chapter will then continue by looking at the meaning of luxury in the various sectors and sub-sectors of tourism, hospitality and events.

First, in Figure 6.1 we will explore the different features that make up a luxury product.

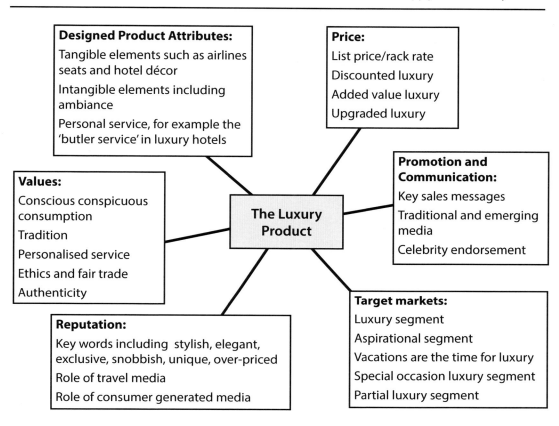

Figure 6.1 : The features of the luxury product in tourism, hospitality and events

Let us now look at thesee six types of features in a little more detail.

Designed project attributes

In terms of the 'designed product attributes', the tangible elements are very important because they are the visible symbols of luxury that attract the consumer. They are also visible to others so that the luxury consumer can gain status when others see the tangible trappings of luxury that they are enjoying. They are equally important in motivating others to aspire to be luxury consumers themselves, so they can enjoy the same tangible luxurious features. Tourism organisations understand the importance of these features and try to encourage consumers to trade up by ensuring that the range of tangible product elements varies between airline classes or categories of hotel room, for example.

On a long haul flight, for example, the designed tangible features include:

■ The seat, in terms of pitch or leg room and width, degree of recline, whether it converts into a flat bed or not, does the seat have a built-in massage facility, and whether there is privacy screening from neighbouring passengers, for instance.

- The onboard entertainment system, in terms of the range of programming available and the size of the screen.

- The food and beverage service, including how much choice of meals there is, can one eat whenever one wants or just when the crew decides, are meals served on china or plastic, and quality of wines offered.

And these are all in addition to the question of check-in and waiting for the flight departure, where tangibles such as exclusive check-in desks and executive lounges are also of great importance.

We could obviously make similar points about the tangible product attributes about hotels, restaurants, cruise ships, concert venues and so on. What is most important about such attributes is they are more objective and measurable than many other aspects of the luxury product in tourism, hospitality, and events, and they are almost wholly under the control of the supplying organisation. Available budget is perhaps the only major constraint facing an organisation, together with the imagination of the senior management and the research they do with consumers when developing new products.

Unfortunately, it is generally very easy for competitors to copy and even improve on tangible product features, so that an airline may spend millions of dollars introducing state-of-the-art 'flatbeds', which may give them a competitive advantage for just a few months. But not improving their offer will almost certainly cause them to have a competitive disadvantage. And with consumer expectations rising constantly, organisations are locked into a process of product development that is never-ending and expensive!

The intangible attributes of the luxury product, such as ambiance, are highly subjective and difficult to measure, yet they are clearly crucial to market reputation. This subjectivity means they may vary dramatically between different market segments. Let us think about a traditional luxury hotel by a lake in Switzerland which was built in the 19th century and still carries five stars today. To an elderly traveller from Asia or the USA, this may seem like the height of luxury with its air of quiet and calm, where restaurants are places of silence and the hand of history rests heavily throughout the property. Clearly this is often reinforced by tangible elements that help create the ambiance, such as heavy old furniture, chandeliers, art works from the 19th century and deep carpets. But to a young traveller from Scandinavia it may simply feel too ostentatious, old fashioned, formal and 'stuffy'. The answer of course for organisations is not to target all segments, but to work out which ones they wish to attract, research their views and then set out to design the property to create a particular ambiance that will appeal to the chosen segments.

Subjectivity is also one of the challenges with the final category of designed product attributes, namely personal service. As we have noted elsewhere in the book, perceptions of what constitutes luxury personal service are not the same for everyone. Some prefer being pampered by large numbers of staff anticipating and meeting needs before those needs have even be communicated by a consumer. Others prefer a more informal, less 'in-your-face' approach to service, while others still prefer to look after themselves if all the facilities they may need are close at hand and personal service is available as an optional extra.

Price

Traditionally this was a simple matter – luxury carried a premium price and the attitude to price was summed up by the phrase: 'if you have to ask the price you probably cannot afford it'. However, this situation has changed and is changing due to a range of factors, from the rise of e-booking to changes in the geography of tourism demand.

We are seeing three main changes taking place as follows:

■ Discounted pricing of luxury hotels, cruises and business class airfares through the rise of online travel agents, where competition is based largely on price, and the rapid growth in supply in all three sectors means that the luxury market is hugely competitive. Even luxury consumers now expect to be offered 'deals'. If ones looks at sites such as Booking.com and Expedia, one will regularly see luxury hotels offering prices, which it is claimed are massively under their normal rates.

■ Recognising that many people aspire to join the luxury segment, even if their income does not put them naturally in that market, many providers are trying to tempt those with more modest budgets to try out high end products by offering attractively priced incentives. On airlines these may be discounted business class fares such as the 'business saver' fares being offered in February 2017 by several airlines from the Gulf States. Hotels frequently offer room upgrades at relatively low prices. Some airlines will now even auction off space in premium cabins to try to increase yield, when there is still capacity as the date of the flights draws close.

■ The plethora of airline and cruise ship loyalty programmes are allowing frequent users to purchase upgrades even if they have bought a ticket in the economy section of the aircraft or cruise ship. Those with enough points can use them to buy a premium priced product without having to spend a cent.

It is interesting to speculate on what all this will mean for the future of the idea of luxury; will it be devalued or even cease to have any actual meaning?

Promotion and communication

Of course, we all know that what is communicated about a product is not always a reflection of reality! If one looks at brochures and websites it seems as if everything today can be luxurious, even camping in a tent! This may reflect a move away from an absolute definition of luxury that automatically excludes many products and experiences, towards one which sees luxury as a relative term where if tent one is bigger, warmer, better equipped than tent two it may be described as 'luxury'.

Again this has to raise questions about whether the term still has any real meaning and is simply yet more marketing hype. Maybe 'luxury' will become the new 'boutique hotel' – a term which through over-use and inaccurate use has become either virtually meaningless or worse has almost become a term, the use of which suggests a lack of sophistication or incredulity on the part of the consumer.

Perhaps in future, even more than now, luxury will not be defined by marketing professionals but rather by what other consumers believe to be luxury and even more so if that consumer is a celebrity!

Target markets

We have already discussed the individual luxury consumer and the luxury market in much more detail in Chapters 4 and 5. There may in reality be a number of ways of segmenting this market which make sense to the supply side organisations, in addition to the established techniques of segmentation such as geographic, demographic and psychographic.

Let us suggest that there are at least five types which require a different approach from suppliers, namely:

- The 'every day is luxury' segment whose wealth and tastes mean that for them luxury is how they live their everyday lives; what is extra special to everyone else is the norm for them.

- The 'luxury as an aspiration' segment who recognise that luxury is not the norm for them but wish it was. These people will be the target market for the various discounted forms of luxury product mentioned above. For these people this approach to purchasing will cover many things not just tourism, hospitality and events.

- The 'holidays are the time for luxury' segment for whom luxury is not the norm either but they see vacations as the time to indulge in luxury, even if this causes them some financial problems most notably 'maxed out' credit cards!

■ The 'special occasion luxury' segment which does not even splurge out on luxury vacations, either because they cannot afford it or are more cautious with their money. However they may make an exception once or twice in their lives, such as for fiftieth wedding anniversary or retirement celebration. These people can be an important segment for round the world cruises and long holidays in tropical climates

■ The 'partial luxury' segment where they cannot afford, or are not willing to afford, a vacation that is luxury from start to finish but instead pick and choose the elements where they will pay extra for a luxury experience. A couple may take public transport to a concert venue and stay in a budget hotel but will then buy the highest price tickets at a concert and pay more for a meet-and-greet experience. Or a group of friends may fly with a budget airline and stay in a basic apartment and then spend heavily on going to fine dining restaurants. Here the industry needs to understand what matters most to the consumer because that will dictate what they are prepared to spend highly to enjoy.

Interestingly, perhaps for the 'every day is luxury' group there may be some who become bored and jaded by having a luxurious lifestyle where they have experienced all the obvious luxury products and services. Maybe for them the ultimate 'luxury' is having little or none of the trappings of luxury, providing it is only for a day or two. Let's remember that many commentators say vacations are often motivated by a desire to try something new. If that is true then perhaps camping can be luxurious providing that it is undertaken by rich people who usually stay in palatial hotels or luxury beachside villas.

Reputation

Reputation is crucial to consumer decision-making as most consumers will be aware of a reputation even if they have no experience of their own of using a product.

Traditionally the reputation of any organisation in tourism, hospitality and events was largely controlled by the organisation itself through its marketing, together with a small group of key influencers that the organisation could at times manipulate and at other times almost control. These influencers included guide book editors and travel writers for example. Limitations of technology meant that most consumer feedback had little impact beyond the walls of the establishment, being limited to customer satisfaction surveys and the *livres d'or* or guest comment books kept by hotels and restaurants for customer comments

Over time, with the growth of the Internet and mobile devices, we have moved to a situation where most reviews that affect reputations are delivered by consumers on sites over which suppliers have little or no influence. However, smart organisations have endeavoured to get some key opinion influencers on their side with various incentives, such as bloggers with large numbers of followers.

The Michelin guide inspectors remain a notable exception to what has been said in the last couple of paragraphs. They continue to have great a great influence on restaurant reputations, yet they are professionals rather than just consumers are cannot really be influenced by restaurateurs.

Values

First, there is a clear link between values and the matter of reputation which we have just been discussing. Some might argue that the only values associated with luxury products and their consumption are greed, ostentation, snobbery and exclusivity. Less contentious terms might include tradition and personal service. However, as we have noted several times already in this book, this may be changing a little as people start to talk about words such as 'ethics', authenticity and even 'fair trade' in relation to luxury.

In Figure 6.2 we will now endeavour to look at the idea of luxury products from three different perspectives.

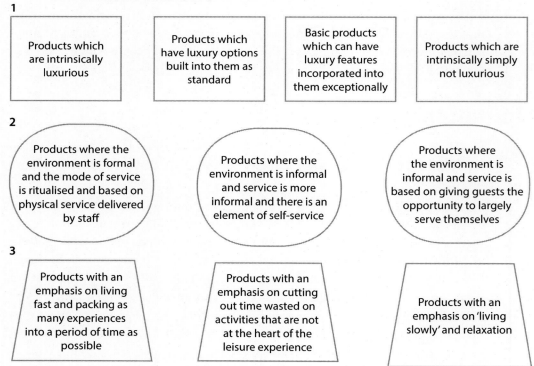

Figure 6.2: Different perspectives on the luxury product

In terms of the ideas covered in Perspective 1, we could consider this in terms of the airline sector. The height of luxury may well be the private jet whether it be owned or chartered. In those airlines which still have first class cabins these cabins will always be intrinsically luxury products. However, in terms of optional luxury, on this same aeroplane options will also probably exist for passengers to buy business class or premium economy classes, that will represent a more luxurious product than that offered in economy class. Interestingly, particularly in the usa, we are now starting to see the emergence of different categories of economy class ticket and experience. In terms of the third category, airlines may offer people the opportunity to purchase upgrades or use loyalty programme points for an upgrade. Finally, in the budget airline sector, luxury is normally not available even as an option, although even there it is possible to board ahead of fellow passengers and pre-select your seat if you are prepared to pay more. However, the on-board service and experience then is generally standardised and would not be considered as 'luxury'.

Clearly many airlines though, even in the budget sector, understand that there is a high degree of snobbery involved in tourism, and that many consumers will gladly hand over more money if they can be convinced that what they are paying for can be seen as 'luxury' and allows them to be differentiated in some way from the other people on the same flight.

Perspective 2 focuses on the type of service which constitutes the product and the environment in which the service takes place. In recent years we have seen a big increase in self-service whether it be online check-ins or serving yourself at the breakfast buffet. This has been driven by industry, particularly by companies operating in high wage economies, as it has helped them reduce labour costs. Yet it has also not been resisted by consumers, even in the luxury sector, where business class passengers seem happy to do their own online check-in because it is convenient, and upscale hotel guests are happy to go the breakfast buffet because they can choose exactly what they want. In some ways this is counter-intuitive to traditional ideas of luxury service, which involved tasks being performed by staff for the guest.

The issue around the service environment is interesting, as traditionally luxury meant formality. However, with changes in society and the rise of a class of young entrepreneurs and new industries, such as IT and e-commerce, a more informal approach to service delivery appears to be gaining ground.

Perspective 3 is based upon the idea that one of the new concepts in luxury is the precious nature of time. It appears that we are now seeing the growth of a bifurcated approach to luxury and time, where luxury can mean either having lots of time to relax and enjoy the experience, or having so little time that as much as possible needs to be packed into as short a time as possible, or removing anything that 'wastes time' from the production process. For suppliers, 'time poor' consumers represent a wonderful opportunity because they will pay heavily for short intense vacation experiences, so that per day spend can be very high. However, it is more difficult, perhaps, to make increased revenue per day from the long stay 'slow travel' consumer, so the return has to be gained over a longer period of time.

Uncontrollable factors and the luxury product

So far in this chapter we have focused on the product and discussed it in a way that suggested it was almost wholly under the control of the supplier, yet we know this is not the case. Indeed it could be argued that the product in tourism, hospitality and events is less controllable than that of most other sectors of the economy. Not least among the reasons for this could be the fact that we have to take consumers to the product as we cannot bring the product to them. This means anything happening in the 'transition zone' between home and the destination, as well as in the destination itself, has a direct influence on the consumer experience. Luxury consumers are not immune from this fact as we can see from the following hypothetical examples:

- The first class passenger on a flight from London to Delhi whose flight is delayed by hours due to fog or snow at Heathrow Airport.
- The guests in a luxury villa who are disturbed by noise coming from a neighbouring villa.
- The honeymoon couple whose trip to the Caribbean is cut short by a hurricane.
- A luxury ski trip to a glamorous resort in Switzerland which is rather ruined by a lack of snow on the slopes.
- A strike that prevents people from visiting a world famous museum or means there are no taxis available for tourists.

Sadly, recent evidence has shown that we cannot even guarantee the safety and security of guests in hotels or walking in the street, in terms of terrorist attacks. While we cannot control terrorism or the other factors outlined above, we can take measures to reduce their potential impact and ensure consumers are aware and prepared for them.

However, in addition to supply side challenges in terms of uncontrollable factors, it is worth noting at this time that there are also demand side challenges that influence the perceptions which consumers have of the luxury products marketed by organisations. These include past experience and expectations together with personality and prejudices. In the case of luxury products I believe that expectations will be very high, which makes it harder to satisfy the consumer. This helps explain why when one looks at the hotels in cities with the best consumer reviews, the top twenty often includes hotels with modest prices that are by no means five star. Consumer expectations for these tend to be quite low so if they are well located, clean and friendly the guest is likely to be satisfied. However, if the hotel carries a world famous brand, nothing short of perfection will suffice or the hotel will have a dissatisfied guest. Many travellers seem to gain an almost perverse pleasure from writing negative reviews of luxury hotels and restaurants. It is also as if by saying that this widely recognised product did not meet *their* expectations they are signalling the superiority of their taste or experience.

Measures of luxury and their meaning today

Luxury is often in the eye of the beholder, a subjective matter that each person judges for themselves based on their own personality, knowledge and experience. Or it is a word used by marketers to encourage consumers to buy products and services at an elevated price.

However, attempts have been made, most notably in the hospitality sector, to produce schemes which flag up for guests levels of quality. In relation to hotels this means star systems, normally comprising of a five point scale starting with one star. Indeed, because of the hotel sector, it could be easily argued that the term 'five star' has now become a byword for luxury around the world and no longer just in relation to hospitality.

Yet while the hotel star system remains rooted in the consciousness of industry and many consumers, its currency has been hugely devalued by two developments as follows:

- First, the fact that the star system is not universal; some countries do not use stars at all, while those that do (including France) may not use five stars, and even those that do use five stars will often have different criteria to each other for the awarding of stars. Furthermore, the criteria are usually measurable and objective, whereas much of the idea of luxury appears to be subjective and not capable of being measured.

- Second, in some countries which have no formally recognised hotel classification system, hotels have given themselves any number of stars so that one famous hotel in the UAE has branded itself as a 'seven star hotel'!

These two factors between them have combined to bring hotel star systems to the point where they are virtually an object of ridicule.

However in the restaurant sector we see a form of quality 'labelling' which appears to have retained its credibility – namely the system of Michelin stars. Michelin stars still have a powerful influence within both industry and the market, and a restaurant which receives three Michelin stars is still imbued with a caché that says 'luxury' and 'exclusivity' and 'exquisite quality' and an 'extraordinary experience'. One reason that the Michelin system of restaurant stars has continued to flourish, is that it has moved with the times and embraced restaurants around the world and establishments that are more diverse than the traditional, rather stiff and formal 'classical' temple of fine dining.

The interesting point about the quality measurement systems we have been discussing is that the allocation of five stars or three stars is in the hands of non-partisan public officials or industry expert inspectors, who go to great lengths to ensure their judgements are impartial.

The big change now is that thanks to the rise of consumer generated media and social media, more and more power is resting in the hands of consumers themselves. These are not experts or professionals and as paying customers they are totally partial! They conform to no rules of conduct or even codes of behaviour. The criteria they use are wholly personal and largely subjective. Yet they have great power in terms of influencing the purchasing decisions of fellow consumers.

For industry the challenge of this phenomenon is that they cannot hope to influence it in any way nor do they have any real recourse against its judgements, no matter how unfair they may be. And if they do take issue with the opinions of consumers, it may simply look like they are unsympathetic or even antagonistic towards the views of those who provide their income.

So I am arguing that in terms of what is being recognised as 'luxury', the key role now is being played by consumers rather than industry experts or professionals. Perhaps the most famous example of this phenomenon is Tripadvisor, which has adopted the five point scale for quality but does not use stars. And the judgements are made by consumers who are not required to justify their judgement in any way.

Yet I would like to suggest that an even more interesting example is Skytrax, the website which features reviews of airlines and airports. This does use a five star system and some airlines have been known to use this 'five star' rating in their marketing campaigns. The website describes them as 'certified five star'. At the time of writing in February 2017 these 'five star' airlines were:

- ANA All Nippon Airways
- Asiana Airlines
- Cathay Pacific Airlines
- Etihad Air
- Garuda Indonesia Airlines
- Hainan Airlines
- Qatar Airways
- Singapore Airlines

However we need to make an important point at this stage, or at least pose an interesting question, about the relationship between luxury and quality.

There is no doubt that with the traditional measures, such as hotel stars and Michelin stars, the top category was associated with luxury. No one would expect to eat a cheap meal at a three Michelin star restaurant. And some hotel classification have traditionally specified a minimum price for hotels based on their star rating. However, with the newer consumer-driven review systems, this correlation is simply not there. In many big cities some of the highest rated hotels on TripAdvisor may well be small privately run hotels in the middle price range which are just well priced and enjoy a stunning location and great service. The top rated establishments may also include bed and breakfasts run by untrained amateurs, and apartments offered on websites, where the only service provided is a box from which you use a code to collect the key!I The restaurants near the top of the rating may also include a simple café on the beach or a famed but low priced fish and chip takeway shop or a 'pop-up' restaurant in someone's house.

Furthermore the airlines which have the highest ratings on Skytrax all offer several classes of travel and the system allows their economy class to also receive five stars as well as just the premier classes.

Therefore it appears that when consumers are asked to rate their experiences, it is not just about the luxury end. This is obviously not surprising as most consumers are not in the luxury segment – they are definitely a small minority.

In that case it may be that some consumers today are, even if they can afford luxury, increasingly much more interested in aspects of the consumption experience whether that be the reliability of an airline, the location of the hotel, or the uniqueness of the places where they eat out, than simply a reputation for being luxurious. After all if you book a first class ticket, but the flight is late is it really a luxury experience, as the economy class passenger who paid a fraction of what you did for their ticket should arrive at exactly the same time as you! We could say the same about the luxury hotel room with noisy neighbours or the high end restaurant where the officiousness of the waiting staff makes the guest feel unwelcome or uncomfortable.

Yet while there may be truth in this point that does not stop many other consumers dreaming and scheming so that they can enjoy those experiences which industry offers that are labelled as 'luxury'.

To bring this chapter towards its end we will stop looking at tourism, hospitality and events as a homogeneous single entity and have a look at its different sectors. Figure 6.3 offers a simplified diagram of the various sectors that make up tourism, hospitality and events.

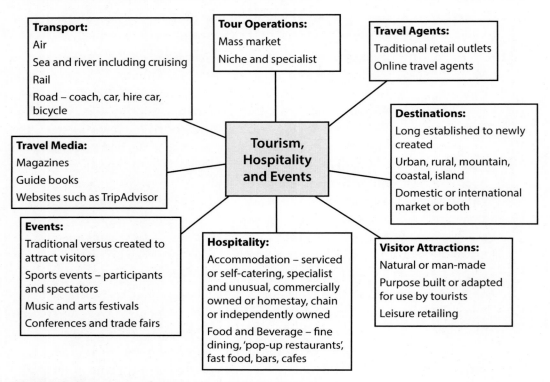

Figure 6.3: The sectors of tourism hospitality and events

■ Transport

In the transport sector, the concept of luxury is largely based around levels of comfort and personal space. Exclusivity is very difficult to achieve unless one is able and willing to charter a plane, boat or train. Otherwise, consumers do not get to choose who they travel with and are often sharing a relatively small space with a wide range of other users. However, those willing and able to pay a premium price are able to enjoy a higher level of comfort and personal service, and are often physically isolated from consumers who cannot afford or are unwilling to pay a premium price, even if the isolation simply means a curtain between one class and another on an airliner.

At the same time, though, transport operators go to great lengths to make their higher spending consumers feel special and differentiate them from other consumers. This may mean more leg room with the seats on trains and planes, more spacious cabins on cruise ships, and better quality meals on flights.

Cruise ships may offer a dozen cabin types from basic inside cabins with no window to the outside to 'President's' or 'Owner's' suites with huge balconies and spacious interiors. Airlines usually offer at most four classes, but again the core product can range from a seat with as little as 75 centimetres of leg room and a very limited degree of recline to a private 'cabin' or suite with 200 centimetres of leg room that converts into a full bed.

In their marketing, both airlines and cruise ships focus on their most luxurious categories of cabin because that is where most income is generated, and by depicting them it is hoped that some aspirational consumers may be persuaded to book a more luxurious (more expensive) class of travel than they had originally intended.

When comparing luxury in the airline and cruise sectors the amount of time spent by the consumers and the profile of users is very important. Most airline journeys are much less than 15 hours in duration and the majority of passengers in business and first class are probably business people rather than leisure travellers, although this is changing thanks to loyalty programme 'miles', where those who acquire 'miles' because of their business travel may then use these for leisure travel for family vacations. The relatively limited journey duration means that the focus of new product development is on comfort and stopping the passenger getting bored, hence the huge investment in airline food and entertainment systems as well as on the seat. Because many premium price service users are business people, convenience and not wasting time is also important, hence the express dedicated check-ins, priority bag delivery at the destination airport and the chauffeur driven car service offered by airlines such as Emirates.

In contrast with airlines which are a means to an end, with the end being arrival at a destination, cruise ships are, for many consumers, a destination in their own right. And of course it could be argued that they should no longer be seen as a means of transport, as few people now use cruise ships to get from A to B these days. However, for the purposes of this discussion, let us assume they are a means of transport. They may be seen as both destination and hotel combined for weeks or even months. It is imperative, therefore, that, they offer a wide range of leisure facilities. In addition to the cabins therefore, cruise lines invest very heavily in everything from onboard theatres, casinos and retail outlets, to adventure sports facilities and spas, to celebrity chef endorsed restaurants. If we were to discuss ferries instead, which are definitely a form of transport, the same points about leisure facilities would apply.

Interestingly though, most of the leisure facilities on cruise ships are rarely for the exclusive use of a particular class of traveller, but are open to all, as would generally be the case in a hotel as well.

Both airlines and cruise companies invest many millions of dollars on developing new physical facilities, particularly for their premium price consumers, in the hope of differentiating themselves from other players and achieving competitive advantage. Yet with every organisation having the same aim, these major invest-

6

ments can give an airline a distinct advantage for as little as a few months or a year or so and maybe a couple of years or a little more for cruise lines.

Cruise companies also have a further dimension to their product, and that is the itinerary and ports of call. These together with the duration of the voyage can be further ways of identifying cruises as particularly luxurious. The 'round-the-world cruise' which is now so popular is, perhaps, the ultimate luxury cruise, regardless of which class of cabin the traveller has booked, because to take the full cruise one must not only have money but also the 'luxury' of months of free time, as such cruises will usually take three or four months and have cabin prices starting from in excess of ten thousand dollars to anything up to over fifty thousand dollars.

On airliners, there are also significant differences in the staff-to-traveller ratio, to ensure that the level of personal service is higher in first class than business and in higher in business than in economy. This is very clear to any passenger on any long haul airliner. A similar phenomenon is to be found on cruise ships.

Road travel is a very interesting contrast with other modes of travel because here consumers have a unique option, in that they can use their own private car. This gives them the freedom to travel where they want when they want rather than being tied to schedules. The car also allows them to choose whom they travel with. This freedom and right to exclusive use is a form of luxury in itself and explains why, by comparison, public transport is less attractive for most car owners. It also explains the rapid growth in recent years of car hire and fly-drive vacations in many parts of the world.

■ Accommodation

The accommodation sector is increasingly diverse, and the concept of luxury is evolving and is longer purely based on high price, opulent environments and staff obliging every whim of the guest, although that certainly still exists in the hotel sector. If we take a broader view of luxury in terms of rarity value and exclusivity, rather than simply cost there are a number of observations to be made.

First, perhaps the most 'exclusive' and 'rare' quality an accommodation establishment can have is its location. A simple 'bed and breakfast' or small modestly priced hotel that has existed for many years in a recently developed destination may have the best location, whether that be on the best beach, on the main shopping street or next to the iconic site for which the destination is renowned. It may not be the most expensive accommodation, but because of its location it may well be the most exclusive.

Exclusivity and rarity value is also offered by 'pop up hotels' that are springing up – and closing down after a while – in cities around the world. Their limited time span is what creates the exclusivity quality in this case.

Another aspect of exclusivity in the accommodation sector is the idea that a consumer chooses a type of accommodation in a particular location that allows them to get 'beneath the skin' of the destination and experience things other tourists are not able to experience. This is much of the appeal of Airbnb, where guests feel they are staying with a 'real' and 'local' person who will be able to let them experience the 'real' destination rather than the packaged, commercialised version. However, it would be wrong to assume that all Airbnb accommodation is modestly priced. In 2015-16 the owners of famous five star hotels in Paris were complaining about 'unfair competition' from owners of luxury apartments renting out their property through Airbnb.

Rapidly growing in popularity in the luxury accommodation sector is the private luxury serviced villa, which the consumer has sole use of and which has a resident staff to provide for all their needs. The ultimate form of such accommodation is, perhaps, the opportunity to rent a whole island, which functions as your own private resort.

■ Restaurants

I would like to suggest that we are seeing a similar evolution of the luxury concept in the restaurant sector. Traditionally, luxury in this field even had its own term, 'gastronomy'. This was designed to distinguish it from merely eating. The Michelin star system provided an impartial service signposting consumers to what were seen as the pinnacles of culinary achievement. And there is no doubt that Michelin stars remain an incredibly important phenomenon within the luxury restaurant and eating out market.

Furthermore we are living in the era of the 'celebrity chef', where great chefs have become television stars, best-selling authors and in effect brands. Indeed it could be argued that chefs such as Alain Ducasse and Paul Bocuse have become luxury brands in themselves. Yet as with hotels there is a broadening of the luxury restaurant concept taking place, with issues of rarity, time and ethics becoming important criteria for somewhere being seen as a 'luxury' place to eat.Interestingly many 'pop up restaurants' have fewer seats than Michelin star restaurants, and in major cities there may be fewer of them, so they are actually a rarer commodity than restaurants recognised by Michelin.

Then we have the phenomenon of the 'slow food' movement where time is the precious commodity, with the 'luxury' element coming from having enough time to enjoy a leisurely experience,when the norm of eating is becoming fast food and sandwiches eaten at the desk while people continue working, or restaurants limiting the time diners can use a table for.

Finally in terms of ethics there are some interesting developments. First, there is growing opposition to what have been regarded as luxury foods such as shark fin soup, on the basis of animal cruelty or the sustainability of stocks. At the same time we have the issues around the fashionable idea of eating organic produce and locally sourced seasonal produce to reduce the phenomenon of 'food miles'.

■ Tour operation

The tour operation sector is interesting in the context of the concept of luxury, for to many people it is represents the absolute opposite of luxury travel. Tour operators are associated with the mass market, economies of scale and standardisation, all of which are anathema to a luxury consumer, according to conventional wisdom. Their growth gave birth to the 'snobbish' value-laden idea that some people are travellers while others are tourists.

However, there are tour operators which market themselves as 'luxury' operators usually based on small groups, exotic locations and often special interests. And, of course, mass market tour operators such as Thomas Cook did start life taking upscale British tourists to new formerly unknown destinations.

■ Travel agents

The link between travel agents and luxury is an interesting one as many people seem to think the traditional travel agent is likely to disappear now that we have online travel agents and consumers are able to make their own bookings directly. However, some types of independent high street travel agents still seem to be doing well particularly those in affluent locations focusing on high end vacations such as cruises, weddings and honeymoons, and trips to remote exotic locations. For those who have money but little spare time, the service provided by a travel agent can be of value, but only if the agency staff are themselves well travelled and well educated.

■ Attractions

The visitor attraction sector is in one way, perhaps, the most important in tourism, because it represents the motivation for most leisure travel. People use transport and accommodation because they want to visit attractions and the destinations in which they are located. Indeed many tourist destinations grow up because of the location of visitor attractions, whether they are theme parks or religious sites, museums or nature sites, unique landscape features or famous retail outlets.

Yet most visitor attractions do not separate 'classes' of consumer in the way that airlines and hotels do with their businesses classes and executive floors. Everyone tends to use the place at the same time as other people, with no control over whom they share the experience with.

Therefore the only ways of differentiating the experience and creating some element of 'luxury' are the pre-purchase of tickets to avoid the need for queuing, for example. But this does not require wealth, just organisation on the part of the consumer. Likewise private tours can be arranged and consumers can feel superior in their knowledge in an art gallery, for instance, by taking a tour with an expert.

■ Events

The events sector is very diverse, covering everything from a professional football match to a religious festival, as well as rock concerts, an exhibition at an art gallery and a celebratory event such as the St Patrick's Day celebration of the kind that takes place in many parts of the world on March 17th.

Like visitor attractions, many events are open to anyone who can buy a ticket, although at many of them consumers will be segregated on the basis of the ticket they purchased, as there are often different categories of ticket based on the seat location. At many concerts now, those willing to pay extra can enjoy the opportunity to meet the performers by buying a 'meet and greet' package. Furthermore, there is often an unofficial 'black' market in event tickets, with a ticket priced at one hundred dollars maybe selling for a thousand dollars, if all tickets have been sold. In this case such tickets could certainly be seen as a 'luxury'!

At the same time some events, over time, attract a reputation for being 'luxurious', based on the nature of the event and who attends. For example, in the UK the Henley Regatta, a rowing event associated with public schools, and the Ascot Races are an example of this phenomenon.

Most of what we have said about events relates to events designed to attract visitors, usually with the aim of making money. However, with traditional events that are religious, for instance, the 'luxury' element may be represented by the opportunity for a foreign tourist to visit a local religious event that would normally only be attended by local people. For them it is part of their everyday life while for the tourist it is a once on a lifetime opportunity to enter into an unknown world that few other 'outsiders' have experienced.

Conclusions

I think we have seen that, as we have noted elsewhere in the book, the nature of luxury is changing in response to changes in society, economic factors and technology. The idea of luxury just being about high prices and opulence, while still partly true, has become wider and incorporated issues ranging from rarity to ethics to the concept of free time. And while rarity or exclusivity has always been a symbol of luxury, it no longer implies a luxury price tag, as we have seen from the case of pop-up restaurants, for example.

In this chapter we have focused on the supply side, the provision of products and services. I would like to suggest that there is something of a 'chicken and egg' situation here. In other words are changes in consumer behaviour leading to changes in the supply side or are changes in the supply side influencing consumer behaviour. The answer is probably both.

One change we have seen on the supply side is the fact that the term 'luxury' is now being applied to virtually every type of product or experience from airlines to hotels but also camping and cycling, walking tours and ferries. Many believe the word is being hyped and over-used and may thus become either meaningless or, worse still, a term that has negative connotations. In that respect it is sometimes compared to the term 'boutique hotel'.

Maybe this trend is inevitable as luxury is an aspirational concept and we have mass markets where everyone aspires to be seen as a luxury consumer. But in doing so we may see the 'de-luxurification' of luxury! The term is also damaged every time a consumer believes that what they experienced has not lived up to the marketing hype. The term 'luxury' brings high expectations which suppliers have to meet or they will face customer dissatisfaction.

For supply side organisations the chang ing nature of luxury is a real challenge as well as an opportunity. It means rethinking products, pricing, promotion and distribution. And as consumer expectations continuously rise as organisations promise more and more the organisations themselves are forced to invest in product development to meet the expectations, some of which are unrealistic.

One could argue that industry has created a 'Frankenstein' customer who expects luxury at a budget price and will punish failure to deliver their expectations through social media reviews.

It is also my view that industry is not keeping up to speed with the evolution of the concept of luxury, particularly in relation to the rarity and value of leisure time and the growing consumer interest in ethical issues, values and authenticity. Even luxury hotels have check-in and check-out procedures that are lengthy in terms of time. You may check in at an executive check-in desk, but it may well be twenty minutes or more from arriving to being in your room with no one hassling you for a tip while disguised as a service deliverer! And luxury hotels are still being designed as kitsch representations of traditional local architectural style.

Having looked at the supply side let us now move our attention to the destination, the place where the supply side organisations and the consumers interact.

7 Luxury Tourist Destinations

Introduction

This chapter will endeavour to identify the characteristics of a luxury tourist destination. It will investigate if there is a 'magic formula' for determining which will be perceived as luxurious, involving traditional criteria such as unique product attributes, for example a world renowned beach or retail offer together with high end hotels and restaurants. Is it important to have a reputation from the past to be seen as luxury today or can a place be seen as luxury from day one, as countries build new resorts from nothing in an attempt to earn 'tourist gold'? Are the presence of celebrities and high prices for everything pre-requisites for anywhere that wishes to be seen as a serious luxury destination?

I will suggest that in many ways the question of whether somewhere is a luxury travel destination is as much a matter of emotion as it is of fact.

We will also consider whether a mass market destination can have small luxury destinations within it, such as a large-scale single ownership all-inclusive resort.

At the end of the chapter I will explore the idea of a fashion cycle in relation to tourist destinations. I will also pose the question of whether the destination is beginning to play a less important part in the vacation experience as it becomes a mere backdrop to the activities of tourists.

Figure 7.1 endeavours to identify some of the key factors that influence the perception of a place as a luxury destination. I believe that all of these factors identified have an impact on perceptions of whether a place is a luxury destination.

Historical reputation

Until recently the historical reputation of a place was very important to its image, but we need to remember that until the last few decades international tourism was focused in relatively few parts of the world. In that situation a few iconic locations became bywords for luxury amongst the tiny minority of the world's population that was able to travel internationally.

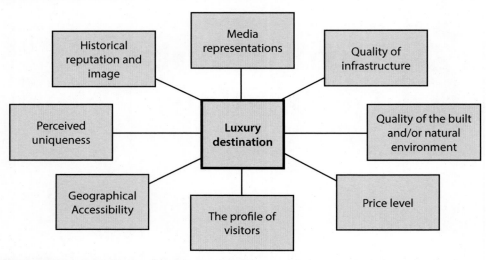

Figure 7.1: Factors that may determine if a destination is seen as a luxury destination

The French Riviera is an example of such a destination and its reputation continues as a luxury destination, in some markets, long after it has probably ceased to be chic and exclusive and inhabited only by rich tourists. Reputations can certainly exist long after the reality as changed. Bali is often seen as a luxurious and exotic destination yet the reality is now that it is a mainstream mass market long-haul destination. Many people might, say a place such as Dubai is a luxury destination yet it has no historic reputation as such for it has only been developed as a tourist destination over the past twenty years.

Media representations

I would like to argue that media representations are today, perhaps, the single most important factor influencing the reputation of a destination. One main reason for this is that unlike some of the factors in Figure 7.1, media representations will have affected the image of a destination for tourists who have not visited it. Media is now truly global and is part of our life through every waking hour. Media representations of destinations can, of course, be both positive and negative, although in relation to luxury they are usually the former. Just some of the ways in which the media may impact on destination image are as follows:

- Celebrity endorsements or visits, e.g. George Clooney getting married in Venice.

- Movies and television shows that feature a particular location.

- Travel magazines and glossy lifestyle magazines that see travel as a vital element in a luxurious lifestyle, for example Condé Nast.

- So-called reality TV shows that feature travel and tourism in any way.

- Consumer reviews of places and vacation experiences placed on various social media platforms.

We need to recognise that destination image today is created much more by the media, than it is by the work of destination marketing organisations who, I believe, generally have only a marginal effect on how destinations are seen by consumers.

Uniqueness

For many commentators, uniqueness is linked to the idea of luxury because it represents a form of exclusivity. But it is a strange idea in tourism because every place and every vacation is in reality unique. Perhaps it is really about the perception of uniqueness, and uniqueness as a positive, for something can also be unique but negative!

Quality of destination infrastructure

I believe that most tourists would say that the quality of infrastructure is vital to any destination that wishes to be seen as a luxury place to vacation. The most important elements of the infrastructure would include:

- Transport links both to and within the destination; these will be judged in terms of criteria including convenience, reliability, comfort and safety.

- The accommodation stock in terms of the star ratings of hotels, locations, and services available.

- The availability of opportunities for eating out, whether upscale fine dining restaurants or 'unique' experiences such as eating under the stars in a desert.

- Retail opportunities, from the gold souk of Dubai to the designer brand stores of London or Paris.

- Upmarket entertainment facilities, including casinos, opera houses, theatres, and fashionable night clubs and bars.

- Visitor attractions and sightseeing opportunities that carry status in the tourism market.

Quality of the built and/or natural environment

The quality of the built and/or natural environment is also seen as an important factor in the luxury market. Most so-called luxury destinations have physical attraction, whether it be beautiful buildings or a stunning natural setting. However this is not always the case. Dubai does not have a spectacular setting and has few beautiful old buildings. However it does have unique ultra-modern buildings and is set in a desert. But it would be hard to imagine anywhere being seen as a luxury destination if it was on a flat featureless plain, with rubbish in the streets, and modest buildings made of concrete within the last fifty years!

Having said that, I will later argue that destinations may becoming less important than what goes on in them; in other words perhaps they are becoming simply a backdrop for what consumers want to do, rather than a focus for their travels.

Price level

To many people the price level is a key indicator of luxury, and high prices are seen as essential to ensure exclusivity, hence the marketing phrase, 'reassuringly expensive' that has been used previously. However, as we noted earlier, many luxury consumers are interested in value for money and countless websites encourage them to believe that discount price luxury is possible. When we look at destinations specifically, the 'luxury equals high price idea' has its own issues.

First, in some places you can enjoy some of the attractions free of charge, such as beaches, views or nature reserves.

Second, price levels vary dramatically between destinations based on their level of economic development. A five star hotel may cost as little as seventy dollars in some places and hundreds of dollars in others. Perhaps one reason why Asia has developed as a destination for Europeans in recent years is that because of low labour costs it can offer the trappings of luxury at an affordable price.

Profile of visitors

The profile of visitors is an important determinant of the reputation of a destination and whether it will be perceived as luxury or not. Let us look at a few possible scenarios to explore this idea further, as follows:

1   A chic island where virtually all the tourists are in the luxury category and all hotels are five star resorts. Everyone would agree this is a luxury destination.

2   An island with enclaves of five star resorts located near to three star all inclusive resorts, so that the two groups of tourists meet in the streets and market but not on the beaches which are private. The five star clients may see their resort as luxury but not the rest of the island, while the three star clients will look at the five star resorts and may well see the whole island as luxury because that also enhances their own feeling of self-worth.

3   A long established coastal resort that tourists have visited for one hundred years. Its glamorous image now attracts a mass market and it still has five star hotels, a marina and a casino. The mass market visitors look at the physical infrastructure and, aware of the reputation of the place, label it as luxury in their own minds. Meanwhile the luxury consumers are 'hiding' from the mass market tourists in their private villas or on their yachts or they visit at quieter times of the year. Or they may even have deserted the destination saying things like 'it's not the place it used to be', yet the luxury image will last long after the last luxury consumer has departed, never to return.

4   A remote place that is hard to get to and where nature is the attraction and infrastructure is limited, which is visited by the classic luxury consumer in search of new experiences and backpackers who are certainly not in the luxury

segment. Given the absence of things to spend money on, there are no obvious ways of demonstrating wealth beyond maybe having a better quality tent! Yet maybe this is still a luxury destination because it is visited by few people and having visited it bestows status on the traveller amongst their peers, whether they be well-heeled tourists or backpackers.

5   Several movie stars and rock musicians have bought villas on a certain island and this has been publicised by the media. Perhaps the island is only a luxury destination when these people are on the island or is it a luxury destination because celebrities have chosen to buy property there?

Geographical accessibility

In terms of the factors that determine whether a destination is perceived as luxury the issue of geographical accessibility is fascinating because there is no simple answer. It needs to be accessible enough to be reached within a day from where the traveller resides, but not so accessible that it is easy and inexpensive for the mass market to visit. Within a destination, of course, accessibility can be restricted physically through walls and fences to give privacy to luxury consumers.

Typology of destinations

Let us now look at a possible typology of destinations that may be described as 'classic' luxury destinations as illustrated in Figure 7.2. There are interesting observations that can be made about each of these types of luxury destination, in respect of the role of tourism and hospitality and their reliance upon it.

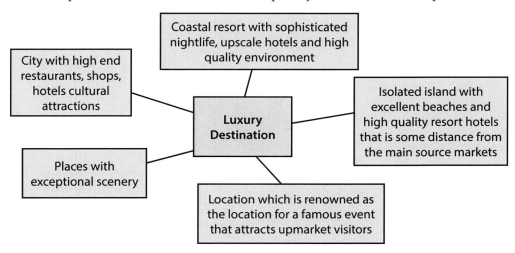

Figure 7.2: Potential typology of 'classic' luxury destinations

Cities

Major upscale urban tourist destinations tend to be places which had a life before the arrival of visitors and still have a life beyond tourism. They are likely to have a well-established resident population that will also include luxury consumers. It is likely that the trappings of luxury tourism, such as fine dining restaurants, luxury shopping and highbrow cultural attractions, will have existed for decades or even centuries to meet the desires of residents. Tourists therefore simply represent a new market for these existing services. Even upscale hotels may have existed in such cities prior to the leisure travel boom to serve the needs of business travellers. This is clearly the case in the case of 'old world' cities such as London and Paris and is now also the case with 'new world' cities from New York to Shanghai.

Given their size, history and economic diversity, cities are rarely economically dependent on tourism in a way that other types of destination can be, although there are a few exceptions such as Venice.

The geographical scale of cities also means that tourists may be concentrated in certain areas of the city, and may have only very limited impact on the majority of the urban area. How far beyond the Ramblas do most tourists stray in Barcelona and how many visit Queens in New York, Lewisham in London, or the outer arrondisements of Paris? However, it is now becoming fashionable to search out the less visited part of cities in the name of authenticity, partly because of the influence of Air BnB.

Coastal resorts

Coastal resorts have existed for a few centuries now and may often have originated as fishing ports or maritime transport hubs and for many years tourism and fishing may have lived alongside each other, with the fishing actually providing sightseeing interest and atmosphere for tourists, particularly artists. In addition to staying tourists, coastal resorts, like coastal cities, have often been able to attract luxury cruise passengers for day visits. Many coastal resorts have become dependent on tourism in recent years due to the decline in traditional coastal industries such as fishing and shipbuilding.

Islands

Island destinations tend to have developed more recently due to the rise of affordable air travel. Even if islands have a long history they tend to find that the luxury market is much more interested in their physical attractions than in their culture. Many islands have sought to attract tourism as their isolation has often presented them with major obstacles to the development of other industries. As a result they tend to become highly dependent on tourism, as can be seen from many islands in the Indian Ocean and the Caribbean.

Exceptional scenery

From the 19th century, places with exceptional scenery began to develop as tourist destinations as rail travel made them more accessible. As well as sightseeing, such places encouraged the development of new adventure sports such as mountaineering and skiing. The Swiss mountains are a great example of this, where names such as Zermatt became synonymous with luxury travel and adventure. Early travellers loved lakes and Switzerland was well placed there too. Lake Luzern and Lac Leman (Lake Geneva) are still today symbols of luxury travel. Top end travellers were not put off by extreme winter weather, providing they had luxury hotels to retire to at the end of the day, with roaring fires and 'gluwein'.

Interestingly, many of the countries that developed early as luxury scenery and adventure sport destinations have never become dependent on tourism for a variety of reasons. Switzerland has had its luxury consumer goods industries such as watch-making and its lucrative banking sector, while Norway has had its oil industry. For such countries therefore tourism has always been the 'icing on the cake' rather than the cake itself.

Special events

Finally, we have the destinations which grew up because of an event that attracted upscale visitors. Here, the visitation is only temporary, and for most of the year luxury tourists will be absent, but the reputation for luxury will exist between events. The kinds of events that, traditionally, were associated with luxury segment visitors, would have included spectator sports such as tennis, grand prix races, horse-racing, golf and arts events such as opera seasons and film festivals. Their temporary nature means destinations tend not to be over-dependent on their hosting of events. However, it is likely that Cannes would attract fewer tourists year round without the glamour bestowed on it by the film festival, for example.

Attractions, hospitality units and destinations

So far in this chapter we have talked as if the concept of a destination is simple and clear cut. I would now like to introduce a complication in terms of the distinction between visitor attractions, hospitality units and tourist destinations. Until recently the distinction was clear. Attractions were the things which motivated tourist trips to destinations, while hospitality units were the services tourists needed to allow them to enjoy their visits to the attractions in the destination. Furthermore, the tourist destination was fixed in space, a geographical location, a place. However, in recent years, the line has become blurred by developments in the supply side in tourism and hospitality

Figure 7.3 seeks to illustrate four ways in which the idea of a luxury destination, and indeed destinations as a whole, has become blurred.

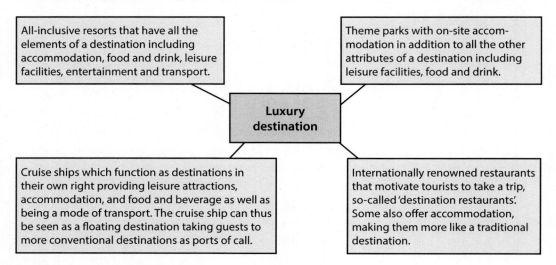

All-inclusive resorts that have all the elements of a destination including accommodation, food and drink, leisure facilities, entertainment and transport.

Theme parks with on-site accommodation in addition to all the other attributes of a destination including leisure facilities, food and drink.

Luxury destination

Cruise ships which function as destinations in their own right providing leisure attractions, accommodation, and food and beverage as well as being a mode of transport. The cruise ship can thus be seen as a floating destination taking guests to more conventional destinations as ports of call.

Internationally renowned restaurants that motivate tourists to take a trip, so-called 'destination restaurants'. Some also offer accommodation, making them more like a traditional destination.

7.3: Blurring the concept of a luxury tourist destination

Of course, I recognise that the contents of Figure 7.3 are quite contentious. However I believe that the idea of what constitutes 'a destination' is changing and that the line between attractions, hospitality units and destinations is changing.

Club Med sites, the pioneers of all-inclusive resorts, were often developed in places where tourism did not exist before, and often in turn became the catalyst for the development of a more traditional destination. Today, many all-inclusive resorts exist in places which have little of the normal destination infrastructure around them. This feels a little like the 'chicken and egg' syndrome. Does the lack of infrastructure create the need for resorts to be all-inclusive or do the resorts stop the development of the infrastructure such as bars, restaurants and so on, because consumers do not wish to leave the resort as everything is included in the price, even at the luxury end of the market?

Theme parks would, perhaps, not be seen as luxury as such, although certain iconic ones are perceived to be so in some cultures. For a Chinese family, for example, a visit to Disney World in Florida, staying in a Disney hotel, enjoying a 'character breakfast' with Mickey Mouse may indeed be a luxury experience.

There are many examples across the world of 'destination restaurants', where a chef sites a restaurant in a remote location, which becomes a tourist destination because of it. For example, the Bras family and their three Michelin Star restaurant, *Le Suchet*, in the Aveyron hills near Lagioule in central France. Or a restaurateur can develop a restaurant in a small village with no gastronomic tradition and create a gastronomy destination single-handedly, as Nathan Outlaw has done with his two Michelin star restaurant in Port Issac in Cornwall. Gastronomic restaurants can even enhance the reputation of a whole city as a destination, as in the case of *NOMA* in Copenhagen or *El Cellier de Can Roca* in Girona.

Perhaps of the four examples used in Figure 7.3, it is the cruise ship which is the most contentious given it is not a geographical location at all! Yet many cruise companies market their products as if they were destinations. Indeed many guests prefer to stay on board, enjoying the facilities, even when the ship is docked in one of its calling ports!

Shortly, in Figure 7.4, I will put forward three models of the development of luxury destinations. Before that I would like to explore another aspect of the luxury destination, namely the 'purpose-built destination'. As we have noted already, most luxury destinations – indeed all tourist destinations – have grown organically over time through a process by which tourism joins existing local activities and land uses, and either lives alongside them or even eventually takes over to the point where the area is almost mono-cultural. However, this is not always the case, as some destinations were purpose-built specifically to attract tourists. Little or nothing existed there before and there is no intention that the place should become anything other than a leisure tourism destination.

In the early days of railways in the UK, entrepreneurs developed coastal resorts from virtually nothing, in places such as Blackpool. Zermatt was created from a sparsely populated upland to a playground of the rich, thanks to the efforts of local entrepreneurs. In recent decades the development of tourist destinations from little or nothing has gathered pace as countries and individuals seek to exploit the dramatic growth seen in tourism globally over the last fifty years or so. In the 1970s the French government created resorts along the Languedoc coast for strategic economic reasons, but these were not luxury destinations. Other governments, such as that of Tunisia, followed suit.

Las Vegas is a perfect example of a different type of purpose-built destination, developed by 'entrepreneurs' motivated purely by commercial and even allegedly criminal motives. The destination in the desert was created to indulge the desire of Americans to gamble, a 'luxury' in a country with very strict gambling laws. Sun City in South Africa, developed during the apartheid era, flaunted the idea of a luxury lifestyle in a country where few could hope to visit not only because they lacked the money but also because of the colour of their skins. And we have Dubai, another luxury destination in the desert, which became a byword for ostentatious luxury with its 'seven star hotel', real snow ski slope, and expensive apartments on an artificially constructed island.

In an era of rapid growth in tourism and impatience it seems likely that we will see more and more purpose built destinations being developed. Whether they will survive as long as those which have developed organically over time remains to be seen but they have certainly made their mark in the world.

In Figure 7.4 I will put forward the idea that there are three main models for the evolution and development of luxury destinations: the 'traditional development', the 'modern incremental development' and the 'modern planned development'. While this is highly generalised, I believe that it does represent reality in many locations around the world, although many destinations are probably a combination of the second and third models.

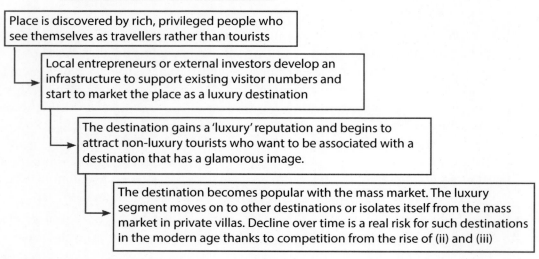

Figure 7.4: Three models of the evolution of luxury destinations. (i) Traditional model

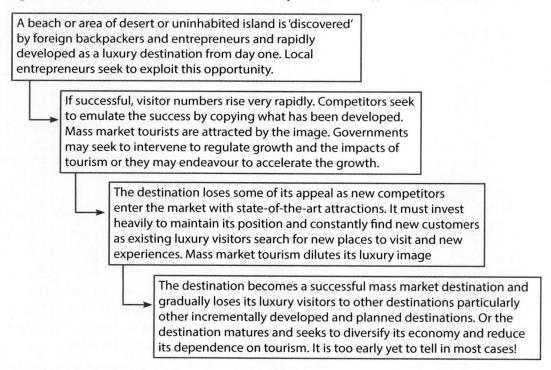

Figure 7.4 (ii): Modern incremental development model

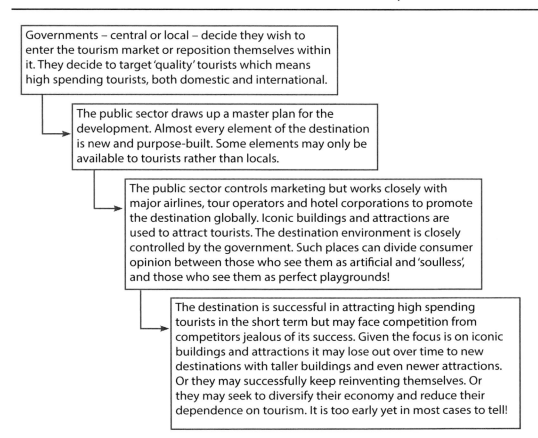

Governments – central or local – decide they wish to enter the tourism market or reposition themselves within it. They decide to target 'quality' tourists which means high spending tourists, both domestic and international.

The public sector draws up a master plan for the development. Almost every element of the destination is new and purpose-built. Some elements may only be available to tourists rather than locals.

The public sector controls marketing but works closely with major airlines, tour operators and hotel corporations to promote the destination globally. Iconic buildings and attractions are used to attract tourists. The destination environment is closely controlled by the government. Such places can divide consumer opinion between those who see them as artificial and 'soulless', and those who see them as perfect playgrounds!

The destination is successful in attracting high spending tourists in the short term but may face competition from competitors jealous of its success. Given the focus is on iconic buildings and attractions it may lose out over time to new destinations with taller buildings and even newer attractions. Or they may successfully keep reinventing themselves. Or they may seek to diversify their economy and reduce their dependence on tourism. It is too early yet in most cases to tell!

Figure 7.4(iii): Modern planned development model

There are a number of interesting points that can be made around this proposed typology, some of which are fundamental to the concept of what the term 'luxury destination' might mean.

First, it is my view, based on observation rather than in-depth research, that the life cycle of luxury destinations is certainly shortening due to a range of factors including economic development, social media and social change, to name but three. Fashion plays a crucial role in the image of destinations, particularly in the luxury sector, and the growth in the number of destinations and the impact of the media is probably leading to a shorter and shorter fashion cycle in other destinations too. It is not that a destination always loses luxury consumers because it is no longer seen as luxurious, but simply that somewhere else comes along which is new and different, and attracts the footloose luxury traveller for whom part of their status comes from visiting places that others have not yet visited.

Second, this leads on to an interesting question as to whether a place that was seen as a luxury destination and then becomes seen as more mainstream can ever be seen as chic and luxurious again. We probably cannot answer this yet as mass tourism is such a recent phenomenon and not enough time has elapsed to give us the evidence of which to base a judgement. It will be fascinating to see what happens with Cuba, which represented decadent luxury for American tourists in the time before Castro, then started to attract mid-level mass market package tourists and may now go in a number of directions. It could continue with mass market beach tourism, try to restore the glamour of the past, albeit the glamour of a time when tourism and criminality went hand in hand, or go for more authentic niche market tourism, and so on.

Third, with the democratisation of travel, it is no longer the rich who are often the pioneers of the new luxury destinations. Instead it may be backpackers or gap year travellers, who have the luxury of time if not money, and are always looking for new places to visit. This encourages entrepreneurs to develop a simple infrastructure, after which major corporations see the potential and invest in the kind of infrastructure that luxury travellers expect.

Fourth, there is clearly a tension between the luxury market and the mass market and luxury segment travellers tend to move on from places once the mass market arrives or to isolate themselves from mass tourists behind their villa walls.

Fifth, the government planned development model for destinations represents a relatively new approach which has been seen most clearly in places such as Dubai. This requires the government to have enormous financial resources and the ability to take decisions quickly, which is probably not compatible with western-style democracy and community participation. It is not surprising therefore that such an approach to development has been seen in relatively few places.

Sixth, competition between luxury destinations is intense, because this market is seen to be particularly attractive, being made up of high spending visitors who are usually people with above average influence. They may even be celebrities, in an age when celebrity is a popular obsession in many countries. Every destination would like to be visited by such people, for some of their glamour will hopefully rub off on the destination and enhance its image. This high level of competition though means that to attract luxury travellers a destination needs to be constantly investing to stay ahead of competitors. These destinations are thus on a roller-coaster that they cannot get off once it starts.

Seventh, as we noted earlier 'luxury is in the eye of the beholder', so one option for a place that is no longer seen as a luxury destination by its traditional markets is to look for new customers who will see it as a luxurious place to visit. This often means people from different parts of the world with no previous experience of the destination in question. When Eastern European tourists began to travel to Western Europe, they were targeted by destinations such as Benidorm. For these consumers, used to the Black Sea Coast resorts, Spanish coastal resorts, at first, appeared luxurious by comparison. And places such as the French Riviera which have lost much of their glamorous image amongst Europeans, are still perceived as glamorous by some tourists from Asia making their first trip to Europe.

Finally, all three models in Figure 7.4 see luxury destinations progressing from no infrastructure to a highly developed physical infrastructure, but based on what has been said elsewhere in this book, we need to recognise that this may be different in the future. Maybe a destination will only be seen as 'luxurious' when it is authentic, with no tourism infrastructure and perhaps even very few tourists. Or it could become a term used for those places that you need the 'luxury' of lots of leisure time to visit, perhaps by overland transport or ships rather than airliners. Perhaps it will be a place where you practice 'slow tourism' rather tha n trying to pack lots of expensive experiences into a short period of time. Could it mean destinations that clearly have an ethical approach to tourism incorporating the principles of 'fair trade'?

Conclusions

So where does all this leave us in relation to the concept of a luxury destination?To begin with, I would like to suggest that the concept of the luxury destination has changed over time for many reasons but perhaps there are two which stand out.

First, is the fact that over the past half century or so, as international leisure travel has gone from being a privilege open to only a few people in a small number of countries, primarily in Europe, to a mass market involving the majority of citizens in those countries where travel was previously open only to a small elite. Perhaps more importantly though, over the same period, outbound international travel has started to grow dramatically in recently developed countries with little history of large-scale outbound leisure travel, including India and China.

Second, and over the same period in tandem, the growth of tourism worldwide has been fed by a constant flow of new destinations coming into the market as places set out to attract tourists to help boost their economies. Many of these 'new' destinations are in Asia the Gulf States and Africa, often in places only visited by Europeans and North Americans because of colonialism or wars.

These two linked phenomena have changed the concept of the luxury destination in a number of ways as follows:

■ Europeans, Americans and Australians have discovered destinations in Asia where low labour costs make a level of personal service the norm which is no longer to be found even in five star hotels in their own countries.

■ For tourists from the newer generating countries, such as India and China, the traditional European 'luxury destinations' are exotic and glamorous because of their history as much as their present. Yet for many Europeans these places have become either mundane because they have been much visited or appear old fashioned as tastes have changed since they were first developed.

■ Instead of destinations acquiring a luxury reputation over time as has previously usually been the case, we have seen the rise of purpose developed luxury destinations, planned or encouraged by governments eager to exploit tourism. Thus the element of history and tradition which has been the basis of many luxury destinations has been challenged by the creation of these new 'instant destinations'.

■ With the rise in the number of places being marketed as luxury destinations, we have also witnessed a decline in 'brand loyalty' to destinations. Instead people are seeking new experiences all the time, which means trying new destinations rather than simply returning to old favourites.

At the same time, and fuelled by the rise in the number of destinations seeking to attract luxury consumers, we have the issue of the 'fashion cycle' in relation to luxury destinations. This does not mean a destination will lose tourists when it is seen as less fashionable as new competitors emerge, but it does mean that the type of tourist may change and the number of tourists may actually increase as the mass market moves in. And one reason why the mass market will move in is because often the reputation for luxury survives long after the reality of luxury has gone. This time lapse between image and reality is well known in tourism, but is particularly fascinating in relation to places with a reputation as luxury destinations.

What we can say, I believe with some certainty, is that the idea of luxury destinations is much more about emotions than it is about rationality and facts. Of course, destination marketers recognise that fact and therefore try to portray pretty well everywhere as a luxury destination in some form or other, because they know luxury is something most people find aspirational. However, there is the risk that in using the word so loosely they risk devaluing the term completely.

Before making one final general comment about luxury destinations I would like to offer a few more thoughts about the evolution of the concept of the luxury destination.

First, perhaps in the future we will see more places developing reputations as luxury destinations for reasons other high prices, five star hotels and luxurious environments. This might mean the 'feelgood destination' where the principles of fair trade underpin the tourist experience such that the tourist in the luxury hotel does not have pangs of guilt about the low wages paid to the staff or the beggars on the streets outside the hotel. Or the basis of the reputation may be based on its authenticity so the visitor feels they have been to a 'real place' rather than a synthetic soulless place. Or it could mean places which you only really appreciate if you have the time to enjoy them 'slowly'. I believe there is some evidence that all of these trends are under way although I would not for a moment claim that they represent the majority of luxury destination demand at present.

Second, it will also be interesting to see if luxury and nostalgia start to become even more closely intertwined with the creation of 'retro resorts', places which seek to recreate in totality a bygone age in every respect. A 1930s themed resort, for example, with no modern technology but lots of style, where the guests can immerse themselves in a version of the lifestyle of the traveller of the 1930s when travel was the preserve of a glamorous elite. Consumption would maybe be by invitation only! This may be fanciful but stranger things have happened, and it is a way of creating uniqueness and exclusivity which remains a bedrock of the idea of luxury in tourism and hospitality.

Third, we need to recognise that the idea of a destination is becoming blurred as we saw in Figure 7.3. as large all-inclusive resort complexes, major theme parks and so on start to take on more and more of the features of a traditional destination.

Fourth, a number of locations, particularly in Asia, are beginning to attract what we might term 'tourist in-migration', particularly amongst retired people from Europe and North America. People who have visited a place as tourists are choosing to move to the destination to live when they retire, and some destinations are encouraging this phenomenon. This tends to take place as a flow of people from places with higher costs of living to those with lower costs of living. Thus a taxi driver who used to drive me to Manchester airport bought a property in India for his retirement, despite having no connection with India apart from as a tourist. But as he explained: "If I sell my small terraced house in England I can afford to buy a huge house in India and my modest state pension and small occupational pension will allow me to even have staff to look after my home in India as I get older." For this man migration to India seemed to represent a chance to attain a luxurious lifestyle he could not enjoy in his own country and he could turn his retirement into a permanent vacation in effect. This phenomenon has seen rapid growth in recent years although it clearly has major implications for destinations, which are by no means all positive.

Fifth, in a world where population growth is continuing and many more affluent people live and work in large crowded cities, worrying about the impact of stress on their lives, it seems likely that solitude and peace may increasingly be valued as a 'luxury' so that destinations that offer such attributes will start to be seen more luxurious, even if their infrastructure is basic or even primitive. This trend is already apparent but I predict that it will grow dramatically in the future.

And now for my final thought on the question of luxury destinations and I think it is a pretty fundamental one. While I cannot point to any concrete evidence I have a clear view that the destination itself is becoming rather less important in

7

the vacation than it was previously. Instead it is becoming more of a backdrop for the experience. This may be because destinations seem to be becoming more standardised in their elements, or travel becomes more common and less out of the ordinary for people, or because most destination investment is in activities and infrastructure. And maybe once you have visited one tropical island or rain forest you become blasé about ones you visit in future and take less notice of the places, and more of the personal experience you have there with family or friends. Or perhaps it reflects the fact that tourists are more and more isolated from the rest of the destinations particularly in the increasingly popular all-inclusive resorts where the tourist may never leave the resort and visit anywhere else in the destination. Whatever the reason, if this is true, it represents a major challenge for the future for destinations if the place itself becomes less important than what you do in it. On the other hand maybe the growth of ideas of authenticity and responsible tourism will reverse this trend.

Conclusions to Part 3

We all know that the tourism/hospitality/events sector is incredibly fragmented and that destinations are an amazingly complex phenomenon. It should come as no surprise therefore to learn that this section is by definition a little more superficial than the other would have wished. Nevertheless, a number of interesting points have arisen from the two chapters.

☐ First, I have suggested that the traditional luxury product attributes, while still having some relevance, are being joined by new attributes which companies need to take into account when developing new products and experiences.

☐ Second, I have suggested, strongly, that the meaning of the term luxury itself is being diluted and maybe even damaged by its over-use by marketing professionals who seem to be affixing this label to virtually everything that is being offered.

☐ Third, we saw that a number of factors affect whether a destination has an image as a luxury destination and that this image and these factors change over time.

☐ Finally, I have put forward the tentative idea that destinations are becoming less important in their own right – that they are often becoming backdrops rather than key players. In other words, perhaps, what is happening and who it is happening to are more important than where it is happening.

In Part 4 we will look at some key emerging themes in luxury in tourism, hospitality and events

Part 4: The Big Questions in Luxury in Tourism, Hospitality and Events

In this section we drill down into five themes which I believe are having, and will have in future, a great impact on what luxury means in tourism, hospitality and events.

In Chapter 8 we focus on how technologies are affecting luxury in terms of everything from how people buy products or experiences to how service is delivered.

Chapter 9 focuses on service, which has always been at the heart of any discussion about luxury and will look at how and why it is changing.

In Chapter 10 we focus on the idea of the 'experience economy' and its impact on the meaning of luxury in tourism, hospitality and events

Chapter 11 looks at the relationship between luxury and sustainability. These two terms have been seen as polar opposites but we will discuss if that is changing.

Finally, Chapter 12 looks at brands and luxury, two words that traditionally go closely together, particularly if the word 'designer' comes just before 'brand'.

8 How is Technology Changing the Meaning of Luxury?

Introduction

Everyone is fully aware in their daily lives of how much technology-driven change has taken place in recent years. This has affected everything from how we communicate with each other to how we shop, and the change is continuous. At the time of writing there is great media interest in the testing of driverless cars. At the same time technological innovation is influencing what we wear, with the advent of smart watches, for instance.

In the world of tourism, hospitality and events, technological developments have had an enormous impact on the consumer experience, the product being offered by the industry, and the ways in which consumers buy the products and services available to them.

In this chapter we will explore specifically how changes in technology are affecting the concept of luxury. I will seek to suggest that the Internet and mobile devices, in particular, are transforming the nature of luxury. I will argue that these developments have democratised travel and that democratised markets call into question the very meaning of luxury. The argument will also be advanced that technological developments have made what would formerly have been seen as luxurious into what is now expected and seen as the norm. Both developments represent a challenge to industry players seeking to position themselves as luxury providers.

Figure 8.1 attempts to represent some of the ways in which technology is influencing both the supply and demand sides in the luxury sector in tourism, hospitality and events.

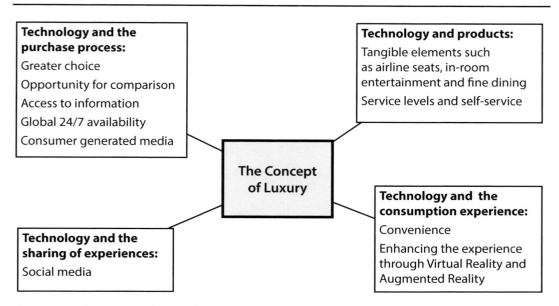

Technology and the purchase process:
Greater choice
Opportunity for comparison
Access to information
Global 24/7 availability
Consumer generated media

Technology and products:
Tangible elements such as airline seats, in-room entertainment and fine dining
Service levels and self-service

The Concept of Luxury

Technology and the consumption experience:
Convenience
Enhancing the experience through Virtual Reality and Augmented Reality

Technology and the sharing of experiences:
Social media

Figure 8.1: The impact of technology on the concept of luxury

Technology and the purchase process

To make any purchase any consumer needs information on what is available to them. Luxury consumers would traditionally have had access to more information than others through personal experiences, word of mouth from well-travelled friends and relatives, and high end travel agents. However, the Internet has democratised access to information with more being available in general and anyone being able to access it from a variety of online sources. Indeed it could be argued that today's 'tech savvy' backpacker on a budget has access to a wider range of up-to-date information on what is available in the market that a rich couple in their 70s who are not confident IT users and whose long-term trusted travel agent has just retired. In the Internet age, perhaps access to masses of information at low cost or no cost is a luxury in itself, and one which is exclusive because many people are not confident or knowledgeable to access the vast quantity of information that is now available.

The other 'luxury' which the Internet bestows on all is the ability for everyone to purchase products and services wherever they are in the world, 24 hours a day without any need for language skills. As such it could be said, again, that technological innovation is rendering the idea of luxury obsolete because it is making a high level of service and convenience available to any consumer regardless of their income.

However, consumers can only enjoy these benefits if they have reliable access to the Internet, and that is not currently the case even in some remote regions in affluent countries let alone in developing countries. And in some hotels, guests are still being charged extra for wi-fi access, not realising that today most guests see this as a necessity rather than a 'luxury'.

The Internet has had another really interesting impact on the purchase process that has profound implications for the luxury sector. Most people use the Internet in terms of tourism and hospitality because they are looking for a 'deal' or a 'bargain' and they have been conditioned to believe that the Internet is where the lowest prices are to be found. We now therefore have a whole new category of 'discounted luxury'. Long gone are the days when it was said that 'if you had to ask the price you could not afford it!'

Today one can find discounted five star hotels, high end cruises and business class air tickets all over the Internet. We are therefore seeing widespread price competition across the luxury market. This is possibly bringing new consumers into the market, who have aspirations to luxury but cannot afford the high 'published' prices for these things. However, over time, this practice of selling luxury primarily on price may serve to undermine the idea of luxury or at least change it significantly.

Technology and products

Technological innovation has been very influential in the evolution of the luxury traveller experience. In the airline sector, much investment has been made in differentiating experiences through the tangible elements of the product. While this has occurred across all classes, it is first and business which have seen the most innovation in this respect. We have seen the development of the seat which converts to a bed and now we have separate cabins. Catering technologies have been used to improve the quality of meals that can be served.

However, technological innovations in aviation, in general, have tended to benefit all passengers, not just those at the front of the aeroplane. That includes planes with longer ranges that no longer need to stop en route to refuel, to improved air circulation systems.

Staying with air travel, an airline may invest many millions of dollars in seats and entertainment systems, but it may only enjoy a few months of competitive advantage before a competitor introduces an even more innovative seat or entertainment system.

Technology and the experience of consumption

In terms of the consumer and consumption, technology has wrought a revolution particularly because in terms of ICT what starts out as rare and expensive rapidly becomes common and less expensive. Therefore, in many cases, everyone can now afford to use technological innovations to enhance their travel experience, whether that be accessing information through their smart phone or taking great holiday photos on their tablet, to sharing their photos with friends on social media. The ability to do this is now much more a function of the traveller being 'tech savvy' than of their wealth. Older wealthy people may not be as comfortable with these things as younger less well-off people. This turns the idea of luxury and exclusivity somewhat on its head.

Customer expectation also plays an increasing role in the use of technology. An airline may not wish to install expensive new entertainment systems throughout all of the classes on the aircraft but once consumers see one company does it they begin to expect it as a norm.

Furthermore, as technology becomes more and more part of everyday life we see that the technology which yesterday was seen as a luxury is today expected as standard by everyone. Wi-fi in hotels, ten years ago, either was not available or was seen as a lucrative extra to be charged for to raise extra revenue. Now a hotel that does not offer wi-fi seems ridiculously old fashioned and guests see it as a necessity that should be freely available.

One impact which technology has had on the consumer experience in travel is increased convenience through online check-in and smart phone boarding passes for airlines, and self check-in kiosks at hotels as well as Ipads with which guests order meals in restaurants. All are very clever in that they also reduce the costs of the airline, hotel or restaurant. At the same time they seem to be popular with many travellers today who see their time as a very scarce and rare commodity, and are happy to go along with these developments because they save them time.

In the meantime, however, from a traveller's point of view there are also severe limitations on what aspects of the experience can be improved by technological innovation. For even the luxury consumer, technology still tends not to get them through immigration any faster than other travellers, nor does it stop them being rained on if bad weather hits a destination. It cannot make the lonely feel less lonely, unless playing with a gadget or a 'virtual friend' can make them feel less lonely! Technology cannot stop your flight being cancelled due to strikes nor does it protect you from the effects of terrorist attacks. Thus technology can, apparently, do little at present to reduce some of the worse aspects of the vacation experience, not even for luxury travellers.

Technology and the sharing of experiences

The inter-twined rise of the internet and mobile devices has stimulated something which is nothing short of a revolution in relation to how tourism, hospitality and leisure experiences are now shared. I would like to suggest that this is perhaps the most important technology-driven change to the vacation experience in the past century, with travellers now able to share their experiences across the world 24 hours and 365 days a year.

There have been a number of really interesting dimensions to this phenomenon, as follows:

- The use of social media between travellers to share experiences and, perhaps more importantly, photographs and videos of their experiences. For many travellers, particularly younger ones, this seems to enhance the enjoyment of the vacation experience. It is the possibility of sharing visual images, literally with the world, which is the most dramatic change from the days when you could only share experiences with a small circle of friends and families through the sending of postcards and the taking of photos which would be developed on paper and kept in an album!

- The rise of social media 'giants,' such as TripAdvisor, which exists solely because of this phenomenon and has become a 'warehouse' for the views of consumers around the world who will never meet each other in normal life. With many millions of reviews, TripAdvisor has become incredibly powerful and businesses know, particularly in hospitality, that consumer reviews can either make or break their business. Tripadvisor has gone well beyond being a travel experience sharing site and is now a place where people go to buy products rather than merely looking at reviews to help them make up their minds. In that respect social media has turned rapidly into commercial media.

- The growth of a plethora of consumer sharing sites, particularly in the airline sector, covering everything from airline meals to airline seats. Travellers are actually spending time taking photos of their airline meals and posting them on sites dedicated to such posts!

- The growing use of consumer experience sharing through reviews on a wide range of online travel agency (OTA) sites and even in the brochures of tour operators where TripAdvisor review scores are now often included on the hotel description pages.

- Some people who are prolific on social media are becoming influencers of tourist behaviour and even gaining celebrity status through sharing their travel experiences through blogs and posts on social media.

So what does all this mean for the concept of luxury in tourism, hospitality and events? In essence, it means that the arbiters of what constitutes luxury are changing. Power is leaving the traditional arbiters such as the guide book and brochure writers and is moving much towards the social media bloggers and posters who are likely to be from a different generation or at least have a more contemporary mind set. And it is likely that their concept of luxury will not be the same as that of the traditional arbiters.

But the desires of a younger, 'tech savvy' leisure market are not just reflected in a greater desire to share their experiences through technology rather than simply by postcard. Their aspirations are also seen in their wish to utilise other technological developments as part of their leisure experience. It is in this context that we will now look at both augmented reality and virtual reality.

■ Virtual reality (VR) and luxury

Virtual reality is not a new technology, but it is one which after it seemed not to have fulfilled its early promise seems to be going through something of a renaissance, particularly in relation to tourism. In essence VR is about creating an artificial environment which is experienced by the consumer through various sensory stimuli facilitated through a computer. It often involves the use of a headset and may be accessed via gloves fitted with sensors. Although interactive, it has traditionally been seen as a solo rather than a group activity although that is now changing.

In its early days it was even suggested that VR might help achieve sustainable tourism by persuading tourists to substitute a VR experience for a 'real vacation', thus reducing pressure on destinations that were particularly vulnerable to the negative impacts of tourism. Today it seems as if the emphasis is on the use of VR to enhance rather than replace vacation experiences. At the same time, VR can play a vitally important role for visitors at historic sites and museums by recreating that which may no longer exist, such as a ruined castle although there will always be debates as to how 'real' such virtual representations can be.

■ Augmented reality (AR) and luxury

Augmented reality is a much more recent phenomenon, whose growth has been largely a function of the development of smart phones and mobile devices. Basically it is a form of technology which overlays a computer generated image on the consumer's actual real time, real world view, providing the user with an amalgamation of both.

An interesting article on the *Augment* blog, accessed in June 2017, identified a number of ways in which AR apps are, in its words, 'revolutionising' the travel experience in the following ways:

- Providing the traveller, who is in the destination, with a range of real time navigation tools.
- Allowing the traveller to enjoy virtual tours of hotels and rooms, before or after a booking is made.
- Providing simple translations of foreign languages terms that the traveller is not familiar with.
- Providing the traveller with a way to look at a range of restaurant menus and book a table, even before they reach the destination.
- Enhancing visits to museums and art galleries, by providing background and further information about exhibits or works of art as well as adding to the enjoyment by adding games and quizzes to the consumption experience.

And, of course, both VR and AR are developing ever more sophisticated applications all the time and as a major industry, tourism is at the forefront of developments in both technologies.

In truth, VR and AR may share a word in their names but they are largely the opposite of each other. The former is about creating artificial environments while the latter is about providing more depth and detail and richness to a environment. But what has all this got to do with luxury in tourism, events and hospitality?

On the face of it both VR and AR could be seen as an 'ultimate luxury', representing as they do an imagined world that does not physically exist or a way of experiencing a destination that goes far beyond what the traveller can actually see. Surely both are marvels which should command a high end luxury price, but that is not the case. Those who develop VR and AR projects, following the normal practice with technological innovations, tend to want to establish mass markets for them. While prices may be high at first, the aim is to use economies of scale to reduce price and grow the market. At the same time, VR in particular, raises questions about the idea of authenticity, which it has been suggested in this book is becoming one of the ideas that may underpin future concepts of 'luxury' in tourism, hospitality and events.

Perhaps what these technologies mean (particularly VR) is that we need to rethink the concept of what authenticity actually means. Just because something does not have a physical form or a 'history' may not in future preclude it being seen as 'authentic'. Or perhaps both VR and AR are useful potential additions to the vacation experience but cannot ever 'tick the box' of authenticity.

Before we draw this chapter to a close I would like to make two further points in relation to luxury and technology in tourism, hospitality and events.

First, most of the major influential technological innovations in recent years in our sector have related to giving consumers more choice and more information. If information is indeed power, as the saying goes, then the ICT innovations in recent years have ensured that anyone who has access to the Internet can get as much information as anyone else (notwithstanding government restrictions on the Internet in some countries). In this respect ICT has created a more 'level playing field' in terms of access to information. However, as we know, access to and levels of use of the Internet, are not identical across all societies. The young tend to be higher per capita users, whereas in terms of income, it is the older generations that tend to have a distinct advantage. Access to technology and thus information, therefore, is perhaps an emerging way of looking at luxury, because ICT technologies provide information about opportunities and experiences that are denied to those who are unable to access these technologies. The privileged 'luxury' segment of the future may be as much about having knowledge others do not, rather than just having more money than others.

Second, there is the issue of time which we have already noted in this book is rapidly becoming a crucial part of the idea of luxury, namely the 'luxury' of having enough time to take and enjoy vacation experiences. On the one hand technology has helped consumers save time spent on utilitarian tasks such as checking in for flights. And while the online booking process is undoubtedly quicker and more convenient than using high street travel agents, the process spent planning has probably been lengthened by the Internet, due to the massively increased choice now available to the consumer.

At the same time, there is a growing concern that ICT that allows us to be 'on call' 24 hours a day, seven days a week, particularly in relation to our jobs, and is impacting on our ability to switch off and truly relax on vacation. For many hard working people, the prime purpose of a vacation is to spend time with family, away from the working environment, yet ICT now means that, if we are not careful, everywhere can become a working environment, even our vacation hotel.

Conclusions

The topic of technology and luxury in tourism, hospitality and events is a fascinating one. Technology has transformed travel and tourism in waves. In the 19th century, the invention of the railway heralded the rise of modern mass domestic tourism, while the introduction of jet powered airliners from the 1950s did the same for international travel. Then little happened until the rise of computer reservation systems which helped the industry process ever larger numbers of bookings. All these technological innovations made travel more accessible to the mass market and thus reduced the exclusivity and maybe the glamour of travel.

The ICT innovations discussed in this chapter have, in themselves, done little to bring new people into the market; they have not reduced the barriers to travel which revolve around disposable income and the distribution of wealth, the availability of disposable time, and physical health, to name but three. But what they have done is democratise choice and access to information, and in doing so have broken down one of the traditional boundaries between the wealthy luxury travellers and the vast majority of citizens.

In both ways, therefore, technology has largely eroded the traditional idea of luxury as being related to terms such as high price, exclusivity, privilege, and rarity. But the rapid developments in ICT have brought with them new opportunities and challenges in relation to luxury, of which perhaps the most significant is around the concept of time.

In the meantime, aside from these major shifts caused by particular technological innovations, less fundamental developments in technologies have generally been raising the quality of the tangible product. Such developments include everything from the flat bed seats in airliners to in-room entertainment systems in hotels. Some of these developments, such as the former, have generally mostly benefitted the more affluent traveller, others, such as the latter, have usually benefitted most consumers.

At the same time innovations, such as more fuel efficient engines and less noisy engines, have helped reduce the impact of air travel on the environment although their effect has been greatly outweighed by the overall massive increase in air travel in recent years.

Finally, technology has also had an impact on the delivery of service which has always been another key element of any definition of luxury in tourism, hospitality and events. The whole matter of service and how it relates to luxury today will be discussed in the next chapter.

9 What Does Luxury Service Mean Today?

Introduction

Ask any student or person in the street to give you a word they associate with luxury and it is very likely they will say 'service' (or high price or exclusivity). We take for granted the fact that luxury and service are two concepts that go hand in hand. Yet we rarely unpick this word and explore what it means, particularly today. That is what I will seek to do in this chapter.

Perhaps there are two kinds of service in tourism, hospitality and events as there are in many other service industries. These are:

■ Physical actions carried out by staff employed by organisations that provide consumers with a tangible product or a beneficial impact, such as carrying their bags upstairs to their room in a hotel.

■ Systems operated by organisations which allow consumers to take actions themselves to enhance their consumption experience, such as the ability to check-in on line for a flight and choose their own seat as part of this process.

Traditionally the focus of the luxury market would have been on the former with the idea that the luxury customer was paying to have others do things for them rather than having to do them for themselves. I will argue that at all levels of the market the supply side providers have been seeking to move the balance of the service they deliver from the former type to the latter, largely to reduce costs.

Attempts have been made to mitigate this trend in the luxury sector but I would still argue that service based on physical inputs from staff has declined in recent years even in the luxury sector, for a number of reasons.

We will also be looking at the rise of non-trained, 'non-professional' providers in the accommodation sector, such as Airbnb, and see how they are changing the meaning of luxury in hospitality.

Before the chapter ends we will also explore styles of service delivered by staff to see how and why these may also be changing or may need to change.

Figure 9.1 seeks to identify five different dimensions of the concept of service in tourism, hospitality and events. An attempt will then be made to explore each of these in relation to the luxury market.

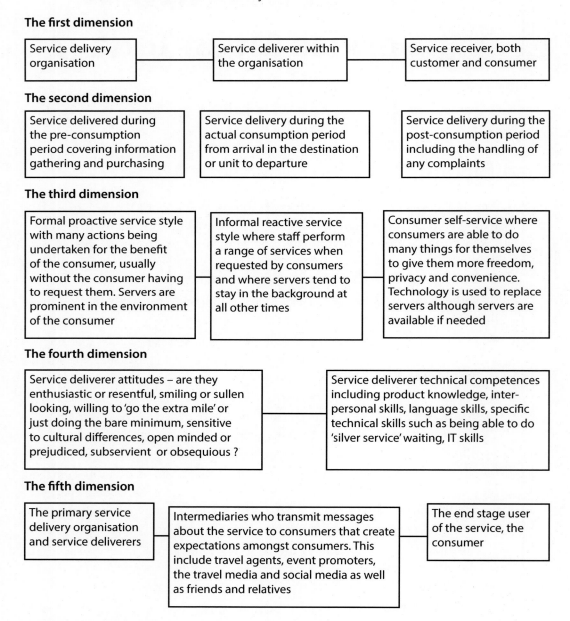

The first dimension

| Service delivery organisation | Service deliverer within the organisation | Service receiver, both customer and consumer |

The second dimension

| Service delivered during the pre-consumption period covering information gathering and purchasing | Service delivery during the actual consumption period from arrival in the destination or unit to departure | Service delivery during the post-consumption period including the handling of any complaints |

The third dimension

| Formal proactive service style with many actions being undertaken for the benefit of the consumer, usually without the consumer having to request them. Servers are prominent in the environment of the consumer | Informal reactive service style where staff perform a range of services when requested by consumers and where servers tend to stay in the background at all other times | Consumer self-service where consumers are able to do many things for themselves to give them more freedom, privacy and convenience. Technology is used to replace servers although servers are available if needed |

The fourth dimension

| Service deliverer attitudes – are they enthusiastic or resentful, smiling or sullen looking, willing to 'go the extra mile' or just doing the bare minimum, sensitive to cultural differences, open minded or prejudiced, subservient or obsequious ? | Service deliverer technical competences including product knowledge, inter-personal skills, language skills, specific technical skills such as being able to do 'silver service' waiting, IT skills |

The fifth dimension

| The primary service delivery organisation and service deliverers | Intermediaries who transmit messages about the service to consumers that create expectations amongst consumers. This include travel agents, event promoters, the travel media and social media as well as friends and relatives | The end stage user of the service, the consumer |

Figure 9.1: Five dimensions of service in tourism, hospitality and events

■ First dimension

In the first dimension, we see two important relationships. One between the service supplying organisation and its employees who perform the actual face-to-face service for the guest. Increasingly, perhaps, senior managers are divorced in space and time from the act of service delivery itself. This creates the opportunity for gaps between company policies and systems, and the service that is actually delivered. This is particularly important in the luxury field where companies often market themselves on the basis of a set of service standards that they promise the guest they will deliver. Any gap here may be the result of everything from poor recruitment and training to inadequate on-site management.

The second relationship is that between the service delivery and the customer and/or consumer. This is at the heart of the luxury experience where the guest expects high levels of technically skilled service to be delivered by people whose smile never leaves their face. Whether this is the reality of the consumer experience depends on training, but also on how motivated employees are and even the local culture.

■ Second dimension

The second dimension recognises the importance of the periods before and after the actual consumption of the luxury experience. During the pre-consumption phase the key to high end service is how easy it is to gather information and make a booking. Increasingly this may be much more a matter of the consumer interacting with an online booking system rather than dealing with a human travel agent, so then it is the convenience and reliability of the system that is the key to consumer satisfaction rather than a smiling travel agent. It is fair to assume that the higher the price to be paid, the more convenient the purchase process should be, but this is not always the case. Some luxury travellers still prefer a real life travel agent to handle the information gathering and booking for them.

During the actual consumption phase the emphasis has to be on seamless service delivery with any problems resolved quickly if they occur. As reviews on TripAdvisor regularly show, expectations from luxury consumers are understandably high and they often will complain strongly about things that seem to others relatively minor issues. Luxury means paying for perfection and being satisfied with nothing less.

Post-consumption service is also important, but not only in terms of handling any complaints quickly. It also means recognising the consumer and thanking them for their custom, as well as seeking to make them aware of other experiences they may be interested in purchasing. If one spends $10,000 on a cruise, perhaps one has a right to expect at least a birthday card from the cruise company! We need to remember that buying luxury is partly motivated by a desire for status and recognituion. Therefore, sending the same cruise passengers a photograph of themselves in their finery at the farewell dinner, which they can display in their home, may be a smart move!

Third dimension

When we look at the third dimension, we see three different approaches to service delivery. There are two important points to make about this category, although they appear to be a little contradictory.

First, I contend that in many ways these three styles can be linked very closely to segmentation. The first category, where service is proactive and formalised, may appeal to those for whom luxury is about being pampered in a way which demonstrates to everyone around them that they can afford this level of service. It suits the traditionalists, as this is the classic view of what luxury service is supposed to be. The servers are in a strong position here, while appearing quite servile, in that they actually are in control of the situation and largely dictating how the service will be delivered. The more informal reactive approach is perhaps more modern and suits those who do not want the server to be a major part of their experience, but to be there in case they, the customer, identify a want at a particular time. Here the customer is in control of the server-served interaction. The self-service model may appeal to a range of consumer from the shy and introvert, to the 'time-poor', to those who value their privacy and 'personal space'.

Second, I contend that the context in which service delivery occurs may influence the preferences of the consumer, so that the same person may prefer different models of service delivery depending on the context, which may include:

- The setting, whether it is a luxury hotel or a safari camp or a secluded luxury villa, for example in relation to accommodation; or a fine dining restaurant, beach café or dinner buffet in the context of a dining experience.
- Whom the consumer is travelling with, whether it be alone, with a partner, with a partner and their children, with a group of friends, with ageing parents, or in a group with strangers.
- If the motivation for the trip is privacy and escapism, or an ostentatious display of wealth, or an attempt to impress someone else, perhaps a new girlfriend or boyfriend.
- Whether the tourist has never visited before or is a regular visitor and therefore more confident in their surroundings.
- The mood of the consumer, ranging from sociable to miserable, elated to

Though these points appear a little contradictory, I believe there is truth in both.

■ Fourth dimension

The fourth dimension in Figure 9.1 focuses on the servers in terms of their attitudes and their technical competences. Of course we always hope to experience service where both are excellent and condusive to a great experience.

I contend that most customers in travel, hospitality and events may forgive lapses in technical competences if the attitude of the server is good. But what is meant here by a good attitude? For most consumers it appears to be around a smiling face and a willingness to please, on behalf of the server. This is particularly the case if the server is young or from a place where tourism is still in its infancy as an industry. On the other hand a superbly skilled waiter who treats his customers as if they are his or her inferiors can be very annoying for consumers.

While this may generally be true, the question is whether this contention is true in the luxury market. One would expect that those paying more would be less forgiving of weaknesses in the technical skills of servers. Sadly while this seems logical, I can find no convincing evidence either way but would suggest it is probably not that simplistic. I believe this is because attitudes towards such issues are influenced greatly by the personality and world view of the traveller rather than simply whether or not they are able to spend a lot of money on their vacation experiences. Annecdotally, I have seen a tourist on a cheap package holiday berating a waiter who messed up the serving of a fish at the table as well as a rich guest at a luxury hotel still leaving a tip for a smiling, enthusiastic young waiter who managed to spill some of the soup course on his new trousers!

Of course, a major problem faced in our industries is how to ensure service delivery matches the promises made to guests, that they will receive technically excellent service from smiling staff. And the fact is they cannot! Training can help with the former but the latter is, at least partly, outside the control of the organisation. Good recruitment of people with the right attitudes can help, but even great staff have bad days when they feel unwell or do not want to smile because of things that happen in their private life.

■ Fifth dimension

In the fifth dimension we are dealing with what we may term the service delivery system, which in most of tourism, hospitality and events involves not only the end use consumer and the primary service deliverer, but also one or more intermediaries.

The primary service delivery organisation creates certain expectations through its marketing activities through both words and images. They may have no direct contact with the consumer until the latter arrives to consume the product, whether that be a concert, hotel stay, meal or flight.

It is highly likely that the consumer will have made the booking through an intermediary, and that intermediary will have sales messages of its own which may not be the same as those of the primary service delivery organisation. There is always the possibility therefore that the intermediary will create unrealistic expectations in the consumer through inaccurate sales messages designed to persuade the consumer to purchase a particular product. Intermediaries can often be a two-way filter though, as they may feed back consumer reactions to the primary service organisation, although these may be biased by their own commercial interests. With the rise of online virtual intermediaries, it is likely that there will be no human interaction between the consumer and the online intermediary so that expectations are being raised through sales messages which are largely remotely generated and cannot be interrogated by the consumer. Messages about the service are also transferred to potential consumers through specialist media such as guide books. Examples such as Michelin can be very important in the creation of expectations amongst consumers.

As we all know, though, consumer expectations of service as with other elements of the travel experience are not just created by the industry and professional intermediaries, other people also act as 'intermediaries' between the product or service and consumer.

Traditionally a major 'intermediary' group were the people you knew, your friends and family, who influenced you through word-of-mouth recommendation. While still important, this channel has probably been replaced in importance by consumer generated media such as TripAdvisor. Here the view of a service or product expressed by a stranger can influence the expectations of a consumer living on a different continent.

So what have we learned from Figure 9.1, apart from the fact that service is a complex concept that can be viewed in at least five different ways? For me, one really important point is about gaps, such as those between:

- the real service delivered to a consumer and their perception of that service;
- the service consumers believe they have been promised and the service they believe they have received;
- different approaches to service delivery which can be vary greatly, as we saw when talking about the 'third dimension';
- the technical skills and the attitudes of service delivery staff;
- the primary service delivery organisations and the staff of these organisations which actually deliver the service;
- the pre-consumption, consumption and post-consumption periods;
- service delivery organisations and their consumers, and the intermediaries who are positioned to bridge this gap.

In all of these cases the gaps are a potential source of dissatisfaction on the part of the consumer and are probably most important in the luxury market, simply because for many organisations it is from these consumers that the bulk of their profits may come.

As we move towards the end of this chapter I would like to make a few other points in relation to service in the context of the luxury segment, that may be of interest.

■ The rise of non-professionals in the accommodation sector

In the accommodation sector we are seeing the rise of competition from untrained 'non-professionals' who appear to be offering better service than trained professionals. For example most international visitors often say the best service they received were in private homes offering 'bed and breakfast'. On a visit to Sri Lanka in February 2016, the best service I experienced was staying at a homestay just outside Kandy. And the phenomenon of Airbnb has transformed the service concept, with literally millions of customers saying how their untrained host went above and beyond to enhance their experience, whether by collecting them personally from the airport or showing them around the destination, for example. Here, the idea of luxury is not a matter of price but rather it concerns the 'luxury' of authenticity and highly personalised service from a 'real person' not a paid employee. Airbnb hosts and bed and breakfast operators have chosen to do this, often as a lifestyle choice and take pleasure in meeting and looking after guests. It is not a job for them and they are in control of the service interaction. In contrast, in many countries, working in tourism, hospitality or events, in a face-to-face service role is seen as a low status job and perhaps even a last resort for those with few other options. It is not surprising, therefore, that the service delivered by these workers is not the stuff of which vacation dreams are made.

■ Consumer expectations and price

There is a real tension between the consumer expectation of high service levels and the downward pressure on prices at all levels of the market. Travellers seem to expect high quality service even when paying high prices. Those paying €20 for a flight from one country to another complain that no one brings them a pillow so they can sleep. I believe that at that price the passenger has received value for money if they simply arrive at their destination on the day they were scheduled to arrive without any injury!

As we have noted elsewhere even in the luxury market there is price-based competition, yet those who pay less still expect the same personal service and range of services as those who have paid full price.

■ Staff costs in different countries

There are substantial differences between countries in terms of levels of personal service based almost solely on staff costs. In a luxury hotel in a poorer Asian country we may have two staff for every guest compared to less than one in a five star hotel in a major European city. This is largely down to the cost of salaries and the social cost of employing labour, which may be ten times or even higher in the European country. Yet in the luxury sector the room price will almost certainly be much than ten times that of the Asian country.

Of course the number of staff is no guarantee of high quality service in itself if the staff are inexperienced or not well trained and managed. However, visitors from Europe to Asia often comment not only on the fact that staff were 'always smiling' and 'naturally hospitable' but that there were so many of them around that the guest never had to do anything for themselves!

■ Is the customer always right?

This latter point leads us to a further issue I would like to explore, namely 'is the customer always right?' Until recently perhaps there has been a view prevalent in our industries that the customer is a virtual god who is entitled to receive almost anything they want if they are prepared to pay. This has been drilled into generations of those serving luxury clientele in everything from hospitality to retailing. Too often this has extended to guests being able to treat staff as they see fit, with the server having no real protection against rudeness or abuse.

As a mature sector needs to make clear to consumers today, no matter how much they pay there are boundaries to their behaviour, and that overt racism, sexism, verbal abuse and so on will not be tolerated. Yet how many organisations, in reality, would warn or even ban a customer who sexually harrassed waiting staff or used racist language about housekeeping staff? Unfortunately, for some people, the power which they perceive they have if they sit in a first class cabin of an airliner or the Presidential Suite in the hotel leads them to behave in an unacceptable manner that should not be tolerated.

Anecdotally it could be argued that such behaviour is, perhaps, found less amongst those for whom having lots of money is an everyday reality than amongst those of more modest means who travel to less wealthy counties where their low to middle income means that for at least a week every year they can 'live like a king or queen'.

■ The rise of self-service

One key trend that needs to be highlighted again, I believe, is the rise of self-service in tourism, hospitality and events, which is happening, even in the luxury sector, with the support of both industry and consumers. On a simplistic level a great example of this trend is the use of minibars in hotel bedrooms. For industry, more self-service means the need for fewer staff, which leads to lower costs and higher profits. Consumers seem happy, in some instances, to serve themselves as it often gives them more convenience and saves time, as well as giving them more peace and privacy. The key is ensuring that the self-service process is as easy as possble for the consumer. And as the minibar example shows, self-service can actually increase consumer spend by making it quicker and easier to buy something.

Conclusions

Yet again, I find myself ending a chapter by saying how complex something is – in this case the concept of service in the luxury market. And not for the first time I find myself suggesting that the whole meaning of the term 'service' is changing in tourism, hospitality and events, in response to a wide range of factors. Also not for the first time, the issues we have been considering do not just apply in the luxury market but are broader.

Perhaps the most important point to make about service in all sectors of our industries, luxury or otherwise, is that service is not an absolute that can be objectively measured. Indeed it is highly subjective and what really matters is not what service is delivered and how it is delivered, but rather how it is received and perceived by the consumer. And as every customer is different in their personality, experiences, attitudes, and situations, they will also have totally different expectations of a service.

This point is important because it puts the emphasis where it should be in a service industry, not on the service deliverer but on the service receiver and their individuality. And that idea underpins the concept of 'experiences' which is the subject of the next chapter, where service deliverers are no longer seen as providers controlling the service design and delivery process, but rather as partners in this process with their consumers, and perhaps junior partners at that!

10 Is Luxury Today all about Experiences Rather than Products and Services?

Introduction

When Pine and Gilmore published *The Experience Economy* in 1999 the world changed! Their ideas challenged the traditional views of both marketing and consumer behaviour.

The concept of an experience focused attention on the consumer and their ability to have something customised to meet their desires rather than having to accept a standardised product designed by industry suppliers. In this respect it shifted the balance of power, in theory, between suppliers and consumers in favour of the consumer.

This desire for customised experiences has also been reinforced by the rise of the Internet and smart devices. These have given far more choice to the consumer in terms of the products and services they may wish to purchase, but also in relation to where, when and how they make the purchase.

Until recently it appeared that only the rich had much choice about what they purchased and were treated as individuals rather than as units in a mass market. This very fact served to clearly identify them as a separate segment, a luxury segment. However, the rise of the Internet and mobile devices has created a new world in which virtually anyone who can afford to travel can customise their vacation 'experience'. In doing so, perhaps the idea of the 'experience economy' has mortally wounded one of the traditional pillars of luxury, namely exclusivity and rarity, by saying what used to be a privilege for a few can now be a reality for virtually everyone.

However, before we get carried away by this idea let us still remember that some travel experiences cost tens of thousands of Euros and/or require weeks of available leisure time or great physical fitness!

Nevertheless, the concept of the experience economy is one which is of particular importance to tourism, hospitality and events, where every purchase is based on a desire for benefits such as pleasure, fun and self-actualisation. None of these purchases are essential for our physical existence or day to day comfort. Indeed it could be said that all tourism, hospitality and leisure purchases are a luxury regardless of how much they cost. This is in contrast to many other purchases which we have to make, whether they be food and drink, clothes, modes of transport, accommodation and so on. While some of these purchases bring pleasure as well as more utilitarian benefits I would argue that, in general, there is much less pleasure involved than there is in a vacation.

In terms of experience there is another characteristic of the consumption experience that sets tourism, hospitality and events apart from most other types of purchase, and that is that most take place over a very limited period of time. Cars, furniture, and clothes should last for years, but in our industries the consumption phase may last several hours, such as a concert, or at most two or three weeks, in the case of a vacation. This makes these consumption experiences particularly intense and rich.

Consumption experiences in tourism, hospitality and events are also distinguished from those in other sectors as they take place away from the home, in places the consumer may never have visited before. This also adds a 'frisson' to the overall experience.

In an effort to catch up with both the theory of the 'experience economy' and trends in consumer behaviour, many suppliers have taken the idea of 'experiences' on board, or apparently so. Perhaps, in reality, most have paid lip service to the idea rather than understanding what is means, and being prepared to immerse themselves in the ideas and take the risk of running with them to their logical conclusion, wherever that might be. Instead the term has often been used as a marketing gloss on a continuation of traditional approaches, designed to suggest empathy with the target market consumers.

In this chapter I will argue that the idea of 'experience' has become a new 'currency of luxury', but one but one which is available to everyone regardless of what they pay and who they are.

Every tourism, hospitality or event experience has always been unique because of the impossibility of homogenising service delivered by human beings with all their moods and inadequacies. Other factors also guarantee each experience is unique, including the expectations and attitudes of each consumer and the people they consume the experience with, such as the other guests in their hotel.

10

The ideas contained in the book by Pine and Gilmore imply a fundamental shift in the role of supply side organisations and their mind-set. They now need to see themselves as the providers of opportunities, not of finished products or standard levels of service. This also means recognising that many consumers no longer wish to be passive recipients of service, but are increasingly seeking opportunities for co-creation, in which they actively participate and cooperate with industry providers to create their own unique experiences. So instead of simply eating a great meal, I can learn to cook the cuisine of the destination as part of my vacation experience.

Finally, the consumption experience does not end when I leave the hotel or finish cooking the meal. Now the memories from the experience and the sharing of that experience with others through social media has itself become part of the overall experience. Organisations that fail to grasp this fact will struggle to achieve success in the luxury market or indeed any other.

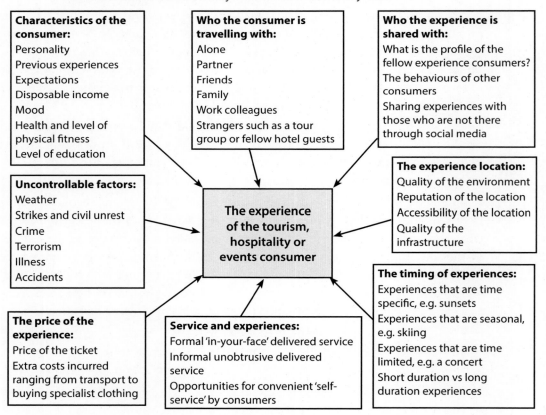

Figure 10.1: The elements of an experience in tourism, hospitality and events

These issues will all be discussed within this chapter, but in the meantime Figure 10.1 proposes a rather simplistic model of the elements of the nature of the experience in tourism, hospitality and events. Figure 10.1 is by no means exhaustive but let us now try to explore what each of these elements means in relation to the luxury market.

■ Characteristics of the consumer

The characteristics of the consumer are vitally important when discussing experiences, because when we focus on experiences rather than products and services we are focusing on the consumer rather than the supply side of industry. If we want every consumer to be able to shape an experience to meet their own needs, we need to understand their characteristics. Given that everyone is different this is a real challenge, hence our reliance on segmentation, despite its flaws. This issue of who is the luxury consumer has already been deal with in detail in an earlier chapter. At this point, therefore, let us just make a few observations relating specifically to the issue of experiences and the characteristics of the consumer.

Intuitively one could suggest that the luxury consumer who consciously seeks out the opportunity to enjoy personalised experiences rather than simply buying standard products and services would fit a particular profile. They would probably be affluent, well-travelled, confident, and educated to an above average level. However, given that the idea of experiences is fashionable, it could also attract those who aspire to be seen as confident, well-travelled and well educated, even if this is not a reality. At the same time a rich, well-travelled individual who now has a disability that limits their mobility or sight, for example, may need to seek out a personalised experience because even the most luxurious product or service does not meet their needs.

And then of course there is the issue of mood so that something the luxury consumer may see as an exciting experience today could be viewed by the same person tomorrow as too much hassle or a waste of money. Consumers are not constant in their attitudes and also change depending on who they are travelling with as we will now see.

■ Who the experience is being shared with

A vitally important element of the experience revolves around with whom the consumer is travelling and sharing the experience – in other words if they are alone or with family, a partner, friends or in a group with total strangers. This clearly affects the experience of a consumer because of their interactions with other consumers, whether these are friends and relatives or total strangers who happen to be sharing with the consumer a concert venue, hotel, cruise ship, or a destination. Those who are strangers can enhance the experience, a romance may even develop, or they can damage it through their behaviour or maybe just by their presence. For the luxury consumer, strangers can be a particularly important element in the experience. Depending on their characteristics – age, wealth, status, and mode of dress, behaviour, and nationality – they may either serve to:

- Reinforce the satisfaction of the consumer by reassuring them that their vacation is truly luxurious because it is validated by the presence of these particular strangers, or

- Reduce the satisfaction level of the consumer, if they feel they are sharing their vacation destination and/or accommodation with strangers that they do not perceive belong to the luxury segment.

At the same time, whom the experience is shared with, is not only about those who are present in the destination at the same time as the consumer. It is also about virtual sharing through social media. Who the consumer is, what they share and whom they share it with will certainly have an impact on the expectations of other potential consumers and will influence whether or not they develop an aspiration to have the same experience. Specifically, if those sharing their experience are influential bloggers or celebrities the impact is obviously magnified.

■ The experience location

Not surprisingly, the experience location is vitally important in terms of both tangible and intangible elements. The perceived quality of the buildings and even their appearance are important attributes for a luxury destination, while visitors will expect to see a range of facilities including high end hotels, fine dining restaurants, designer brand outlets and specialist shops, as well as leisure attractions such as casinos, spas, and fashionable art galleries. Guests in supposed luxury destinations will expect exemplary levels of cleanliness, safety and security. However, intangible factors are also important, although far harder to measure, such as atmosphere, as well as reputation.

On the other hand, if I am correct and the idea of luxury is changing to embrace issues such as rich experiences, authenticity, sustainability and so on, then the luxury destination of the future could also be an island with no infrastructure, or a village with no other tourists present, or a resort with none of the usual trappings of luxury, such as air conditioning and a golf course.

■ The price of the experience

Traditionally the price of the experience would have been the prime identifier of a luxury experience. However, as we have seen earlier, this simplistic idea that luxury is expensive has been changing due to a number of factors including:

- The rise of online travel agencies, so that even luxury accommodation is being discounted and some luxury hotels are indulging in price wars, albeit rather discreet ones!

■ Likewise new discount websites have grown up offering cut price business class tickets, while loyalty programmes allow regular customers to upgrade from economy to business or even purchase business class tickets in exchange for loyalty points with no payment required.

■ Many of the destinations that have appeared on the scene in recent years are in poor countries with a very low cost of living and low labour costs. This has meant they are often able to offer a five star experience for the price of a three star experience in Europe.

■ The service element of the experience

Through much of this book, and specifically in Chapter 9, we have focused attention on the service element of the experience, which has traditionally been one of the differentiators of a luxury experience. However, I have suggested that the type of service is changing and is no longer just about a rather formal style of service. Instead it can now embrace more informal service or even self-service designed to increase convenience for the traveller.

■ The timing of the experience

In the context of luxury experiences the issues relating to the timing of the experience can be highly significant. Some elements of an experience can be time-specific such as sunsets, but that is not unique to luxury experiences. Seasonality is an important factor, in that some destinations are only perceived as luxury at certain times of the year, particularly if these are the times when major events occur, such as art festival or major sporting event. And being in a fashionable ski resort, such as Aspen or Zermatt, in summer will not carry the same status as being there during the ski season. Time of year can also impact on the idea of a luxury experience, if a place is packed with mainstream mass market tourists in August but is quieter and more beautiful in June.

Disposable time is becoming another factor in whether an experience can be seen as a luxury experience. Perhaps, in future, the time dimension will create two polar opposites in relation to luxury experiences, namely:

■ Short duration high intensity experiences where consumers compensate for a lack of leisure time by packing a lot into a short time and spend a lot of money doing it! This segment is likely to be those in employment in the 30 to 50 plus age range, who are cash-rich but time-poor.

■ Very long vacation experiences that may be measured in weeks and months, as people who have disposable time use it to truly relax and/or explore somewhere in depth. This segment is likely to be retired people aged 50 plus, choosing a round the world cruise, for instance, but it may also include young people and students from affluent families with a continuation of the idea of a 'gap year', where it is the time element which is the luxury rather than, necessarily, the level of spending.

And in between might well be 'family quality time vacations', where hard-working affluent parents who feel guilty about the time they spend away from their children working, endeavour to partially correct the imbalance through vacations where the emphasis is on family activities and family togetherness.

■ Uncontrollable factors

Of course, no discussion of luxury experiences within tourism, hospitality, and events would be complete without a discussion of the uncontrollable factors that affect the consumer experience of all travellers.

Even a luxury consumer, despite what they have paid, can have their experience affected, ruined or even terminated by a wide range of factors which are beyond the control of the industry, ranging from terrorist attacks to natural disasters, labour disputes to extreme weather. In these instances it is vitally important that the industry is seen to respond well to the challenges to try to mitigate the effects of the uncontrollable factors as much as is humanly possible.

The rise of co-creation

Alongside the concept of the experience economy we have seen the rise of the concept of co-creation in tourism, hospitality and events. In general, co-creation is a general term covering activities where industry organisations try to work in cooperation with customers to create outcomes which satisfy consumers as well as helping the organisation meet its objectives.

Co-creation also represents another step in the apparent transfer of power from producers to consumers, which is explicit in terms of the impact of the Internet and implicit in the concept of the experience economy.

In the manufacturing sector, where producers and consumers are usually separated by both time and space, it can mean, for instance, involving consumers in the design and development of a new product such as a car. However, in a service sector such as tourism, hospitality and events, where there is normally no temporal or spatial separation of producer and consumer, it offers more intriguing opportunities. For one thing something in our industries can be co-created in minutes or even seconds!

Co-creation is not new, for example cookery classes have been offered for years by some restaurants, so diners cannot just eat food created by professional chefs but can also learn to cook the dishes themselves in the restaurant's kitchen.

And with the rise of customer databases and loyalty programmes, industry organisations are at pains to point out their desire to proactive 'passive co-creation' at least by using consumer data to personalise their experience to some extent.

The scope for co-creation in tourism, hospitality and events is enormous and can encompass:

- Pop-up restaurants established by professional chefs in an office or home.
- A new micro tour operator trying to raise finance through online crowd-funding.
- Consumers working with industry suppliers to decide on priorities for sustainability practice at a hotel

We also have the phenomenon of Airbnb, which is a variation on the theme of co-creation where hosts, who are not trained tourism and hospitality professionals, give paying guests access to their home and sometimes show them around their own home area free of charge and interact with guests far more than would happen in a 'normal' hospitality business.

Of course, what is great about co-creation is that a small group or maybe even a single traveller can create their own unique experience in collaboration with an industry organisation. This must be seen as a luxury experience as uniqueness and personalisation lies at the heart of almost all concepts of luxury.

However, we need to be careful not to always see co-creation as a problem-free 'win-win' situation, for as we will see with the 'volunteering' market, in Chapter 11, it can lead to negative impacts and questions about its value and even a morality especially where tourists are asked to pay companies for the opportunity to work as volunteers!

The end of product-led marketing?

10

So, does the rise of co-creation, as part of the experience economy, really represent an end to the idea of product-led marketing whereby companies produce goods and services and then try to find customers for them? Certainly industry organisations are all lining up to claim that they are consumer-led and that their sole purpose in life is to meet the needs and desires of consumers.

But perhaps they have not yet fully appreciated what this means in reality rather than in the land of hype. This means a further transfer of power from them to consumers. It also means that all they now offer are opportunities rather than finished products and customers do not want to pay for anything that they do not use to create their own experiences. Likewise this means that segmentation, based on lumping people together according to shared characteristics, will become increasingly obsolete as everyone is unique and is now being promised that they will be treated as an individual.

In this context perhaps it no longer matters if a company believes it offers a luxury product or experience; perhaps what will matters from now on is if the consumers see it the same way. This has major implications for the way in which tourism, hospitality and event organisations communicate with the market.

Finally, if the experience is more than the sum of the parts of the product, and if it transcends the mere product through the value added by each consumer to form each experience, then the implications are potentially quite far-reaching. This may include a greater role for ICT companies, rather than tourism, hospitality and event organisations, as they can directly facilitate experience creation and sharing, and allow travellers to personalise their experiences without input from organisations in our own sector. This means that industry organisations will be forced more and more to justify their existence in a world where boundaries between industries, and between consumers and suppliers are becoming increasingly blurred.

Conclusions

I will now try to pull together some threads from this disparate chapter.

First, it is my contention that the concept of the experience economy doesnot relate to a new phenomenon, but is rather about identifying and labelling something which has always been present in tourism, hospitality and events, given their nature as a set of activities, service-based, not essential to daily life and all about the pursuit of enjoyment.

Second, while industry seems to have been converted to the idea of selling experiences rather than products in its marketing communications, it seems not to fully understand the situation. It still talks of selling experiences, which is just wrong; it is now the consumers who believe they are using the products offered as raw material from which they will construct their own unique experience.

Personalisation and uniqueness has often been seen as a touchstone of luxury, so if all this is true then the concept of the experience economy is suggesting that this personalisation is within the grasp of a much wider cross-section of society than merely the rich. Yet again this seems to suggest that the luxury paradigm is shifting significantly. However, before we get carried away by all this talk of customisation for all, let us reflect on a couple of issues, namely:

■ Consciously developing an experience for yourself requires a fair amount of confidence, and perhaps this confidence is more likely to be found amongst experienced frequent travellers who are likely to come from higher socio-economic groups in societies.

- Maybe some people are still happy to enjoy standardised products which bring reliability, safety and consistency and prefer not to spend valuable leisure time planning 'experiences' or taking responsibility for their own vacation experience rather than paying a tour operator to do it for them.

However, in the specific context of luxury, it is worth noting that Figure 10.1 does suggest that the concept of 'experience' in tourism, hospitality and events is evolving in some interesting ways.

I have often discussed in lectures, and occasionally in print, the idea of a 'feel-good tourist', someone who wants an enjoyable experience but does not want the feelings of guilt that can come with believing that their pleasure has been at the expense of someone else's misfortune. Following a theme already identified in this book I would like to suggest that this is all about the consumer experience, and has been recognised by a small number of industry players, who have sought to make the vacation products they offer rather more responsible. It has to be said that this has occurred more at the higher end of the market, in the adventure travel sector for instance, rather than in the mainstream market, but perhaps it is coming there too. Companies want to be seen to be working with the concerns of their consumers and asking their consumers to accept certain limitations on their behaviour for the good of the planet or local communities. If properly communicated this can enhance the consumer experience, give them a sense of doing something worthwhile, and help differentiate the organisation from competitors!

This brief discussion rather nicely leads us in to the next chapter which is concerned with the relationship between sustainability and luxury.

10

11 Are Luxury and Sustainability Compatible?

Introduction

We live in a world where we are constantly bombarded through the media with messages about the threats facing the future of the planet, from climate change to water shortages. Citizens are exhorted to 'do their bit' to save the planet, whether that be by doing more recycling or taking the bus to work rather than using their own car for their daily commute.

As industries concerned with fun, rather than the necessities of life, we are under particular scrutiny about the impacts we have through everything from the carbon emissions of airliners, to the use of water resources, to the impact of tourism on wildlife.

Considerable efforts have been made by NGOs and these industries to communicate with consumers about sustainability issues in tourism, hospitality and events. People have been exhorted to buy locally made souvenirs, but not bits of animals, not have their towels washed, and think about offsetting their carbon footprint by funding the planting of trees with an additional voluntary payment.

Most commentators have doubted very much whether the luxury segment would respond positively to these messages. After all, is luxury about opulence based on ostentatious and excessive consumption – that is almost its definition. And on a positive note, high spending tourists create more jobs and sustain more livelihoods per head than other tourists, so there is an up side to their existence.

However, it is the luxury sector that flies in private jets and rides in large limousines, has villas with private pools on the edge of deserts, eats highly priced rare and endangered species and so on, making this sector perhaps the major threat to sustainability in tourism. Therefore if we are to make tourism, hospitality and events more sustainable, we need to get the luxury consumer on board and willing to modify their behaviour. But will a high end consumer tolerate the absence of air conditioning in a hot climate or other changes to the product that will reduce the quality, or indeed the glamour, of the experience?

In this chapter I will suggest that at least some luxury customers could be persuaded to modify their expectations and behaviour, if such modified behaviour could be made fashionable and status-enhancing. Throughout this discussion the widest possible definition of sustainability will be used, encompassing environmental sensitivity, economic viability and social equity.

Figure 11.1 sets out some of the dimensions of sustainability that we will then look at in the context of luxury.

Sustainability in tourism, hospitality and events

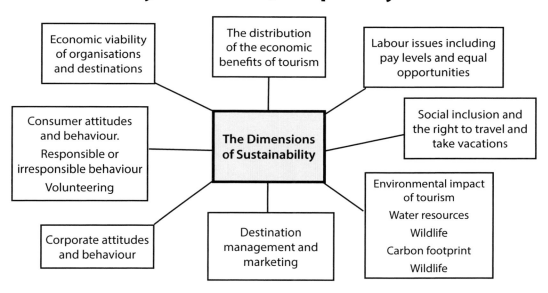

Figure 11.1: Dimensions of sustainability in tourism and hospitality that are relevant to the luxury market.

Let us now discuss what some of the issues identified in Figure 11.1 mean in relation to the concept of luxury in tourism, hospitality and events.

In terms of the economic viability of organisations and destinations, the luxury consumer is very important given their level of spending. For this to happen the organisation or destination needs an offer which is attractive to such consumers and this segment is becoming increasingly demanding. However, as we noted earlier in this book, luxury is not an absolute and is to some extent 'in the eye of the beholder', so that any organisation or destination that can persuade consumers that it offers luxury will be able to grow its business and thus ensure its viability.

At the same time, though, the distribution of the economic benefits of tourism is an important issue in relation to sustainable tourism. If a luxury consumer spends three thousand dollars for a stay at a foreign-owned resort where all labour and food is imported, the local economy may benefit less than a budget tourist who spends five hundred dollars to sleep in a homestay and eats in local restaurants which use produce from the surrounding area.

The issue of who benefits from tourist spend is also at the heart of the debate over all-inclusive resorts, many of which target the luxury market. In this case the questions relate not only to 'leakages' from the local economy, but also from the suggestion that all-inclusive resorts mean there are few opportunities for local entrepreneurs to find customers for their beach bars, restaurants and leisure activities. If tourists pay an all-inclusive price, they are dissuaded from leaving the resort to buy locally things that are already included in their vacation package.

Given that tourism and hospitality is a labour intensive sector of the economy, the economic benefits of the spending of luxury consumers can be limited if the majority of the jobs are low paid. But in terms of sustainable tourism, the labour issues are concerned with more than just wage rates; they are also about the opportunity for local people to receive training that can help them rise to management positions. It is also about whether they are are dependent on tips to earn a living wage and so believe that they need to behave in a subservient manner in order to earn a living.

One topic that that is often overlooked in debates about sustainable tourism is social inclusion, the idea that everyone should be able to enjoy a vacation whatever their circumstances. Given that money is perhaps the most important barrier to social inclusion in tourism, it would seem that social inclusion and luxury travel share no common ground, and there is much truth in that. However, even within the luxury segment there are those whose ability to enjoy a vacation is affected by factors such as a disability or health issues, or responsibilities as a carer, although they may have the means to overcome some of these due to their wealth.

In terms of the environmental impacts, it is perhaps fair to say that this is where a major challenge exists with the luxury segment in several respects. First the carbon footprint of the luxury consumer is likely to be larger than that of other tourists due the likely frequency of their trips and the fact that they may be more likely to make long haul journeys.

Second, it is likely that their per capita water consumption figures will be higher than that of other tourists, with their desire for villas with private pools and lush gardens, amongst other things.

They are also likely to be statistically over-represented in the market for wildlife experiences, which are often highly priced, whether it be a safari or a whale-watching trip.

The policies of destination management or marketing organisations are vitally important to the issue of sustainable tourism. The focus of many of the organisations is to target the high spending luxury segment so, hopefully, the same income can be realised from a smaller number of tourists. This would make it seem as if destination sustainability and the luxury market could be ideal partners, although it does not help at all with the issue of the impacts of mass market tourism.

The attitudes adopted by tourism and hospitality businesses are also important and traditionally the promotion of luxury experiences has had little to do with responsible consumerism. Indeed it has often seemed as if luxury consumers were being encouraged to believe that they had no responsibility for anything apart from their own hedonistic enjoyment. However, now, at the top end of the market, we are starting to see a change, but the motive for this change is the idea of how to differentiate the luxury experience from non-luxury and one company's product from that of another. Tourists are told it adds to their vacation experience to meet local people in their own homes, buy authentic local foods and souvenirs, and support local 'good causes' or charitable projects, rather than emphasising that this is 'responsible behaviour' because it brings the benefits of tourism to those who need them most.

This brings us to considering consumer attitudes towards luxury and sustainability. To many consumers, whatever their income level, a vacation is a time to forget everything and just enjoy themselves, so it is a real challenge to get them to think about sustainable tourism while they endeavour to forget the dullness of their everyday lives and their mundane home environment, and hurl themselves into pleasure-seeking. In theory, this should be less of an issue for the luxury consumer whose lifestyle is less constrained by money, so that they have more say in where they live and how they spend their days, at least.

In terms of the relationship between luxury travel, consumer behaviour and sustainable tourism there are two interesting points to be made as follows:

- We now have 'volunteering tourism' where tourists spend their vacations working on a project and usually paying for the privilege – sometimes quite a lot of money. This fascinating phenomenon on the face of it seems like a good thing, an altruistic act, and often is. But it can be pure self-indulgence, where the main motive is to make the tourists feel good and give them status with their peers, and the projects are of little or no value to the host community

- Many tourists seem to equate luxury with irresponsibility, and also believe the adage that 'the customer is always right' and the idea that 'I have paid to visit a destination and can therefore do what I like there regardless of the fact that one person's destination is another person's home!'

Still focusing on consumer attitudes, let us now turn to a subject we have discussed before, *authenticity*, and the idea that we are entering an era when sustainability is increasingly defined in terms of authenticity. This is linked, in my mind at least, with the evolving concept of luxury. In the retailing and fashion fields this is all about luxury brand products being the 'real thing' rather than fakes.

In hospitality it is somewhat different. It is about the provenance of ingredients used in the restaurant kitchen. In tourist destinations it means 'real places' that have not been changed or 'spoilt' by tourism – an odd idea that tourists want to think they are visiting places that have not been changed by the activity they are engaged in!

The idea appears to be that as our industry develops and globalisation contin-ues, 'authentic experiences' are becoming rarer and this increasingly gives them the air of exclusivity, which has always been at the heart of the concept of luxury.

Sustainability and tourism destinations

In terms of tourist destinations the link between sustainability and authenticity is presented in relation to tourism in Figure 11.2. We will then go on to discuss how this relates to the concept of luxury. I believe that what is presented is based on a fairly widely agreed concept of what constitutes authenticity and how this relates to the idea of sustainable tourism.

If luxury is about authenticity and small scale tourism, which is thus exclusive, then the early stages of this model are the only ones during which luxury, authen-ticity and sustainability can truly exist. Yet, to date, we know that more often luxury destinations have often been perceived to be very different places, in that it is often assumed that to be a luxury destination a place needs to have, at least:

- Highly developed infrastructure.
- A range of upscale accommodation with high levels of professional service.
- A variety of leisure experiences tailored to meet the needs of luxury clients such as spas.

Indeed, we can go further and say that many of the destinations now associated with luxury have not even followed the model of organic development set out in Figure 11.2. Instead, they have been purpose-developed as playgrounds for the luxury segment and those who aspire to be seen as part of this segment.

This model also assumes that tourism development begins with a number of local small-scale entrepreneurs who are new to the tourism and hospitality sector. Yet many of these modern purpose built luxury destinations have been developed by governments and/or major international corporations. As such, we can safely say that to date the development of luxury destinations has not largely followed a model that could be perceived as being based on any idea of authenticity or sustainability.

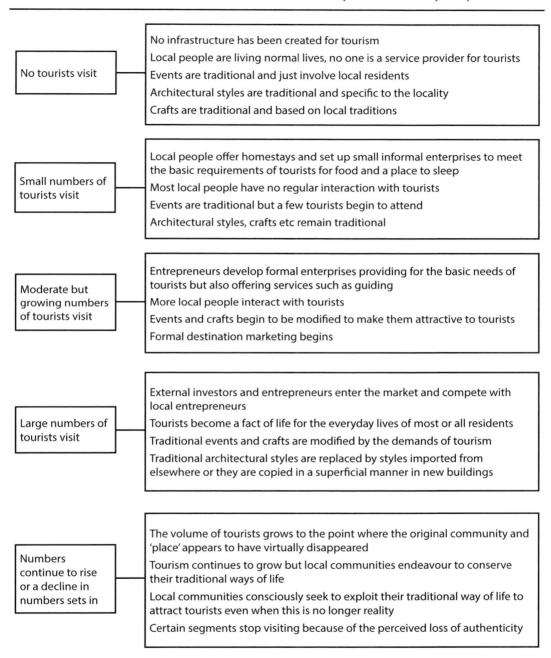

Figure 11.2: The continuum of authenticity and sustainability in tourist destinations

11

Luxury and sustainability

My contention is that things are changing and even many luxury consumers are becoming aware of, and interested in, ideas of responsible travel and authenticity. Indeed it could be argued that these are now fashionable concepts in this segment, although the nature of the luxury product may make it difficult to turn this consumer interest into reality in the supply side.

At this point, let us be careful; the luxury markets has its own segments, some of whom appear to have no interest in either authenticity or sustainable tourism, and are motivated almost solely it appears by the desire to be totally pampered, or consume ostentatiously, or pursue pleasure regardless of the consequences.

We also need to recognise that for decades debate has gone on about what authenticity actually means in tourism, and whether consumers can recognise it, let alone go looking for it. Nevertheless, the growing interest in sustainability and responsible consumerism amongst some luxury consumers gives us a real opportunity to move forward the sustainable tourism agenda.

Rightly or wrongly, celebrities and luxury consumers are major influencers of behaviour in the mass market, whether we are talking about fashion, interior, design, food and drink or vacations. If their behaviour were to change it could lead to change throughout the whole tourism market and that would be important as tourism will only become more sustainable if all types of tourists begin to behave more responsibly. This idea, and it is certainly a very idealistic one, is illustrated in Figure 11.3 with the label of a 'virtuous circle'

For this to happen, authors such as Xavier Font would suggest – and I would largely agree – that we need to change the way in which sustainable tourism is communicated to consumers, focusing less on lecturing them about what they should do and, instead, suggesting that doing 'the right thing' can enhance the quality of the vacation experience. This is the idea that underpins the success of companies such as Responsible Travel in the UK. In other words, responsible tourism will grow if we can give tourists, luxury or otherwise, a 'feelgood' effect if they behave more responsibly.

I would argue that this idea of those at the top end of society, financially speaking, behaving responsibly is not without precedent. The rich philanthropists of the USA and Asia who provide endowments to educational institutions or buy works of art for public museums come to mind. Likewise the tendency for many rich people in countries across the world to generously support charities because it makes them look and feel good.

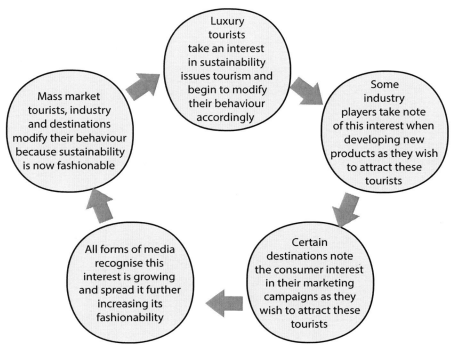

Figure 11.3: Sustainability and luxury: a virtuous circle?

We need to make promoting and supporting more responsible forms of tourism and hospitality as attractive as supporting 'good causes'. However, while these ideas sound great we need to be realistic and take the following into account:

- Tourism is not the only agent of change in any community, so even if we can make tourism more responsible this may still not guarantee sustainability.

- The growing markets of Asia, where modernity is equated with progress and luxury consumption is still a novel experience, may not embrace the ideas of authenticity, responsibility and sustainability that we have been discussing for some time.

- Older generations, wedded to traditional views of luxury, may be less open to 'the virtuous circle' than younger generations.

- Making this 'virtuous circle' a reality will require the media to pick up on these fledgling trends and disseminate them widely.

- The tourism, hospitality and events industries will need to be proactive and develop and promote genuinely responsible vacation experiences more than they do now at all levels of the market. This is important because, despite what traditional marketing theorists may say, many trends in the market are led more by developments in the supply side offer than by explicit consumer demand.

11

Conclusions

To conclude, I would like to reinforce some points made previously and add a few new ones about the relationship between luxury and sustainability in the context of tourism, hospitality and events.

First, I believe that the changes that are occurring in the concept of luxury – which have been discussed since the first chapter of this book – are creating an opportunity to bring together the concepts of sustainability and luxury, and that has not been the case before. This includes the growing interest of parts of the luxury market in issues such as fair trade, values and authenticity.

Second, I have suggested that tourism can only become more sustainable if the luxury market and those who supply it become more responsible.

Third, if sustainability means better salaries for employees and modifications to the product, which in turn will mean higher prices, then at least the luxury market should have the ability to pay a higher price, perhaps unlike tourists who are less affluent.

Fourth, we need to recognise, however, that making luxury travel more sustainable will be a challenge, because of the likely resistance of many parts of the market to attempts to lower the level of comfort they enjoy, as we endeavour to reduce the negative environmental impacts of tourism. If sustainability also means restricting access to vulnerable places, this may be particularly difficult to 'sell' to luxury consumers who are used to people not denying them anything.

Fifth, if industry suppliers recognise there is a growing interest in sustainability in the luxury market and seek to exploit this, they will need to do so properly and not in a tokenistic manner or they may face a consumer backlash and media criticism. Likewise they will face criticism if they focus just on the environment and ignore issues around human rights.

Sixth, much of the sustainable tourism literature focuses on islands, natural areas and remote regions, all of which are popular with luxury travellers. However, much luxury tourism consumption takes place in cities. Although these places may appear rich they almost always contain areas of poverty and many people who are severely disadvantaged. Any discussions about sustainable tourism and the luxury market, therefore, needs to look at how tourism can benefit the poorest urban citizens. This is particularly important with the growth in anti-tourism demonstrations in places such as Amsterdam and Barcelona, where people seem to be rebelling against both the type of tourism and numbers of tourists their cities are attracting. Tourism needs to work much harder to be a 'good neighbour' in cities than it is currently, and that includes the luxury market.

Finally, we are beginning to see the growth of a 'slow tourism' segment following the growth of the 'slow food' movement. Here the emphasis is on taking your time to enjoy the place you visit and explore it in depth, getting under its surface to discover the 'real place'. This kind of tourism is likely to be more sustainable, with the economic benefits of tourist spend being greater and spread more widely than with traditional tourism. It should also be less environmentally harmful. Throughout the book to date we have made reference to the fact that in today's busy world leisure time itself is becoming a luxury commodity. Therefore if 'slow tourism' continues to grow, it may be an excellent bridge between sustainable tourism and the idea of luxury, as we seek to get people to realise that spending time is as important as spending money.

To end this chapter let us return to the original question that is the title of the chapter, namely, 'are luxury and sustainability compatible?' The simple answer to this question is that they not only can be compatible but they must be compatible if tourism is to be sustainable in the long-term.

11

12 Are Luxury Brands a Contradiction in Terms?

Introduction

We live in the age of brands and branding, where you are judged by the name and the logo on your phone, your trainers and your handbag. The price of a product can be inflated dramatically beyond the cost of its production if carries a particular name or logo.

In a way brands are the opposite of luxury for they are often purchased by consumers who do so because they are standardised in appearance and function and are also reliable. This seems to be diametrically opposed to the idea of luxury products, as things which are differentiated from other products and largely standardised. Then we have what are termed 'designer brands' particularly in the fashion sector. These can carry great status yet often they are made in relatively large numbers, often with little personalisation. The fact therefore that relatively large numbers of such products, which are generally very expensive and high quality, are made must surely affect the idea of what constitutes luxury. Our consumer world is currently full of products which purport to be, and are accepted by consumers as, luxury brands, despite them being produced in large numbers.

There are some other interesting dimensions to this discussion around branding and luxury that we may wish to discuss briefly at this point.

First, in the field of manufactured goods there is the interesting phenomenon of fakes – lower quality copies of luxury products that, nevertheless, on the face of it have the same appearance of the 'real thing' and carry the appropriate name or logo. Everyone seems to recognise that these fakes will not be of the same quality as the original, but many buy them anyway suggesting, that the status acquired by being associated with these labels is very important to some people who may be unable to afford the authentic article.

Of course, in tourism, hospitality and events, this faking of the tangible product is almost non-existent, although copying elements of the product of a leading brand is not unknown! And while no destination can be seen as a fake there is considerable debate around the authenticity of destinations and 'inauthentic' could be seen as an alternative word for fake!

Second, in many sectors of manufacturing we now have everyday brands which would, by no stretch of the imagination, be perceived as luxury, developing products and marketing them in ways designed to make them appear to be a 'luxury purchase'. This is often done by developing so-called 'limited editions', which suggests a rarity value which is often synonymous with luxury, yet the production run for these 'limited edition' clothes, soft drink, chocolates and so on could run into millions of units! In relation to the tangible elements of the product in tourism, hospitality and events, such 'limited editions' are not so obvious although they could be said to be represented by the opportunity to pay to upgrade to a better hotel room or a higher class of travel on the aeroplane.

Third, and most intriguingly perhaps in the context of tourism, hospitality and events, is the issue of services. Branded hotels, airports, casinos and so on may create luxurious physical environments and seek to impress consumers with lavish tangible goods such as food and drink, entertainments systems, and comfortable beds, but they are also service businesses where a big part of the experience comes through intangible service delivery.

Here I would suggest that the whole idea of branding begins to break down somewhat, or certainly that element of it relating to the service being of a similar standard and style time after time after time – in other words consistency. It is impossible to fully standardise a service delivered by a human being, despite all the training in the world. Service delivered by people is never the same on any two occasions because of changes in the relationship between three sets of factors:

- The server, even if it is the same person, has moods which change, feels great or feels unwell, is enjoying their working day or is hating it.

- The consumer has the same issues around mood and feeling well or not, but also brings other variables to the service interaction, including their personality, previous experiences and expectations.

- The context in which the service takes place, which covers everything from the number and identity of other consumers within the service delivery location, to how busy the operation is, to the physical environment, to the quality of the tangibles – such as food and drink – that the server is given by the rest of the team to provide for the consumer.

Furthermore, the idea that branding ensures a certain standardisation and consistency is also increasingly not true in the hospitality sector. Here the widespread use of franchising and management contracting in relation to hotels and restaurants leads to issues around the implementation of brand standards and values in every single unit operating under a particular brand.

12

Given that luxury is sometimes seen in terms of rarity value or uniqueness, one could argue that all service encounters in tourism, hospitality or events are 'luxury' based on that simplistic view! That is obviously not my view, and it is clear that many famous brands which see themselves as being at the luxury end in these industries go to great lengths to ensure that the service is as good as the tangible elements of the product. In my experience, Michelin starred restaurants are perhaps best at achieving this marriage of service and tangible elements. In the hotel and sectors, this seems harder to achieve; indeed in the accommodation sector the best service seems to be seen in so-called 'bed and breakfasts' where the service deliverer is also often also the proprietor and host.

The characteristics of luxury brands

We will begin, in Figure 12.1, by outlining the main characteristics that consumers might expect of a product which was labelled as a luxury brand. These will then be discussed in the context of tourism, hospitality and events.

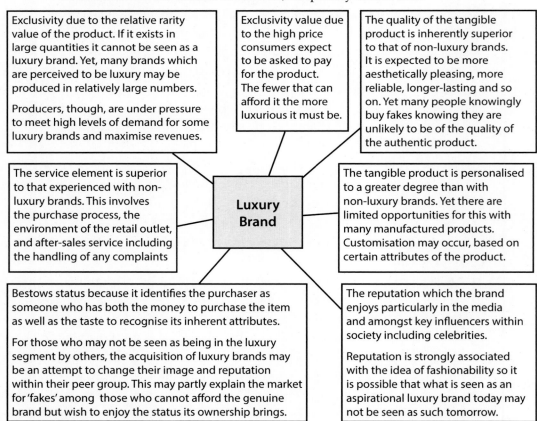

Figure 12.1: Expected characteristics of luxury brand products

Let us begin by recognising that in our sector the issue of luxury brands has two elements, namely the products offered by industry, and the destination where the vacation is located. Destinations can be seen as brands in their own right although this view is contested by some commentators.

■ Exclusivity through price

The idea that luxury is about exclusivity, achieved through a high sales price, is clearly evident in our industries through everything from first class air fares, to 'Presidential Suites' in hotels, to 'Owner's Suite' cabins on cruise ships. However, virtually no product in tourism, hospitality and events is priced so high as to be beyond the means of all but the richest, although for poorer people it may mean saving for many years, rather than being able to afford it instantly, as would be the case for the mega-rich. But only a tiny minority of the less well-off could ever aspire to own a luxury home or Monet painting, for instance.

Furthermore our industries tend to focus on cost-plus and competitor-based approaches to price, and even at the high end they may see little advantage in being the most expensive. Furthermore, even at the high end, margins are modest. In other sectors there can seem to be an idea that luxury means the more expensive the better, regardless of the cost of production and distribution. At the same time, if we focus on the destination as the heart of the vacation, we can see that some elements of the experience are actually free and in most cases cannot be taken over by private interests and made the subject of charging, including views and weather, but not beaches where private interests, if permitted, can charge people to use a natural attraction that they did nothing to create!

■ Exclusivity due to rarity

The other way of ensuring exclusivity is through the rarity value of the commodity, whereby the supply is limited in some way, for example by the capacity of a workshop or the availability of a raw material,. Obviously the former can be increased through expansion, although the latter may be more difficult to change.

In our industries it is slightly different in several ways. First, a workshop producing a luxury product is unlikely to be also producing low end products at the same time. However, in hotels, concert venues, airliners and cruise ships each unit will be offering a range of options from luxury priced to economy priced. Furthermore, the supplier can, with a little effort, in some cases, modify these options to match demand, changing the configuration of an airliner for example.

And while natural resources such as diamonds are only available in certain places, it seems that most places in the world can attract tourists if they get the product and the marketing right. While the most special may be expensive to reach, almost any are available for tourists, with usually no entrance fee beyond

12

the cost of a visa. Only in those rare privately owned island resorts do we see examples of destinations with fixed capacity, controlled by industry players.

■ Superior quality

It would normally be argued that luxury consumers would expect the quality of tangible products labelled as 'luxury brands' to be superior. This is, indeed, usually the case although there may be differences between countries. A hotel room sold as 'luxury' in country Y may be seen as that within the country, but could seem far from that in country X, where general standards are higher.

Quality can apply to everything from aesthetics to reliability, features to performance. Nevertheless, I contend that the expectation of superior quality in terms of the tangible elements of the experience is as prevalent in tourism and hospitality as in other sectors.

■ Personalisation

It is often suggested that one definition of luxury is that the tangible product is more personalised than is the case with non-luxury products. I suspect that this is also the expectation of luxury sector consumers in tourism, hospitality and events. Yet, as with other industries, the scope for personalisation of the physical product is limited. Even in first class on an airline, there may be twelve identical 'cabins', very luxurious but identical in terms of the physical elements. Personalisation is about the service element, rather than the physical environment, but that can also be done, theoretically at least, in business class too or even economy class.

■ High reputation

Another dimension of luxury brands is the idea that the product enjoys a high reputation, particularly amongst those whose opinion matters most, namely celebrities, including well-known bloggers. This is also true in our industries but there are no equivalents in tourism, hospitality and events of famous luxury brands such as Louis Vuitton, Prada, Jimmy Choo, Rolex, and Ferrari. There are high end brands which have an excellent reputation but, in general, they attract far less media attention and generate much less marketing hype themselves.

Interestingly, destinations can also have a high reputation, perhaps more so than individual product brands, although this reputation may become outdated and no longer reflect the reality, as was discussed in Chapter 7.

■ Status

For many who buy luxury brands, their motivation probably includes an element of the idea that purchase bestows status on the consumer. In the case of the rich, it may be a matter of buying to maintain the status they already enjoy, while for others it is a matter of hoping the purchase will elevate their status in the eyes of 'society', which might just mean friends or neighbours. As we noted above, as the profile of brands in our industries tend to be lower than in other industries, a Prada outfit or Rolex watch will probably bestow more status than flying first class or having the best seat at a concert. One reason for this may be that the flight and concert only last a few hours, and most of our industry's products are of very limited duration, so after a short time all one has is a memory, whereas the outfit or watch can last for years and be shown to everyone one meets!

■ Superior service

Finally, many organisations promote the fact that their product should be seen a luxury because the service element is of a superior quality, to what could be seen as normal service. This relates to everything from the purchase process through consumption to post-service and the addressing of any complaints. Yet, in tourism, hospitality and leisure this is challenging, not least because of the short duration of consumption experiences, which give a very limited time to resolve problems. Even at the purchase end of the process, luxury clients may be using the same channels as other consumers, unless they have some form of priority status with the organisation through its loyalty programme, for example. Further relevant issues around service are discussed in Chapter 9.

Further observations about branding and luxury

I would now like to make a number of further points about the relationship between branding and luxury in respect of tourism, hospitality and tourism.

First, many major corporations in our sector will have brands at different levels in the market, such as Accor which includes both Ibis and Sofitel for example. And most airlines offer business class and economy class products in addition to possibly first class and premium economy often too. Tour operators also may have mixed portfolios of luxury end and mass market products.

Second, the highest profile and best known brands in our sector today tend not to be at the luxury end. In the UK, for instance, Ryanair is possibly the highest profile airline and the budget chain Premier Inn the most high profile hotel brand.

Third, often those brands which are perceived as luxury are not part of large organisations but are, instead, single units in private ownership. This is particularly the case in relation to luxury end hotels and restaurants.

Fourth, some brands have chosen to challenge the traditional indicators of quality and luxury, particularly in the hospitality industry. Once the Burj-el-Arab

12

hotel in Dubai described itself as seven stars, it pointed out that the star system is now obsolete.

Fifth and almost in contrast to point four, some strong brands have developed in our sector not as providers of tourism, hospitality and events products, but rather as arbiters of what constitutes luxury and quality. These brands include names such as Michelin and Skytrax and media such as Conde Nast Traveller.

Sixth, faking of luxury brands is much more difficult to achieve in tourism, hospitality and events, not least because the product is delivered and consumed at a particular location at a specific time.

Seventh, celebrity endorsement is at the heart of brand marketing these days, particularly at the luxury end, in areas such as fashion, cosmetics, and so on. However, as yet, we have seen relatively few campaigns for luxury brands or aspiring luxury brands in tourism, hospitality and events that feature celebrity endorsement. One notable exception was Mandarin Hotels in 2016. Turkish airlines has also used famous footballers but to promote the whole airline rather than using the association to promote an image of it as a luxury end carrier.

Eighth, a brand which is low status in one country may be seen very differently in another. We perhaps all recall the splash which MacDonald's made when it first arrived in Russia. In poor countries with national airlines which have very poor reputations for service or safety, a European airline may be seen as a 'luxury' option, while within Europe it might be seen as unexceptional or below average.

Finally, there is the question of whether a destination can be seen as a luxury brand or even a brand at all. My view 'no' because:

- A destination is not a product, but rather a set of opportunities, from which the traveller builds their own 'product'. It is like a Lego set, from which anything can be constructed providing the necessary bricks are in the box to begin with!
- Destinations are not controlled or managed by any one entity, and the public sector which is the nearest they have to this entity has little control over two and maybe three elements of the Marketing Mix, in most cases, so true 'destination marketing' and 'destination management' are largely self-delusions in most parts of the world except in totalitarian states, ironically.
- Destinations have a function well beyond tourism, hospitality and events and the vast majority do not exist primarily to service the desires of consumers within these industries.
- Destinations are unbelievably complex and changing by the second, and they are, largely, organic rather than having been created as destinations.

This has not stopped many destinations from having branding strategies and brand identities and there is no doubt, as we saw in Chapter 7, that some places do have a reputation for being luxury destinations which they seek to exploit.

Conclusions

I will now attempt to conclude by making a number of general points and by revisiting the question which forms the title of this chapter. The easy answer to the question 'are luxury brands a contradiction in terms?' is, of course, that it depends on how you define the words 'luxury' and brands'! For what it is worth, my conclusions are that 'luxury brands' is a problematic term if we think luxury is about rarity value or even uniqueness and personalisation, because generally brands are about standardisation and consistency. However, if one takes a very simplistic view of a brand just being an identity, whether that be a name or symbol, then you could say anything could be a luxury brand if the name or symbol was recognised as such within the market.

Turning specifically to tourism, hospitality and events, there are a few final points to be made by the relationship between luxury and branding.

First, the term 'luxury brand' is highly subjective and is not an absolute. Traditional ways of defining it around high price and rarity no longer tell the whole story and it as much about perception and feelings as about facts and reality. This is also being driven by the rise of social media and the replacement of formal arbiters of quality such as star systems in hotels with much more fluid evaluations based on consumer opinion rather than on the views of professionals.

Second, I am not convinced that any brand which has more than one unit and is part of some form of 'chain' will be seen as a luxury brand in future, as consumers widen their definition of luxury to include matters such as authenticity and the opportunity to enjoy truly personalised service and unique experience.

In terms of the service element in destinations and hospitality, the real touchstone of 'luxury' may well become much more about sincerity and informality and encounters with 'real' local people, rather than highly formalised service delivered on a large scale by trained staff.

The idea of luxury brands still suggests very much a product and supplier led approach, based on 'marketing speak', which seems at odds with the idea of the experience economy and co-creation as we discussed in Chapter 10. So, perhaps, we should stop looking at this from the supply side and start talking about it from the demand side; after all throughout the book we have discussed how power appears to be moving from the industry to the consumer. Fanciful though it might seem, maybe one day in future, consumers will each be their own brand, demanding products and services rather than buying what organisations wish to offer them.

In the meantime, back to reality, in some sectors like fashion, cars and watches, luxury brands are easy to identify, thriving and have consumers who are hungry

12

for the opportunity to buy them. In tourism, hospitality and events they are less easy to identify, have a lower profile and do not seem to attract the same level of excitement as in some other sectors. That does not mean that our consumers are not interested in luxury; but it may mean that they do not believe that luxury is simply about buying particular brands. It is far more complicated than that.

Conclusions To Part 4

Well, we have looked at the 'big questions' but have we found any answers? Probably not but I believe we have discovered some interesting points

☐ First, it appears that while these five issues are very different, there are significant links between them. For example, new technological developments are having an impact on what service means in tourism, hospitality and events. The rise of organisations such as Air BnB is a direct result of the concept of the experience economy and technological innovation that facilitates its existence

☐ Second, technology is putting more power into the hands of consumers and is allowing them to have more control and less reliance on professionals if they wish to spend time planning their own trips.

☐ Third, the concept of service is undergoing a transformation currently with the rise of self-service, where consumers may forgo some personal service delivery if that gives them more choice or greater convenience.

☐ Fourth, we have seen that the idea that tourists are looking for personalised experiences rather than standardised products and services is subtly changing the relationships between industry and consumers.

☐ Fifth, sustainability and luxury may be compatible but it may also be true that we cannot have sustainability in tourism, hospitality and events unless we can persuade luxury consumers to become more sustainable in their behaviour.

☐ Sixth, I have questioned whether brands can ever be truly luxury, although this seems a very radical view in the world of today.

In Part 5 we will attempt to draw everything together with three chapters looking at a research agenda, overall conclusions and, most difficult of all, the future.

Part 5: Conclusions and the Future

The most difficult part of a book to write is this section where one attempts to pull everything together and then make prophecies about the future.

In Chapter 13, I will endeavour to discuss the weaknesses of academic research in relation to the idea of luxury in tourism, hospitality and events and then go on to suggest a brief research agenda.

Chapter 14 seeks to identify key themes that have arisen from the text and I attempt to offer a model of the changing nature of luxury in tourism, hospitality and events.

In Chapter 15 an attempt is made to look into the future and suggest how the concept of luxury may evolve in the future. I will set out a number of possible scenarios for you to consider.

13 Towards a Research Agenda for Luxury in Tourism, Hospitality and Events

Introduction

Whenever I write a book about these three sectors I am struck by the lack of good academic research, and this book has been no exception. Indeed the luxury end of tourism, hospitality and events seems to have been largely ignored despite the fact that, per head, it brings the highest economic benefits to both organisations and destinations. And 'luxury' is also a term used freely in the marketing communications of most organisations in these sectors – even at the lower price levels.

Perhaps the reluctance to research in this area relates to the fact that it is seen to be about elitist travel and this elitism may carry a stigma of its own. Furthermore it only covers a tiny minority of those travelling around our planet in their leisure time, so is perhaps felt to be of less importance than mass tourism. This is unfortunate as luxury travel has a disproportionally high per capita economic impact, and its environmental impact is intensified as these are the travellers who can afford to visit some of the most isolated and fragile ecosystems in the world.

Or it may be that the lack of research may simply reflect the fact that the term is difficult to define and place within a simple conceptual structure. Luxury is also a term that cannot be easily contained within a box labelled 'tourism, hospitality and events', as it spreads across a much broader canvas that encompasses everything from retailing to fashion, media to technology, lifestyle to personality. Furthermore, in terms of academic disciplines it crosses many including history, psychology, sociology, geography and economics not to mention the huge 'discipline' of management, that catch-all phrase covering a range of subjects such as marketing, finance, human resource management, and so on.

Whatever the reason behind the lack of research I hope in this chapter to highlight where research is needed, and in doing to motivate researchers to start to look more deeply at the subject of luxury in tourism, hospitality and events.

Figure 13.1 sets out the main areas where research is required in this field and each of the points identified will be discussed later in this chapter.

Figure 13.1: The scope of a research agenda for luxury in tourism, hospitality and events

Let us now look at the factors identified in Figure 13.1 in a little more detail.

■ Definitions of luxury

First, let's begin by looking at the issue of definitions of the meaning of luxury in tourism, hospitality and events. There is no single accepted definition of luxury in our sector – it is as if people do not think it necessary to define it everyone understands what the term means. But as this book has hopefully shown, this is simply not the case, for it is a complex matter. And if its meaning has been clear in the past, I have suggested, throughout this text, that the meaning of luxury is changing and will continue to change so old definitions will become increasingly irrelevant. We need to interrogate the idea that luxury means the same in tourism, hospitality and events as it does in other sectors such as fashion, retailing or cars. Maybe it does and maybe it does not. We also need to develop definitions that are based on the perceptions of consumers and that recognise that there may be national and cultural differences in these definitions. Finding realistic and usable

13

definitions of luxury will allow us to gather data on the luxury market which is reliable and provides a sound foundation for the segmentation of the luxury market. This could potentially involve the development of new terms to replace the word 'luxury' of course – who knows!

What does luxury mean?

Second, we need to look 'under the skin' of tourism, hospitality and events and explore what luxury means in the various sectors of these industries, such as airlines, cruise ships, hotels and villas, restaurants, visitor attractions, sporting events, cultural events and so on. We need to establish if there are common threads between them in relation to the meaning of luxury and identify clear differences between these elements. Some may be because some relate to the journey to the destination while others are firmly based in the destination. Some may be the motivator for taking a trip while others are the things needed during a trip, such as a bed and meals, yet at times it can be the hotel or the restaurant itself which can be a major motivator for the trip.

What is luxury service?

Third is the question of what the term 'luxury service' means. While there is a plethora of really interesting papers about service in our sector, little attention has been paid to typologies of service in the luxury market. Yet it is clear that across tourism, hospitality and events the concept of luxury service is evolving as we saw in Chapter 9. This research needs to focus not only on how service is delivered but perhaps more importantly on how it is received by the consumer. It also needs to focus on the three stages of service, namely the purchase process, the consumption phase and after-sales service and complaint resolution.

The supply side of luxury

Fourth, we need more research on the supply side of luxury, particularly in relation to the following;

- Product development, in terms of how long it takes and costs, and the extent to which it takes on board ideas such as experiential marketing and co-creation.
- The pricing of luxury products, and decisions to discount so-called luxury products and experiences, particularly in the hotel sector.
- Loyalty programmes and the opportunities they provide for those regular business travellers, who may not normally be luxury travellers, to access luxury services such as flight and hotel room upgrades free of charge through the accumulation of points or miles.

■ The messages which suppliers communicate to the market, that create expectations amongst consumers and the influence these messages have on consumer perceptions of luxury.

■ Consumer decision making

In the fifth place, as with other markets in tourism, hospitality and events, we need further research on the decisions made by individual consumers in terms of their motivators and determinants and how they make their purchases. We need to understand more about the role which status plays in decision-making, and the major influencers on their behaviour. It would be particularly interesting to know how they make decisions, and how the factors which influence them relate to behaviour in other parts of the market which are not seen as 'luxury'.

As well as looking at the behaviour of individuals, it is particularly important for more research to be conducted on luxury markets as a whole, especially in respect of the following;

■ How many people there are in the luxury market at any one time; how many of these are 'habitual' luxury consumers, for whom luxury is a fact of everyday life; and how many are occasional or once-in-a-lifetime luxury consumers, for whom luxury is not a normal way of life.

■ Accurate measurement of the spending of luxury consumers, including per day spend and per category spend, e.g. transport, hotels, eating out, sightseeing, retailing and so on.

■ The demographics of demand, particularly in relation to age and gender, as conventional wisdom about the luxury market seems to make assumptions about both which I believe are becoming obsolete with social change

■ Ways of segmenting the market and particularly the importance of psychographic segmentation, given that the concept of luxury seems to be closely tied to both personality and lifestyle. And in the context of lifestyle we need to look at three types: the lifestyle the consumer actually lives, the lifestyle they wish they lived, and the lifestyle they hope other people will think they lead!

■ Trends that are relevant to the luxury market including, as noted elsewhere, everything from attitudes towards sustainability, to the idea of authenticity, to people feeling stressed and 'time poor', to concerns over terrorist threats.

13

■ National and cultural differences

Following on from the need to do more research on markets is the issue of national and cultural differences in the concept of luxury. We need to explore this and use empirical research to either challenge or validate some of the stereotypes that are clearly present in the market. These stereotypes may include:

- The idea that for certain Asian markets luxury means travelling to purchase international designer brands.

- The suggestion that ostentatious displays of wealth are the norm amongst the rich in some countries, whereas in other countries the wealthy play down their wealth and keep it more private.

- The so-called more egalitarian societies, such as the countries of Scandanavia, where even the wealthy seem to take pleasure in simple non-luxury activities and where it is hard to detect a distinctly 'luxury market'.

Furthermore, we need to understand differences not only in the size of the luxury market in different countries but also the potential for further growth in those markets.

■ The concept of luxury in different sectors

The next area for research, and a fascinating one, is the comparison of the concept of luxury in tourism, hospitality and events, with that in other sectors of the economy. What are the similarities and differences in the concept of luxury consumption between our sector and high end retailing, luxury fashion, and exclusive car brands, for example? Is there anything unique about luxury in tourism, hospitality and events, based on the fact that:

- Unlike most industries our consumers have to travel to consume the product, it cannot be brought to their place of residence or local town?

- Our products and experiences are not part of everyday life but indeed represent a desire to break away from everyday life.

■ Future evolution

Finally, if we are to understand the meaning of luxury in tourism, hospitality and events and be able to predict how it will evolve, we need to understand the factors which will determine its future evolution. In saying this we have perhaps left the most difficult area of research until the last, for here it is not only about understanding individual factors but how they combine together to shape change. And these factors themselves are incredibly diverse, ranging from social change to economic development, terrorism to the impact of climate change, technological innovation to new product developments from industry!

Research now

Before we go to identify some final challenges in relation to research and luxury in respect of tourism, hospitality and events let us say a few words about the researchers themselves, their methodologies and their results.

First, as with all areas of research in our sector, it appears that there is not enough truly inter-disciplinary work going on involving specialists bringing different areas of expertise to research projects. Instead we tend to get tourism researchers looking at the psychology of consumer behaviour although they have no real background in psychology, while psychologists publish papers about tourism in which the level of knowledge of tourism is worryingly low. The result is work which lacks real quality or value in terms of the creation of new knowledge.

Second, much of the research being conducted in tourism, hospitality and events is increasingly quantitative, not least because of the career need for academics to get their work published. Not only do the practical limitations of time and money mean that such work often involves very small samples, but perhaps more importantly it denies the complexity of the subject that requires sophisticated qualitative approaches.

The third point I would wish to make relates to the lack of longitudinal studies that are vital in order to identify trends in the luxury market or the meaning of luxury itself.

At the same time, there is too much research being done in countries and cultures where the researcher is 'foreign' and lacks the cultural awareness or language skills to truly understand what they are seeing and hearing.

Sadly, there are also many areas of the world where potentially fascinating research is not being conducted or reported for a variety of reasons including:

- The relatively low level of higher education development in the country.
- The fact that tourism, hospitality and events are not seen as legitimate research fields in some countries.
- The dominance of English as the medium of communication for refereed journals which means that some excellent research may not reach a wide audience if the researchers are not able to publish their work in English.

In most countries we also have the problem that most of the best data collected is gathered for commercial reasons by private interests and is confidential and unavailable to researchers.

I would now like to make a number of general points about research, the idea of luxury and tourism, hospitality and events.

■ Destinations

One area where research in our field is different to that in pretty well any other is in respect of the phenomenon of the destination. Luxury in our sector can relate to the journey to the destination but always relates to what is consumed within the destination. However, when researching what signifies a luxury destination there are a number of points to be borne in mind, including:

13

- Destinations are places which people live in as well as just visit, and many are not wholly or largely focused upon delivering luxury experiences to visitors.

- Most destinations grew up organically and only developed as tourist destinations over time, whereas today we are seeing the creation of more purpose-built destinations that have no real 'history' as destinations or even as settlements! This could be said of some of the resorts developed in Tunisia in recent decades or Sharm-el-Sheikh in Egypt or even Las Vegas for matter!

- Destinations have images which either encourage or discourage visitors, and these images are based on perceptions rather than any objective reality. Furthermore an image or reputation can live on long after the reality has changed. One might use the French Riviera as an example of this, although at the time of writing a new TV series '*Riviera*' is showing on Sky, which may just reinforce its image of glamour and luxury.

- Destination images are increasingly influenced by external forces, such as the media and tour operator marketing rather than by internal stakeholders such as local government or locally owned hotels.

- Destinations can have different images with different audiences such as domestic tourists, long-haul travellers, business travellers and so on.

- In destinations it is normal for luxury travellers, mass market tourists and budget travellers to share the same public space, which can be confusing when one is researching the idea of a 'luxury destination'.

- The fact that destinations not only offer the opportunities for enjoyment for visitors, but also provide a source of risk for the traveller, whether that be through crime, terrorist threat, extreme weather events or accidents.

There are other complications around researching luxury in tourism, hospitality and events that are worth mentioning briefly.

■ Consumers

In the first place, as we have noted already in this book, luxury is a relative concept rather than an absolute, a feeling as well as, or perhaps rather than, a fact. It is about meeting and exceeding expectations so we need to recognise that the expectations are affected by a myriad of complicated factors from personality to life experience, who your friends are, what media you use, together with your past experiences. They change over time and are sometimes simply unrealistic. If your romantic relationship is failing even a flight in first class and a stay in the Presidential Suite at the swishest hotel in a city stay may not be able to change that fact!

Moving on, I would contend that the idea of luxury does not just relate to a vacation, hotel stay or concert. Perhaps equally important, at least, with a luxury experience is the pre-consumption anticipation as well as the post-consumption memories and the sharing of these memories with friends and family and social media contacts.

One thing which is always difficult when researching tourist behaviour, or other consumer behaviour for that matter, is getting to the 'truth'. People may not always be aware of their motives or be willing to discuss them, even if they are aware. For example, few would readily admit that the desire for status motivates them to purchase luxury products, but do we believe those who say that it plays no part in their decision?

We also need to be careful to recognise that what people buy may not necessarily reflect what they would like to buy, and this is not just a function of disposable income. It can also be a result of other factors such as state of health, caring responsibilities, lack of confidence, fear of flying and many others besides.

Consumers in tourism, hospitality and events are also increasingly facing challenges over their choices and finding themselves almost having to defend their behaviour. Luxury market customers tend to be under pressure because of the number of trips they make and their environmental impact, not only of their flying but also their holiday lifestyle and desire for things that come with environmental costs, such as air conditioning and golf courses in deserts! Those luxury travellers with a more sensitive disposition may be feeling that far from being something to be proud of, their behaviour may be irresponsible in today's world.

There are suggestions that we are seeing significant shifts in the idea of luxury and there is plenty of evidence from respected observers that this is the case. However, it is all so new that there still remains little empirical academic research and very few refereed papers talking about this change. As ever, academic research is struggling to keep up with the pace of change 'in the real world'. This is particularly clear in relation to the idea that, particularly for the younger generation, values and experiences are becoming seen as well as things as being part of luxury consumption. Also that some luxury consumers are recognising the need to be responsible travellers rather than just hedonists.

Conclusions

So let us now try to gather some of the threads from this chapter together.

We have noted that academic research in the field with which this book is concerned is weak and under-developed but we have also recognised that this is generally true in tourism, hospitality and events. As we have seen we even lack the basics such as generally accepted definitions without which research is extremely difficult. At the same time I would like to suggest that there is a particular need to undertake research around the areas where there are particularly interesting developments taking place in relation to the meaning of luxury.

- The impact of technological innovation, particularly in terms of mobile devices and the consumption experience.
- The meaning of luxury service today, including new styles of less formalised luxury service and even consumer self-service.
- The idea of the 'experience economy' and the shift this implies in power from suppliers to consumers.
- The growing concerns over sustainability and responsible consumerism in tourism, hospitality and events.
- The issue of branding and luxury, and the apparent contradictions between these two terms.

As an over-arching theme I would also like to make a plea for more research effort to be focused on the issue of time and its relationship with the idea of luxury. In many countries after decades of economic development it often appears today that many people are wealthier than their parents' generation but feel they have less free time, are more pressurised and as a result more stressed. If that is the case, we need to explore if time availability and the way we use time may be as important to our concept of luxury in future as wealth and disposable income.

Our research needs to focus on what is likely to happen in the future rather than what has happened in the past. Furthermore to be effective, we academic researchers need to work with governments and industry partners rather than in isolation, and our research needs to be truly interdisciplinary and based on working with experts in other fields.

And our research needs to be willing to be radical, indeed we may decide as a result of our research that the word 'luxury' is already obsolete, misleading or simply unhelpful, carrying negative connotations. In a world facing so many problems such as shortage of water, climate change and terrorism, to name but three, it may well be that luxury starts to appear a bad thing, an unjustified self-indulgence that the world can no longer afford. If we cannot achieve 'luxury' for all maybe we should not have 'luxury' for the few!

14 Conclusions

Introduction

As always there is a need to seek to bring things to a neat end with an attempt to distil the ideas contained in many pages into a couple of thousand words. This involves trying to identify key thoughts and facts that encapsulate the main achievements of the text in terms of advancing our knowledge of the subject.

Writing conclusions implies that something has been completed or achieved but often the only outcome of a book is a new set of questions and I fear that this is the situation I am faced with here.

In this chapter I will endeavour to pull together threads that run through the whole book. At the same time I will revisit some of the ideas and definitions that were explored in the first chapter. I was surprised by how many of the apparently diverse subjects touched upon, from technology to sustainability, service to brands, geography to the 'experience economy' appeared to link together easily and naturally under the umbrella of luxury.

Perhaps, first of all, it would be a good idea to look at the main points which emerged from each of the chapters.

The first chapter suggested the existence of traditional definitions of luxury that revolved around high price and exclusivity. It was also noted that in our sector the concept of luxury was born in Europe and had since been adopted globally, not least due to the domination of the international travel market by Europeans, at least until recently. However, I suggested there was evidence from within tourism, hospitality and events that the meaning of luxury was changing due to a range of factors from technological developments to terrorism, economic development to social change. I also used the views of commentators from the wider consumer world to suggest that a fundamental shift in the concept of luxury was taking place, including two particularly interesting ideas. The first of these was a contention that for some consumers, particularly younger people, luxury was becoming more about experiences than the possession of things. And the second suggestion was that perhaps the term 'luxury' is now being used so widely that its very meaning is being diluted.

In the second chapter we took a historical perspective of luxury in tourism, hospitality and events. Here the point was made that until the mid-20th century virtually all international tourism was by definition luxury travel, as only a tiny proportion of populations were able to afford to travel internationally. Since then travel has become democratised, and in developed countries has become a mass market. In that context it has become possible to distinguish between luxury and less luxurious forms of tourism. However, the domination of Europe in terms of what is seen as luxury has continued, despite the rise of important new markets in recent decades in Japan, India, China and the Gulf States. Travellers from these countries have, so far, largely followed the ideas of luxury first developed in Europe, although this may change as these markets mature.

Chapter 3 had the very difficult task of trying to identify the factors that are shaping the changes, which we are seeing globally, in the concept of luxury. There was a suggestion made that the most important factors included:

- Technological developments, notably the Internet and mobile devices, which have given more choice and convenience to all consumers regardless of wealth.

- Demographic change and the rise of a global class of young entrepreneurs, often working in new technologies, whose ideas of what constitutes luxury are often very different to those of the older generation who have traditionally dominated the luxury market.

- The idea of the 'experience economy' with its suggestion that everyone should and could have a personalised experience, regardless of wealth.

- The increasing power of the globalised media linked to the growth of celebrity culture.

- The growth of terrorism, which means 'luxury' may now mean, first and foremost, being safe and secure.

- Rising consumer expectations and the fact that yesterday's luxury quickly becomes today's necessity.

- Consumers feeling increasingly pressurised and short of 'free time', so that time itself becomes a 'luxury commodity'

In Chapter 4 we looked at the luxury market as a whole. The first point made was that the lack of clear definitions of luxury meant it was virtually impossible to measure the global size of the luxury market in tourism, hospitality and events. We also noted major geographical differences which have an impact on our understanding of what luxury means. When looking at 'net high worth individuals', i.e. rich people, the USA still dominates with sixteen million people in that category compared to around one million in China. In the USA, HNWIs represent 7% of the population, whereas in China they represent only 0.1% (EuroMonitor 2015). However, this data was reported in 2015 and it is likely that the number in China will grow much faster than it will in the US. It is also likely to rise much faster in India which, according to Euromonitor, did not even have one million HNWIs in 2015. However, it is not just about how many rich people live in a country, it's also about how they spend their money. And it is clear that in emerging markets such as China and India, international high end travel is still a novelty and one which bestows great status on the traveller within their own society. We also noted from the same report, differences in what luxury travellers from different countries spent money on. Chinese tourists spend far more, for example, on shopping and activities than the global average, but less on food and drink. This has made them an attractive target market for cities with thriving retail and entertainment sectors.

In the same chapter we also looked at the market for luxury in different sub-sectors of tourism, hospitality and events, together with what constitutes a luxury destination. These issues were taken further in two subsequent chapters.

Chapter 5 focused on the behaviour of individual luxury consumers, whose aggregated behaviour makes up the market. I suggested that the idea of luxury and purchase decisions in our sector are strongly linked to the idea of lifestyle or rather three versions of lifestyle namely:

- The lifestyle the consumer actually lives
- The lifestyle the consumers wishes they lived
- The lifestyle they hope other people will think they live.

I also discussed a number of other factors relating to consumer behaviour, including the idea of time as almost a luxury commodity, the question of the status bestowed by being seen as a luxury consumer and the importance of being able to share luxury experiences through social media. We also began to explore what could be seen as a continuum of luxury in tourism, hospitality and events, and this is illustrated in Figure 14.1. I put forward a number of other proposed typologies of luxury consumer behaviour in tourism, hospitality and events and made a number of other points including:

- The concept of time as a precious commodity, almost a luxury in its own right.
- Luxury is about unique or rare experiences, but these do not always have to be highly priced.
- Safety and security are highly prized but can no longer be taken for granted with the rise in terrorism and the apparent increase in natural disasters, extreme weather incidents and outbreaks of disease .
- Some consumers prefer a more informal approach to luxury service delivery than the more formalised style which has been the norm in the luxury market.
- The vacation experience is greatly enhanced by the ability to share experiences through social media.

14

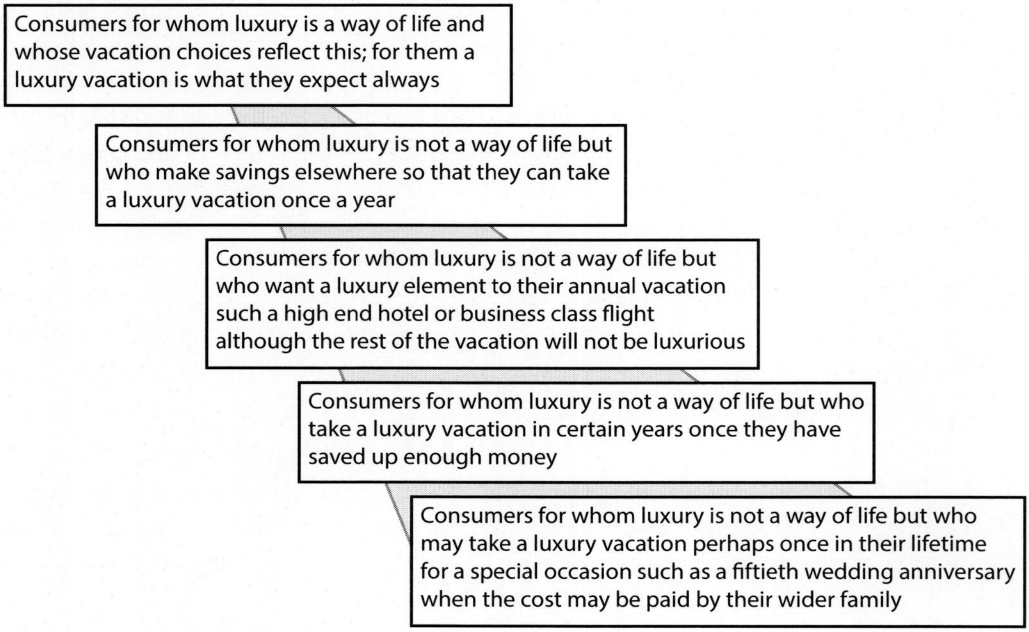

Consumers for whom luxury is a way of life and whose vacation choices reflect this; for them a luxury vacation is what they expect always

Consumers for whom luxury is not a way of life but who make savings elsewhere so that they can take a luxury vacation once a year

Consumers for whom luxury is not a way of life but who want a luxury element to their annual vacation such a high end hotel or business class flight although the rest of the vacation will not be luxurious

Consumers for whom luxury is not a way of life but who take a luxury vacation in certain years once they have saved up enough money

Consumers for whom luxury is not a way of life but who may take a luxury vacation perhaps once in their lifetime for a special occasion such as a fiftieth wedding anniversary when the cost may be paid by their wider family

Figure 14.1: The luxury consumer continuum

Chapter 6 focused on the supply side and looked at the tourism, hospitality and events industries and their approach to luxury. At an early stage I noted that it appears that in its marketing, the whole sector is using the term 'luxury' liberally, even in relation to products such as camping, because it believes that the word 'luxury' sells products. But this over-use of the term may be debasing it to the point where it becomes meaningless. I went on to suggest that the industry has also been responsible for democratising luxury by offering people the opportunity to upgrade from basic products to luxury ones at a reasonable non-luxury price, and by engaging in price-based competition online, particularly in the hotel sector. Issues were raised such as whether a large branded hotel with hundreds of rooms can be seen as luxury, if luxury is about exclusivity, and the problem of being competitive in the delivery of luxury service in Europe where labour costs are far higher than those in Asia.

In the next chapter we focused on the question of what makes a destination a luxury destination. We looked at the power of reputations based on the past which live on long after the reality has changed. I also explored the idea that luxury resorts go through life cycles, and suggested that while most grew organically we have seen a trend in recent years towards purpose-built luxury destinations, as governments and corporation seek to exploit demand for vacations in places perceived to be luxury destinations. It was noted that a luxury destination normally needs not only at least one or two exceptional attributes

– scenery, beach, man-made attraction, famous event etc – but it also needs a first class infrastructure embracing everything from transport services, to hotels and restaurants, to a clean environment. Yet it was also noted that if a place is truly unique, and particularly if it is fairly inaccessible, it may be seen as luxury even with very little infrastructure. Indeed the lack of a sophisticated infrastructure may actually be part of the appeal for some high end travellers.

The following five chapters were designed to examine five particular issues I believed were at the heart of changes taking place today in the meaning of luxury.

Chapter 8 focused on technology and suggested that it was transforming the idea of luxury by putting greater choice and convenience in the hands of consumers or at least those consumers who are 'tech savvy'. It was argued that as this group is more likely to be younger than older it is changing the balance of power in the debates over luxury. It means a young traveller with limited money can use technology to find unique experiences which they can then share with the world through social media. I also suggested that technology is raising standards in hotel rooms and airliners in terms of seats and entertainments systems, for instance, but while these may originate at the higher end of the market it they can quickly become an – expensive – expectation from mass market consumers. In other words, the overall theme of this chapter was that technological developments have served to democratise travel and in doing so may have undermined the traditional notion of luxury.

Chapter 9 focused on service, one of the cornerstones of traditional ideas about luxury. I noted that luxury consumers no longer all seem to expect or want the highly formalised, very proactive, form of service that has been the norm in the luxury market for over a century. Some seem to be more comfortable with a more informal reactive approach, where service deliverers are in the background, not the foreground, of the vacation experience. Others even seem happy with technology facilitated self-service, if it gives them greater convenience or privacy. And through the bed-and-breakfast movement, AirBnB and pop-up restaurants, high end consumers seem to value the personalised service offered by people who are not trained at all in hospitality service.

In the next chapter we looked at the idea of the 'experience economy' and saw that, like technology, it was changing the power relationship between suppliers and consumers, as well as perhaps diluting the concept of luxury. Suppliers have been happy to embrace the language of 'experience' rather than 'products' but perhaps without realising that this has created an expectation amongst consumers in general, not just luxury travellers, that they can have the kind of personalised vacation experience that might previously only have been the preserve of the rich. But whether suppliers can actually satisfy that expectation remains to be seen.

14

In Chapter 11 we examined the link between luxury and the idea of sustainability, two concepts that would traditionally have been seen as polar opposites, with luxury travel being seen as being focused on personal gratification in the present rather than the future of the planet. I suggested that sustainable tourism would be impossible to achieve unless luxury travel could be made more responsible. And I believe there was some evidence that elements within the luxury segment were beginning to recognise this, and that being seen to behave more responsibly could bring status and a feel-good factor for the consumer, akin to that normally sought from traditional luxury experiences. This is allied to a trend noted in other sectors, where luxury is being seen now as embracing values as well as the possession of things, and where authenticity is becoming an important aspect of the appeal of these things.

Chapter 12 focused on brands and their relationship to the concept of luxury, given that one of the most prevalent images of luxury in today's world are products carrying designer labels and famous brands. Yet in our sector I suggested a contradiction between brands, which are large scale and have a business model based on standardisation, and the idea of luxury as exclusivity and personalisation.

Finally, in Chapter 13, I set out ideas about how luxury in tourism, hospitality and events should be researched, given how little good research has occurred to date and much change I believe is occurring in the concept of luxury today.

In Figure 14.2 an attempt is made to provide a simple model that identifies some of the key points that have emerged during the course of this book up to now, in relation to the concept of luxury in tourism, hospitality and events. Chapter 15 will build on the points made in Figure 14.2 when it seeks to look at how the concept of luxury may evolve in the future.

Before looking at the points in Figure 14.2 in more detail, let us begin by making the point that we are currently in a fascinating period of transition between an old fairly simple traditional idea of luxury and an emerging modern concept of luxury which is more subtle and diverse. We can see the complexity of the concept of luxury clearly from Figure 14.2. The key points from it are probably that:

■ It is an idea which is highly subjective, with each person seeing it slightly differently, depending on their circumstances and experiences. For a rich, frequent traveller, only the most exceptional vacation will be seen as luxury whereas to a carer who spends every day looking after a disabled relative, even a day trip to a coastal resort fifty kilometres away will feel like luxury.

■ Industry has leapt onto the 'luxury bandwagon' because it believes attaching this word to a product attracts customers and/or may justify a higher price tag.

■ The idea of what constitutes service – which is at the heart of most concepts of luxury – is changing rapidly due to a number of factors ranging from technological developments, to labour costs, to social change, to name but three.

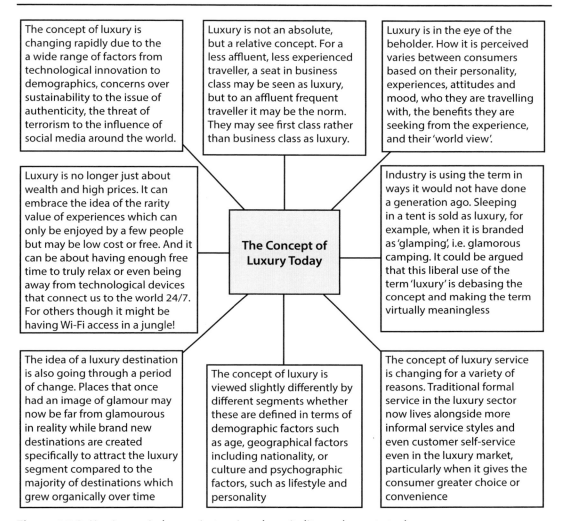

The concept of luxury is changing rapidly due to the a wide range of factors from technological innovation to demographics, concerns over sustainability to the issue of authenticity, the threat of terrorism to the influence of social media around the world.

Luxury is not an absolute, but a relative concept. For a less affluent, less experienced traveller, a seat in business class may be seen as luxury, but to an affluent frequent traveller it may be the norm. They may see first class rather than business class as luxury.

Luxury is in the eye of the beholder. How it is perceived varies between consumers based on their personality, experiences, attitudes and mood, who they are travelling with, the benefits they are seeking from the experience, and their 'world view'.

Luxury is no longer just about wealth and high prices. It can embrace the idea of the rarity value of experiences which can only be enjoyed by a few people but may be low cost or free. And it can be about having enough free time to truly relax or even being away from technological devices that connect us to the world 24/7. For others though it might be having Wi-Fi access in a jungle!

The Concept of Luxury Today

Industry is using the term in ways it would not have done a generation ago. Sleeping in a tent is sold as luxury, for example, when it is branded as 'glamping', i.e. glamorous camping. It could be argued that this liberal use of the term 'luxury' is debasing the concept and making the term virtually meaningless

The idea of a luxury destination is also going through a period of change. Places that once had an image of glamour may now be far from glamourous in reality while brand new destinations are created specifically to attract the luxury segment compared to the majority of destinations which grew organically over time

The concept of luxury is viewed slightly differently by different segments whether these are defined in terms of demographic factors such as age, geographical factors including nationality, or culture and psychographic factors, such as lifestyle and personality

The concept of luxury service is changing for a variety of reasons. Traditional formal service in the luxury sector now lives alongside more informal service styles and even customer self-service even in the luxury market, particularly when it gives the consumer greater choice or convenience

Figure 14.2: Key issues in luxury in tourism, hospitality and events today

- There is evidence that the idea of luxury is fragmenting and that we may need new techniques for segmenting the market, covering criteria such as age, nationality, personality, attitudes to risk, views on sustainability and ethical values and perceptions of free time and its value.

- The idea of luxury destinations is also changing as some places lose their glamorous image, new places are purpose-built to be luxury resorts and simple unsophisticated places gain luxury status because of their inaccessibility or rarity value in an increasingly accessible and developed world

- Luxury is ceasing to be just about high prices and things and is, for some consumers at least, also a matter of intangibles such as values and beliefs or experiences, which may cost nothing but which are unique and fulfilling.

14

■ The concept of luxury is being changed by a bewildering range of factors over which, by and large, the suppliers have little influence, let alone control.

It is now time to try to put some of my thoughts into the form of a table. In Table 14.1 I will try to suggest that a change is taking place currently from traditional ideas of luxury to more diverse and contemporary ways of viewing luxury, in relation to tourism, hospitality and events. Where all of this may lead in the future will be discussed in detail in Chapter 15, where this text will draw to a close.

Table 14.1: The changing meaning of luxury in relation to tourism, hospitality and events

Luxury and ownership	
Traditional meaning	Luxury means owning tangible goods, possessions which are highly priced and bestow status on the owner amongst peers in their own locality
Agents of change	Social change and growth of a class of entrepreneurs gaining wealth at a younger age. Technological developments; changes in lifestyle and the pressures of everyday life; growing disquiet about the corporate world and its behaviour; concerns over sustainability.
Emerging meaning	Owning possessions is still important but the type of possessions may have changed. And owning possessions is no longer the only criterion. It is also about experiences which may be free of charge but exceptional and which can be shared globally. Values are also increasingly important with consumers keen to buy products from organisations that appear to share the consumer's own values.
Comments and implications	This trend is occurring at varying speeds in different cultures and countries. It is more evident in countries which have been developed longest and where general living standards are high and large numbers of citizens have been travelling internationally for several decades. It is much less developed in recently developed countries whose citizens are relatively new to the international tourism market
Access to luxury	
Traditional meaning	Luxury consumption is an option only available to a small minority of the population with the exclusivity being based solely on price and wealth. For these people luxury is a fact of everyday life, the norm.
Agents of change	Economic development, social change, the Internet, and the media, together with the marketing messages of suppliers have created an aspiration to luxury amongst a wide cross-section of societies. Consumers' expectations have risen generally.
Emerging meaning	Access to luxury is now more 'democratic' and not just based on wealth. It can now be based on access to information about options which may be a function of access to, and knowledge of, the latest technologies. Luxury may still mean exclusivity and experiences only enjoyed by a few but the basis of that new exclusivity may be access to information or personality and so on rather than just wealth. Luxury can be indulged in from time to time, or on every vacation, even if it is not the norm for their everyday life, if the consumer makes sacrifices elsewhere in their everyday expenditure.

Comments and implications	Industry is also working hard to 'democratise' luxury to boost its revenue. This includes discounting luxury hotels, offering upgrades to business class at low prices and so on.
Service	
Traditional meaning	High levels of face to face proactive service delivered by trained professionals in a formalised, often quite servile, or alternatively aloof, manner.
Agents of change	Social change, consumer culture, rising labour costs in developed economies, new technologies that can replace staff, the growth of phenomena such as Airbnb.
Emerging meaning	High end luxury service can mean different types of service. Not only formalised professional service but also friendly informal service, and even self-service which brings greater convenience for the guests. And service does not always need to be provided by trained professionals as the popularity of bed-and-breakfast operators in the UK and Airbnb shows
Comments and implications	Suppliers need to recognise that, even at the high end, attitudes towards what constitutes luxury service are changing, though some will continue to prefer the old style formalised service. We need to recognise that there is an important cultural dimension to the issue of both delivering and receiving service which complicates the picture.
Personalisation	
Traditional meaning	The luxury product is personalised for each and every consumer and this is viable because of the high price being paid by the consumer.
Agents of change	The growing scale of demand, the rise of brands that are large-scale even at the top end, technological developments, rising consumer expectation and desire to be treated as an individual, the idea of the 'experience economy'.
Emerging meaning	Consumers at all levels of the market, not just the rich, may increasingly enjoy the benefits of personalisation, at least in theory. Luxury now begins to mean the ability of virtually every consumer to create their own personalised vacation experience and share it with people around the world.
Comments and implications	Industry now has to persuade true luxury end consumers that they are being treated as individuals even when the hotel has 500 rooms, an apparent contradiction. Otherwise why would they pay $500 for a night in a big 'five star' hotel when the person staying in an Airbnb apartment on the beach is having a unique experience for $50 a night. This is one of the future challenges facing the purveyors of luxury.
Time	
Traditional meaning	Time is not an issue for the rich have plenty of it available if they so choose. They can take plenty of time to indulge their interests or relax, whenever they feel like it.
Agents of change	The perceived increases in time pressures in daily lives, stress, work demands and 24/7 connectivity to the workplace; more younger people with high disposable income but demanding jobs.
Emerging meaning	Time is now a luxury commodity for many people, even the most affluent, unless they are retired. Having time gives a consumer a luxury benefit even if they are not rich.

14

Comments and implications	Industry needs to offer vacations that allow people to get the maximum value out of each hour whether that be packing in lots of activities or guaranteed true relaxation to help recharge the batteries.
Security	
Traditional meaning	Safety and security are taken for granted
Agents of change	The rise of terrorism and crime against tourists, media coverage of such things as well as coverage of natural disasters, extreme weather events and so on
Emerging meaning	Being safe and secure becomes a 'luxury' rather than something expected
Comments and implications	Industry and destination governments need to be more active in developing measures to protect the safety of their consumers and this will become a key issue in consumer decision-making. However it will remain outside the control of either government and industry and thus a risk
Customer behaviour	
Traditional meaning	The customer is always right and they do not need to worry about the impacts of their actions.
Agents of change	Concerns over sustainability, and media exposés of irresponsible behaviour in tourism.
Emerging meaning	Luxury means being responsible and concerned about issues such as resource utilisation, fair trade and authenticity. This gives the consumer a 'feel-good' benefit and may increasingly also bestow status on them.
Comments and implications	To make tourism, hospitality and events more sustainable, luxury consumers need to modify their behaviour as their impacts, both good and bad, are higher per head for a variety of reasons. This is a concern for industry, as it fears sustainability may signal lower quality and less comfort to this crucially important group of consumers
Destinations	
Traditional meaning	A relatively small number of established luxury destinations with high profile reputations featuring outstanding attributes, plus a highly developed infrastructure, high levels of formalised professional service and an upscale visitor profile.
Agents of change	Reduction in the real cost of international travel, growth in the number of destinations, huge increase in the volume of international tourists, growing interest in authenticity and getting away from places dominated by tourism.
Emerging meaning	A luxury destination is a place where you can enjoy an exceptional, unique experience but that could mean a desert with no infrastructure, trekking in virgin rain forest carrying your own equipment, or camping on a beach with amazing sunsets, as well as the more traditional types of luxury destination which are still popular.
Comments and implications	Some traditional luxury destinations have already lost most of their luxury visitors and glamour, and are attracting a lower spending mass market attracted by the destination reputation rather than the reality. Luxury, for some, may mean isolation from other tourists and going 'off the beaten track' as much as going to a long established destination with a luxury reputation.

Long though it may be, Table 14.1 cannot incorporate all the ways in which I believe the concept of luxury is changing in general, and specifically in tourism, hospitality and events. A few other comments are necessary to complete the picture.

First, I am not suggesting that the traditional concept of luxury will disappear; indeed I am confident that it will still be present many years from today. But it will no longer be a simplistic concept, with few if any nuances and variations. Instead I believe that in the short term the idea of luxury will splinter into various ideas of luxury, each with a different emphasis. Several major factors will play a significant role in determining what these different perspectives on luxury might be in the future, including:

- The geography of tourism demand, as national and cultural differences are integral to any understanding of the diversity of attitudes to luxury we will see in the future. And we will need to research how the process of globalisation may weaken these differences or not.

- Technological innovations which may put more power into the hands of consumers vis-à-vis industry and how industry responds to this, together with the extent to which technology empowers younger travellers.

- Demographic and economic change, which may affect the distribution of wealth and attitudes towards wealth, particularly wealth that may have accrued from what are seen as unethical activities.

- The influence of the media in shaping opinion and as arbiters of both fashion and taste.

- Lifestyles, including how people respond to the challenges of sustainability in their daily lives, concerns over well-being and the stresses of everyday life, and possible disillusionment about material possessions from a younger generation that may find it harder than their parents to buy cars and houses and other material possessions due to unemployment, insecure employment and needing to fund the pension payments of the older generation!

Second, even if the concept of luxury broadens, as outlined in this book, there will still be those who stick to the traditional view, not least because they believe that is where status lies. This may be pure 'snobbery and may not even be accurate but it is still a powerful draw for many people. Older people born into wealth will continue with their view of luxury and 'look down their noses' at the behaviour of those they regard as 'new money' or the young affluent who they disparagingly see in both cases, perhaps, as having lots of money but no taste!

Third, the democratisation of travel has put things that would previously have been regarded as luxury within reach of people of relatively modest means. This in itself will force us to re-examine the concept of exclusivity which underpins most modern ideas of luxury.

14

Fourth, as we have seen, luxury is not so straightforward these days in tourism, hospitality and events, in that the market is fluid with people entering and leaving it through decisions to make a once in a lifetime trip, forgo a luxury vacation to buy a house, or bid online for an airline upgrade, and so on. Perhaps therefore we should no longer talk about a luxury market, but rather patterns of luxury behaviour, and devise segmentation techniques based on this idea.

Conclusions

Well, how do we conclude such a chapter and draw together the threads of where we think we are today before we go on to look at the future in the final chapter?

The meaning of luxury in tourism, hospitality and events is changing and becoming more diverse. I acknowledge that this change is not being seen equally across all countries, cultures, demographic groups and sectors of our three industries. And I accept that this change is so far limited in the case of the mega rich.

However, I would add that one of the major changes we have seen in recent years has been the 'democratisation' of the so-called luxury market, with the aspiration to join it now extending well beyond the mega rich class, thanks to the marketing messages of the industry, social, economic and technological change, and the influence of the media.

Furthermore, younger generations, buoyed by their skill at using new communication technologies but concerned about their futures in an era of climate change and terrorism, appear to be embarked on a journey to find alternative ways of fulfilling their desires, and in doing so are creating new ways of viewing luxury. Unconsciously perhaps, they are shifting the emphasis from the ownership of expensive tangible goods to intangible experiences that may cost nothing. For this generation in a hurry, time is a luxury commodity and has to be filled with as many pleasurable experiences as possible. Their grasp of technology also makes them rich, not in money terms, but in terms of access to information and the ability to share experiences with people on a global scale. All of this represents a major change in the meaning of the word 'luxury'.

Perhaps the world is changing so fast that the era of luxury is over! Maybe we need new concepts and a new word that will be meaningful for the world of the future. Luxury is a term rooted in history with many connotations, both positive and negative, that seem less and less relevant in our time.

15 The Future of Luxury in Tourism, Hospitality and Events

Introduction

I have argued throughout this book that after centuries when the concept of luxury was quite simple and easily understood by all, it is now undergoing rapid and radical change which is changing it forever. This has been a result of the interaction of a wide range of factors ranging from economic development to terrorism, from technological innovation to social change. Furthermore these factors are continuing and new ones are emerging all the time. Many of them are to date little researched and imperfectly understood as we noted in Chapter 13.

In the last chapter I suggested that we are currently living through a transition period where traditional ideas of luxury are living alongside those which are emerging literally every day.

Tourism, hospitality and events has always been a sector with a high profile due to its nature, and each sector has its iconic elements which are globally recognised as symbols of luxury. But the size of the global markets for all three have increased enormously in recent decades and are continuing to do so. As a result, the markets have increasingly become democratised so that what was once a luxury product only available to the few is now available to hundreds of millions of people. This requires a major re-think of what the concept of luxury, as defined in terms of rarity, exclusivity and so on, means today and indeed if it still has any meaning.

It is in this context that I will now seek to make predictions about the future of the idea of luxury in tourism, hospitality and events, based largely on trends which I believe can be identified today. This attempt to predict the future is a brave, or rather a foolish thing to do in such volatile times but here goes!

Let us begin by identifying the factors that will, in my opinion, shape the future of the luxury concept in general and specifically in tourism, hospitality and events. These factors are presented in Figure 15.1.

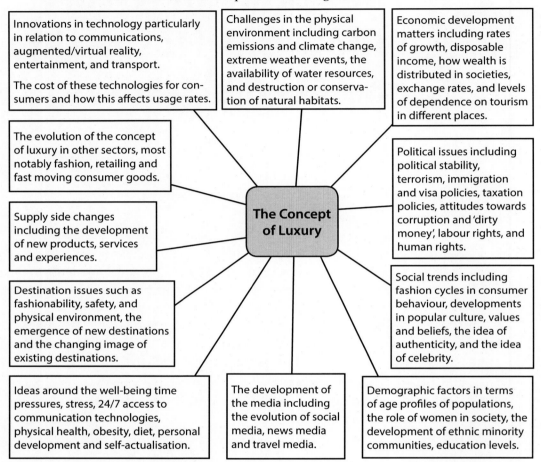

Innovations in technology particularly in relation to communications, augmented/virtual reality, entertainment, and transport.

The cost of these technologies for consumers and how this affects usage rates.

Challenges in the physical environment including carbon emissions and climate change, extreme weather events, the availability of water resources, and destruction or conservation of natural habitats.

Economic development matters including rates of growth, disposable income, how wealth is distributed in societies, exchange rates, and levels of dependence on tourism in different places.

The evolution of the concept of luxury in other sectors, most notably fashion, retailing and fast moving consumer goods.

Supply side changes including the development of new products, services and experiences.

The Concept of Luxury

Political issues including political stability, terrorism, immigration and visa policies, taxation policies, attitudes towards corruption and 'dirty money', labour rights, and human rights.

Destination issues such as fashionability, safety, and physical environment, the emergence of new destinations and the changing image of existing destinations.

Social trends including fashion cycles in consumer behaviour, developments in popular culture, values and beliefs, the idea of authenticity, and the idea of celebrity.

Ideas around the well-being time pressures, stress, 24/7 access to communication technologies, physical health, obesity, diet, personal development and self-actualisation.

The development of the media including the evolution of social media, news media and travel media.

Demographic factors in terms of age profiles of populations, the role of women in society, the development of ethnic minority communities, education levels.

Figure 15.1: Factors that will influence the future meaning of luxury

Before we begin to examine the contents of Figure 15.1 we need to recognise that some of the factors that influence the future of the luxury concept may not even be known yet! Nor does the diagram include every single factor that might influence the future of the idea of luxury in tourism, hospitality and events.

However, notwithstanding what has just been said, there is plenty that is known and more than enough to give us food for thought!

Almost all of the factors identified in Figure 15.1 seem to represent challenges to traditional ideas of luxury. In Figure 15.2 we will look at how these factors are likely to affect the meaning of luxury in the future. In the meantime we will simply make some observations about the factors themselves.

First, they will be felt differently in different parts of the world and of course what is important in the tourism, hospitality and events market is how these factors work in both the country the consumers live in and the countries they visit in their leisure time. In Figure 15.3 we will try to explore these issues further when we look at the geographical evolution of the meaning of luxury in the future.

Second, there is the question of timescales as some of the factors which are already highly visible will be short-lived while others may become almost permanent features of our world. Others that are hardly recognisable yet may become major phenomena in the next few years. And some may be cyclical, assuming great significance for a while and then apparently disappearing again for a period of time before re-emerging. I believe that the challenge will be how difficult all this will be to predict, anticipate and plan for. Once we expected economic downturns on a regular cycle of, say, eight or nine years, yet we have now been in some form of recession for ten straight years. In microcosm, this gives us an insight into the difficulties of predicting the future in this more uncertain world.

Third, there are some 'mega factors' at work which far outweigh the others in potential importance for the planet, as well as for tourism, hospitality and events. I would like to suggest that these include three in particular namely:

- **Environmental** challenges including climate change and water resources in particular.

- The growth in **international terrorism**, in which consumers of tourism, hospitality and events appear to be prime targets. While thinking about and researching this book there have been attacks on concert goers in Manchester, airport users in Brussels, nightclub users in Istanbul, hotel guests in Egypt and tourists strolling around London and Nice

- **Technological innovation**, particularly in terms of those which provide information for travellers and those which make it easy for consumers to share their experiences

Fourth, what is frightening for industry is that not only are these mega factors totally outside their control, but so are most of the factors featured in Figure 15.1. Tourism, hospitality and event organisations are used to having to cope with the impact of uncontrollable factors such as bad weather and strikes. But the uncontrollable factors shown in Figure 15.1 are on an unprecedented scale. To anticipate and plan for them, industry needs to be proactive and take decisive action but the great uncertainty and sheer scale of some of these factors may sap the self-confidence of organisations so they become like 'rabbits in the headlights' on the road to change and fail to take the decisive action that is required!

Fifth, there is the power of another uncontrollable factor, the media. The traditional travel media, which was sympathetic to the industry and often existed in

15

a symbiotic relationship with it, is losing influence to the new generation of blog-gers and online reviewers who may even be antagonistic to industry. Much of this 'social media' is an example of power without responsibility. At the same time we now have global 24/7 news so that if anything – largely bad things – happen, people around the world are instantly aware of them.

Sixth, these factors will be heavily influenced by political decisions, but what these decisions might be is increasingly difficult to predict. Over the time this book has been thought about and written we have seen the Brexit vote in the UK, the election of President Trump in the USA, the election of a President with little political experience in France and the ousting of a President in Brazil. In the week in which this is being written violent anti-government demonstrations are taking place in Venezuela, President Zuma has survived an eighth confidence vote in South Africa, and the USA and North Korea are threatening each other in a way that seems more like two drunks in a bar rather than two heads of state. The point I am making is that, apparently, there is change taking place in politics in many countries. Voters are challenging the democratically elected political elites who it seems are out of touch with popular opinions in their countries, and this challenge may in itself be a good thing. However, in the short term, it is creating uncertainty and bringing divisions to the fore. And at a time when countries need to be working together to solve global issues we appear to be seeing the rise of nationalism and populism which makes this more difficult.

Perhaps the main theme to come out of any consideration of the factors likely to affect the future meaning of luxury in tourism, hospitality and events is uncer-tainty, with the only certainty being that these factors will change this meaning in significant ways in future.

In Figure 15.2 I will endeavour to predict how the concept of luxury may change in the future in tourism, hospitality and events in response to the fac-tors identified in Figure 15.1. Of course, I can only do this by looking at trends which are already visible in some way; others may well emerge over time that will change the picture.

Figure 15.2 suggests that in future seeking to define luxury will become more complex and that future perspectives on luxury will incorporate both traditional ideas of luxury and new and emerging ideas, some of which may not even be visible. The diagram offers perspectives rather than definitions as such, differ-ent ways of viewing the idea of luxury in the context of tourism, hospitality and events.

We can also quickly see that some of the perspectives put forward in Figure 15.2 appear to be, or actually are, contradictory.

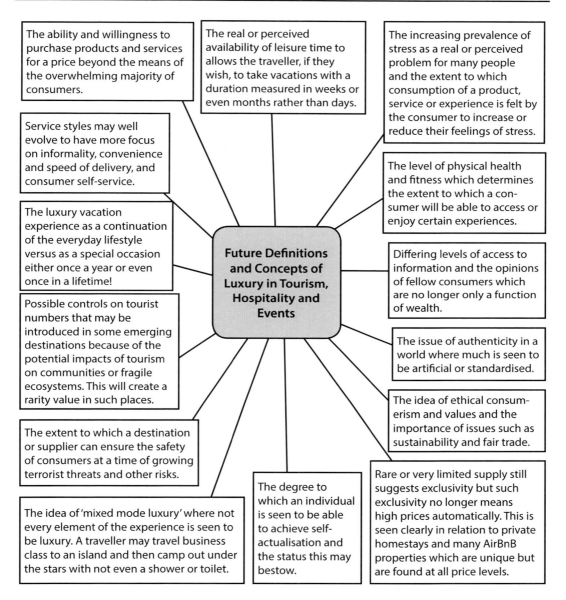

The ability and willingness to purchase products and services for a price beyond the means of the overwhelming majority of consumers.

The real or perceived availability of leisure time to allows the traveller, if they wish, to take vacations with a duration measured in weeks or even months rather than days.

The increasing prevalence of stress as a real or perceived problem for many people and the extent to which consumption of a product, service or experience is felt by the consumer to increase or reduce their feelings of stress.

Service styles may well evolve to have more focus on informality, convenience and speed of delivery, and consumer self-service.

The level of physical health and fitness which determines the extent to which a con-sumer will be able to access or enjoy certain experiences.

The luxury vacation experience as a continuation of the everyday lifestyle versus as a special occasion either once a year or even once in a lifetime!

Future Definitions and Concepts of Luxury in Tourism, Hospitality and Events

Differing levels of access to information and the opinions of fellow consumers which are no longer only a function of wealth.

Possible controls on tourist numbers that may be introduced in some emerging destinations because of the potential impacts of tourism on communities or fragile ecosystems. This will create a rarity value in such places.

The issue of authenticity in a world where much is seen to be artificial or standardised.

The idea of ethical consum-erism and values and the importance of issues such as sustainability and fair trade.

The extent to which a destination or supplier can ensure the safety of consumers at a time of growing terrorist threats and other risks.

The degree to which an individual is seen to be able to achieve self-actualisation and the status this may bestow.

Rare or very limited supply still suggests exclusivity but such exclusivity no longer means high prices automatically. This is seen clearly in relation to private homestays and many AirBnB properties which are unique but are found at all price levels.

The idea of 'mixed mode luxury' where not every element of the experience is seen to be luxury. A traveller may travel business class to an island and then camp out under the stars with not even a shower or toilet.

Figure 15.2: Potential future perspectives on the concept of luxury in tourism, hospitality and events.

The ability to pay for luxury

A classic traditional definition of luxury travel would have been the **ability and willingness to purchase products and services for a price which is beyond the means of most tourists.** Being seen to be able to pay a very high price brought status and, until recently, the market was polarised between high volume lower price and low volume high price.

15

I have noted throughout this text that this traditional view of luxury is changing for the following reasons and I see no prospect of this trend being reversed:

- The Internet has focused largely on the price of products and experiences rather than their quality, and so five star hotel beds and business class seats have become the subject of discounting thus, perhaps, debasing the idea of luxury based on high price and exclusivity

- Given travel is discretionary and not something we buy everyday, some who do not normally live a luxury lifestyle make sacrifices so they can enjoy a luxury vacation once a year or even once in a lifetime. These people do not belong to the old cosy luxury club whose members were clearly identified by their wealth.

- Those on more limited income can also temporarily join the 'luxury club' through the medium of the upgrade. Thus a regular business traveller on a modest income can take their family on vacation business class because of the 'miles' they have accumulated from their business trips. Or you can now even bid online for upgrades, which mean you are paying a fraction of what others in the business class cabin have paid for their seats. This can cause bad feeling amongst the higher spenders and a belief that 'business class is not what it was' and 'is going down market'!

- Of course, in terms of many destinations, the 'the best things in life are free' as the classic Flying Lizards song, *Money*, says whether it be the beach, the sunsets or the views, so once in the destination rich and poor travellers can share them alike in most cases.

- Thanks largely to the Internet there is now status to be gained from paying the lowest rather than the highest price for a product or service, even at the luxury end of the market. It makes the purchaser look like they are smarter than others; this is particularly true for those elements of the experience which are necessary but are not the object of the trip, such as the flight to the destination. This may also help explain why the demographic of budget airlines, for instance, is not all poor people by any means; many are frequent flyers and second home owners.

Perhaps, also, the lengthy economic downturn the world has been experiencing has made everyone more cost conscious. Certainly there is anecdotal evidence that even wealthy consumers want value for money in many cases.

Availability of free time

The real or perceived availability of leisure or free time is an important prerequisite for all tourism and leisure experiences. Traditionally we talked of the 'idle rich' – people with inherited wealth or who had other people managing their businesses leaving them free to enjoy themselves. For them time was not an issue and this created a polarised market where for some every day was a holiday while others worked long hours and had a holiday for a week or two if they were lucky.

Again things seem to be changing and I believe that this trend too will continue. Around the world business is more globalised and competitive than ever, and successful entrepreneurs, managers and professionals all seem to be permanently busy, partly due to ICT which now connects them to the world every second of every day. While those with inherited wealth for whom leisure is their daily routine still exist, but they have now been joined by those who are working incredibly hard so they are truly cash-rich but time-poor.

In this situation, time can be a rarer commodity than money and for such people any leisure time has a high rarity value which tends to lead to two diametrically opposed responses. They either want to totally relax and do nothing on vacation or they want to pack as much as possible into their short vacation period and enjoy some really intense experiences. The latter group is perfect for destinations as their per head spending can be incredibly high.

Ironically, as the proportion of people in higher education grows across the world we have seen the rise of the 'gap year traveller' and the backpacker, who often have limited money – although they are often subsidised by parents – but have the luxury of large blocks of leisure time allowing them to take trips measured in months rather than days. And because they tend to come from more affluent countries and travel to poor ones, they can indulge in a quality of life that would be impossible in their own countries. Interestingly, in some countries we are also seeing an increase in such long but low per head spend vacations amongst older people who have retired early from work and have private pensions and endless leisure time.

Increased stress

The increasing prevalence of stress as a real or perceived problem which is no doubt linked to the last point. Many people seem to feel that life is stressful and even leisure experiences can be stressful, particularly in terms of travel to and from the destination. Again there is nothing on the horizon that looks likely to reverse this trend.In this stressed world therefore luxury in tourism, hospitality and events could be seen in terms of:

- The services offered by the industry which take the stress out of the journey to the destination

- The products and services offered in-destination that are designed to reduce stress and improve mental well-being. This may help explain the high status which spas seem to enjoy in the hospitality sector.

15

Health and fitness of consumers

The level of physical health and fitness of the consumer is important as it determines their ability to participate in experiences. No matter how much money someone, has their leisure opportunities will be adversely affected if they have certain diseases, mobility issues, sight difficulties or hearing problems, for example. Improvements in health care in many countries have made the 'luxury' of good health accessible to more people than would have been the case a generation or two ago.

However, ironically, while health care is improving, increasing affluence in a number of countries is leading to an increasing number people being obese and unfit, as they eat too much of the wrong foods and live sedentary lives. This is happening at the same time as more and more people are joining gyms and dieting; there is a real dichotomy between these two segments which has implications for tourism, hospitality and leisure.

Access to information

Differing levels of access to information about opportunities is becoming a key factor in the idea of luxury in tourism, hospitality and events. Traditionally the rich, who were more often older people, had access to most information through their travel agents and the conventional travel media. However, today there is far more information available online for downloading through mobile devices than ever there was through travel agents and the travel media. And, of course, social media is allowing users to share information for their mutual benefit.

We know that, although it can be exaggerated, it is younger people who are much more skilled and comfortable at using the new media to plan trips, make reservations and make decisions about what to do when they are in the destination. These media are widely and inexpensively available and so no longer do the mature rich segment have an advantage in terms of access to information; indeed it is the younger generation that has this advantage. It could be argued that even if the young person is not rich, the access to information gives them the luxury of choice, laying before them more options than older rich people who are not confident technology users will ever have. If knowledge truly is power then access to information is a way of gaining status and could therefore be seen as part of the idea of luxury.

What remains to be seen is whether the younger 'tech savvy' consumers will keep up with technology as they age, and whether this issue will disappear or will they – relatively at least – still not keep up with technology to the degree their children will.

Authenticity

The issue of authenticity is an interesting one in relation to luxury in tourism, hospitality and events. In a world where much of the offer in these sectors appears artificial and standardised, even when it is priced highly and marketed as luxury, it is interesting that we are seeing an increasing interest in the idea of authenticity. No one seems able to satisfactorily define it, but everyone seems to be searching for it as can be seen from the use by marketers of phrases such as 'discover the real X' and 'see the Y that the tourists never see'. Tourism itself is seen as the problem with experiences being created specifically for tourists who other tourists reject as they search for a 'real experience' that may be an illusion or a piece of wishful thinking. There is certainly a feeling that authenticity in tourist destinations is rare, and if you find it, you are amongst the privileged few. That seems to me pretty much akin to two of the traditional ways of defining luxury.

■ Ethical consumption

The idea of ethical consumerism and values would, until recently, have been very unlikely to appear in a sentence which also included the word 'luxury'. Indeed they would have been as polar opposites, sworn enemies. The idea was that being a luxury consumer meant having the right to be irresponsible, a chance to enjoy your own privileged position. This is particularly true in tourism and hospitality where the idea is that a vacation is a time for hedonism when one forgets temporarily all of one's responsibilities.

As I noted earlier in the book, this is in stark contrast to the case with the behaviour of the rich in many countries who gain status by supporting charities and good causes, endowing scholarships, and sponsoring cultural events.

In recent years, however, we have begun to see the rise of interest in responsible or sustainable tourism and hospitality, even in the luxury segment. It is now fashionable to eat street food cooked by local people, buy locally produced rather than imported souvenirs, avoid controversial foods such as shark's fin soup or foie gras, and support local good causes through community tourism projects and donations to local schools. Of course there is a 'feel-good factor' at work here, for doing these things makes the consumer feel more worthy and brings them status amongst their peers.

However, industry is still wary of pushing luxury consumers too far; they may still resent a lack of air conditioning and a golf course in a hot destination with electricity and water supply challenges!

On the other hand, the luxury segment travels more often than most and spends the most, so it is hard to see how we can get close to achieving sustainable tourism unless we get luxury travellers to play their part.

15

Rarity and exclusivity

Rarity or limited supply and the idea of exclusivity is an intrinsic part of the traditional view of luxury but again this is becoming much more complex today in tourism, hospitality and events. Today, rarity or limited supply does not automatically mean higher prices in our sectors any longer. I am aware of a three star Michelin restaurant in Europe with forty covers which serves meals twice a day, six days a week for seven months a year. They are thus able to serve some 14,000 customers a year at an average of €120 per head. I also know a pop-up restaurant in Europe that opens for seven nights a year with ten covers and can thus serve 70 customers per year at an average of €25 per head. The latter is a much rarer commodity in terms of the supply yet the price is much lower. At the same time I know of a five star hotel that charges $500 per night for one of its three hundred rooms while I am also aware of a single luxurious apartment in the same city, owned by a private citizen, uniquely furnished, sold through AirBnB, where the owner, a well-known artist, greets guests personally and even gives them a quick tour of the neighbourhood for less than $200.

The point here is not to claim that the Michelin starred restaurant and the five star hotel are not worth their price tag or are anything other than excellent quality. The point is that they are their capacity is much larger than that of the pop-up restaurant or the apartment, so they are less limited in supply. Maybe that makes them less exclusive too in some way?

Whatever the answer, there is no doubt that it is increasingly trendy to use accommodation and restaurants that may not be very expensive but may be in very limited supply or even unique. It also fits neatly with other issues discussed above such as authenticity and ethical consumerism. If this fashion for the unique, the quirky, the locally owned, the service delivered by people who are not trained professionals, and prices that represent value for money continues it will certainly have a profound impact on the idea of luxury in tourism, hospitality and events.

These new kinds of 'luxury experience', if that is what they are, have been made possible by technological developments, and seem in some ways to be a reaction against the somewhat stuffy and stolid luxury products on offer from the mainstream hospitality industry.

Personal development

The degree to which an individual is seen to achieve self-actualisation could also be seen as an indicator of a 'luxury lifestyle' perhaps, and it is not just about income. It about reaching your potential, which could be either your real or your perceived potential. The idea that an individual appears to have reached a level of personal development to which that others aspire could well bring status as well as personal satisfaction. This links to points made previously about stress and values, for self-actualisation is inextricably linked to things such as spirituality and well-being. Importantly it not only goes beyond material possessions, but is almost the antithesis of materialism. And as the Mash Blog noted in 2016,

> "as more and more people have started to access amazing experiences, travel to hard-to-reach destinations, stay with locals, and visit pop-up dining events – experiences in themselves start to become common currency, and therefore not as desirable to an emerging class of high-end luxury consumers…For them the most desirable experiences are the ones that provide them with unique skills or new knowledge, enable them to express their creativity or do good for other people on the planet. Today's luxury consumers, seeking to stand out from the growing mainstream affluence have started to move into a quest for self-improvement, personal growth and self-actualisation." (Mash. UK 2016)

Yet I would like to suggest that this is not restricted to luxury consumers. At a time when some younger people, particularly in Europe and North America begin to realise that their material wealth may be less than that of their parent's generation for various reasons, some of them are reacting by rejecting materialism and instead seeking alternative roads to satisfaction whether that be spirituality, creative arts or health and well-being.

Mixed mode luxury

The idea of 'mixed mode luxury' seems well established now, and likely to continue as a trend, I believe. In this not every element of a vacation experience is luxury, where luxury is defined in terms of high prices and great comfort. However this may be for one of two reasons, namely:

- The consumer lacks the financial means to buy an experience where every element is luxurious although they are prepared to spend heavily on one or more elements that matter most to them whether that be the flight to the destination, the accommodation or fine dining, for example.

- The consumer can afford a wholly luxurious experience with lots of comfort and pampering but as this may what their everyday life is like they seek a contrast on their vacation. So they may fly business class to a remote destination where they stay in a tent and cook their own meals. For them the very simplicity of their accommodation is a rarity in their lives and represents something therefore that could be seen as a 'luxury' because of this rarity value.

Safety

The extent to which a destination or supplier can ensure the safety of consumers. In this respect my view of the foreseeable future is simple. As travellers perceive the world to be becoming a more dangerous place in which to travel due

15

to terrorism, natural disasters, epidemics, extreme weather events and so on, then safety and security will move from being expected to being seen as a 'luxury' that cannot be taken for granted. Perhaps a premium price will need to be paid for vacation experiences which appear to be the safest. This is ironic given how much some adventure tourists pay to indulge in risky activities on vacation!

We have noted at various points that luxury is often about rarity value and exclusivity. In that context **possible controls on tourist numbers that may be introduced in destinations** could artificially constrain supply. Thus some places could attain luxury status because only a certain number of visitors are permitted to visit them. This could be seen particularly in remote fragile environments or wildlife habitats which are under threat from the impacts of tourism – the kind of places that often appeal to a certain type of luxury consumer. Such action has been advocated in Venice too and the current debate about so-called 'over-tourism' in cities and towns may be the shape of things to come. Perhaps the key question will be the basis on which the limited capacity is filled. If it is first come first served, that is one thing but if it is sold to the highest bidder that will be something else.

Finally on this point we also have the growing fear that some places, such as the Maldives, will actually disappear due to climate change. If this were to be the case the ultimate luxury might be to be amongst the last tourists to visit these islands – a chilling thought.

Whether or not **the luxury vacation is a continuation of everyday lifestyle** or is something out of the ordinary is a theme explored too many times throughout this text to require much more discussion. But it is an important trend that looks set to continue, whereby those who do not live in luxury at home every day, save up or use their credit card and use the Internet smartly to ensure that for a or two weeks a year, or once in a lifetime, they can enjoy a luxurious vacation. For the industry these people represent a specific segment which is well worth targeting.

Service styles

Service styles may well evolve in luxury sector of the future, or perhaps it would be more accurate to say continue to evolve as I have already identified trends which I believe will grow stronger in future due to everything from social change to labour costs. I believe we will see an increase in the following:

- More service being delivered by 'non-professionals' and people not trained in tourism, hospitality and events, with AirBnB a portent of things to come as consumer desires to meet 'real people' in destinations combines with ICT developments and other factors to drive this trend

- More informal service styles will grow as travellers become more experienced and younger generations reject the traditional rather stuffy formal service of the kind for which parts of Europe are famous, or should that be infamous?

■ Self-service where even luxury consumers will be able to do some things for themselves if it gives them benefits of cost, choice or convenience

Before we move on, a few further words are required on Figure 15.2.

First, it is very unclear, as yet, how the factors considered in Figure 15.1 will actually lead to the changes outlined in Figure 15.2. You could be forgiven for thinking, based on Figure 15.2, that the concept of luxury will change completely for everyone in coming years. However, my view is rather more nuanced than that. I believe that the idea of luxury will become more heterogeneous and fragmented, with significant differences based on factors such as age and gender, as well as social, technological, political and economic factors. Furthermore, I contend that attitudes to the concept of luxury will be diverse enough to justify using them as a basis for new approaches towards segmentation.

At the same time though, I would like to suggest that in ten or twenty years' time there will still be many people whose attitudes to luxury will not have fundamentally changed and whose behaviour patterns will be similar to those they have currently. But these more 'conservative' consumers will no longer be the dominant view, and they may be found largely or wholly amongst the elderly so that their views will become less and less representative of the market as a whole as they literally die!

The geographical dimension

So far in this chapter we have talked of the idea of luxury largely as if it had no real geographical dimension, but I believe this is not an accurate picture. We noted above that the concept of luxury is evolving in response to changes in economic, social and political factors and the point about such factors is that they vary from place to place; they are not common to the whole world. Furthermore, the pace at which these factors shape change also varies between countries and regions.

However, little real empirical evidence exists to allow us to make categorical statements about how the concept of luxury may vary today, and in the future, between different regions of the world.

Foolishly perhaps, given that fact, I am going to endeavour to make some tentative suggestions about the geographical dimension of luxury which will be illustrated in Figure 15.3. These thoughts have no empirical underpinning and are presented simply in the hope that it will stimulate research because this subject is fascinating and vitally important for the industry.

The ideas in Figure 15.3 are, in theory, generic and not overtly geographical in concept. However, in reality, the countries in these five categories do tend to be concentrated in particular geographical regions around the world.

15

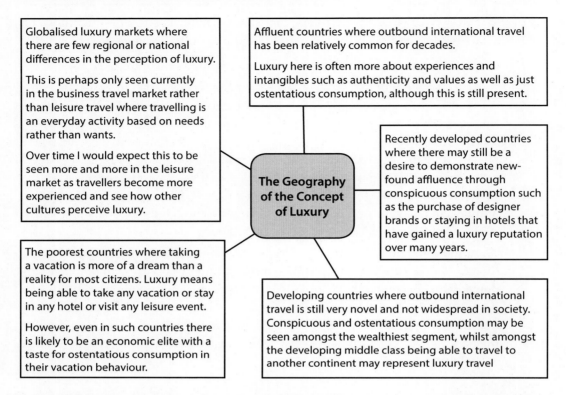

Figure 15.3: The evolving geography of the concept of luxury in tourism, hospitality and events.

We do, of course, need to be acutely aware of the danger of stereotyping and producing sweeping statements based on little or no empirical evidence. And if we do not discuss the issue of the geography of the luxury concept at all we risk misunderstanding what is happening and what seems quite clear from anecdotal evidence and observation. This is a fascinating subject for further research and another of the research challenges in this area that was discussed in Chapter 13.

I am not suggesting that people in some cultures are more inherently inclined towards ostentatious displays of wealth. Instead I see these apparent current behaviour traits as a function of the level of maturity of markets. I note that similar phenomena were seen in Europe and the USA in the 19th and early 20th century as their industrial revolutions produced a new class of mega rich who had worked for their wealth rather than merely inheriting it. The parallels with the economies of countries such as China and India are too obvious to need pointing out.

In many emerging tourism markets, therefore, the early stages are marked by the use of foreign airlines which are perceived to be more prestigious than domestic ones. Famous brand hotels and restaurants are used and foreign designer label goods make up the bulk of retail purchases. It seems to be all about convincing the travellers themselves and their neighbours and peers that they have 'arrived', they have 'made it' onto the world stage of luxury travel. This is very similar to the behaviour of the those entrepreneurs in the Europe who desperately bought art, big houses and private educations for their children in an attempt to demonstrate the same thing to the aristocracy, namely that they had 'arrived' and 'made it'.

Inevitably, perhaps, as Europe was the birthplace of modern international tourism, it is not surprising that travellers from this newer markets look to Europe for the symbols of luxury in tourism, hospitality and events. Hence the presence of so many Asian guests in the 19th century ultra-traditional hotels in the ski resorts of the Alps and the classic five star hotels of Paris and London. However, just as Europe is losing its position as the main generator and receiver region of the world for international tourists, it is slowly losing its place in terms of the perceived luxury brands in tourism, hospitality and events. For example the airlines which are perceived to be at the top end of the market are neither European or American but rather from the Gulf States or Asia. Indeed many in the luxury market in parts of the world are increasingly looking to these same two regions as the emerging suppliers of high end consumerism in our sectors.

This trend is at the heart of the geographical evolution of luxury and reflects the question of reputation versus reality. It is Europe which has the reputation, but the reality of the supply of luxury products and experiences is that Asia and the Gulf States are setting the pace now, in response to both inbound tourism and growing domestic demand.

Interestingly much of this supply is artificial and created, and has been developed over years rather than decades or even centuries. Dubai is a perfect example of this with its ski slope, artificially constructed islands and high rise hotels like the Burj-el-Arab. Often it seems there is a rush in Asia and the Gulf States to forget where they came from and focus only on where they are going. It is the polar opposite of Europe which seems obsessed with nostalgia and where it has been, with the USA in the middle but looking more and more like Europe.

One might expect that as outbound international travel becomes more common in the emerging markets, the need or desire to make ostentatious displays of wealth by buying that which is perceived as luxury simply because it has that label will diminish. As travellers become more confident and experienced the markets they come from could be expected to become diverse in their perceptions of luxury with more focus on things like authenticity, ethical consumerism, and self-actualisation. But the fact is we do not know; it is all new ground.

And what of the other regions of the world: how, if at all will they shape the future of the concept of luxury across the world? Africa, the sleeping giant of tourism, South America which was seen as the height of glamour in the years between the first and second world wars, and Australia with its amazing natural environment and huge mineral wealth.

15

Eleven predictions for the future

Unwisely perhaps given the volatility of the world, I will now endeavour to make ten predictions about the meaning of luxury in the future in tourism, hospitality and events. I do this in the certain knowledge that by doing so I am creating hostages to fortune, but here goes anyway!

1   The luxury market will evolve and with the changing meaning of luxury we will see new approaches to segmentation. In 2016, Amadeus AIT published a fascinating report entitled *Shaping the Future of Luxury Travel – Future Traveller Tribes 2030* in which they explored the issue of the segmentation of the future luxury market.

First, they suggested that there were six segments or tribes in the travel market as a whole, but that only three were really relevant to the luxury market, namely *reward hunters, simplicity searchers* and *obligation meeters*. Three other groups were not so relevant to the luxury market; they were *ethical travellers, cultural purists* and *social capital seekers*. (Amadeus AIT, 2016). Based on the wider view of luxury I have taken in this book, I would suggest that while this has been true to date it may not be the case in the future.

The report then went on to identify six *'luxury travel tribes'* and sought to put a number of the size of each segment, based on a survey of 204 consumers. The results were as follows:

- *Cash – rich, time poor 4%*
- *Strictly opulent 18%*
- *Independent and affluent 3%*
- *Always luxury 4%*
- *Special occasion 20%*
- *Luxury 31%*

[Amadeus AIT, 2016]

I may not fully agree with this segmentation of the future luxury market but I am delighted to see high quality empirical research being undertaken to endeavour to anticipate the future composition of this market.

My own view is that the segmentation of the market will be more complex and will need to take on board a range of issues, from age and gender, to lifestyle, to values and to personal circumstances. Of course, if segmentation becomes too complex it becomes unworkable, or at least not cost effective, at some point in marketing terms. We can reach a point where everyone is a segment of one person! Perhaps, instead of seeking to segment people, we should segment behaviour patterns and recognise that people will move between these in response to changing circumstances.

2   If international travel continues to grow and embrace more and more people around the world, we should see a reduction in the national and cultural differences in the behaviour of luxury consumers that were suggested in Figure 15.2, amongst the more experienced travellers at least, whose self-confidence will grow with this experience. Over time all segments we may identify in future should be visible in all national and cultural markets, albeit maybe in varying proportions.

3   Security and safety will start to become seen as a luxury rather than the norm, particularly in relation to terrorism and natural disasters. In respect of the former it is now very clear that terrorist groups are specifically targeting travellers, hotel guests and those attending events. People in future may be prepared to pay a premium to visit places which are perceived as less risky and may also start to favour hotels, for example, which seem to have exceptionally good security measures in place. Instead of current practice, which seems to be to try not to talk about safety, it might become a potential source of competitive advantage for destinations and companies, although a very risky one

4   I have no doubts that time may come to be seen as *the* defining idea of luxury in future in tourism, hospitality and events, as life becomes ever faster-paced and when more and more people feel themselves to be cash-rich but time-poor. These people will be prepared to pay a high price to make the most of their limited leisure time, which will normally mean intense experiences. Likewise consumers will be prepared to accept changes in the way service is delivered to them if it gives them greater convenience or saves them time. At the same time, those with lots of leisure time may start to be viewed as a type of luxury consumer, even if they have only limited spending power, whether they be students or retired people. Time to relax and time to develop new skills or knowledge may become a new 'luxury differentiator'.

   Perhaps 'slow tourism' will become a new concept of luxury in tourism and hospitality?

5   While the whole luxury market will not change any time soon, I believe we will see the rise of a substantial segment of 'responsible luxury consumers' seeking the 'feel-good factor' from behaving in ways which are seen positively by their peers and society. That could mean everything from buying locally produced goods, to supporting good causes in destinations, to boycotting destinations and attractions which exploit wildlife, and so on. Such responsible or ethical behaviour could be seen as the antithesis of traditional ideas of luxury tourism which was about self-indulgence and throwing off any idea of responsibility. But society is changing and being a responsible citizen is starting to be more fashionable, and is a source of admiration rather than mild ridicule!

   If this does not happen there is a danger that 'luxury' could start to become a dirty word making luxury consumers a group not only to be jealous of but to

15

blame for the state of the world, whether it be climate change and water shortages, the growth of terrorism, or the exploitation of labour and destination communities, for example.

6 The future meaning of luxury in our sectors will not be decided by the tourism industry, the traditional travel media of guide books or by governments with their hotel classification systems. Instead, I would like to suggest, it will be determined and shaped by others, notably:

- Social media and the large-scale sharing of ideas and photos shared between travellers.

- Consumer-generated review sites which are becoming the new classification agencies, seeking to allocate a number of stars in a system of their own devising to suppliers, with no reference to official government classification systems.

- The growing 'lifestyle media', including glossy magazines focused on leisure activities including travel, and the increasing number of satellite and cable channels which have shows just about travel and particularly cruises.

- The global news media which 24 hours a day is making consumers aware of ethical issues they should be concerned about, safety and security issues and the lives of people living in tourist destinations. This forces even luxury consumers to confront moral dilemmas and make choices about their behaviour, without being able to claim they were ignorant of the issues

7 I am convinced that the meaning of luxury in future will not just be about the ability and willingness to spend large amounts of money. While I think the ideas of exclusivity and rarity will still be relevant to the concept of luxury, this will not always mean ultra-high prices. Instead I believe this exclusivity and rarity may also come from having access to information on opportunities that others do not have, or enjoying experiences whose availability is very limited, such as eating at a pop-up restaurant or staying with a local family. Indeed given the financial challenges facing the younger generations and future generations in many parts of the world, people will need to find new experiences that feel luxurious but do not cost huge amounts of money.

8 Following on from this, I think that some future consumers will seek things that are increasingly difficult to find in their everyday lives, which will increasingly be in busy towns and cities, with a fast pace, noise and a busy working life with lots of stress. The 'luxury' then is probably for many going to be about seeking simplicity and solitude on vacation as the antidote to these pressures of everyday life. Maybe Scandinavia is a pointer towards the future in this respect. These countries which have high levels of affluence give their citizens the means to afford traditional luxury vacations in far flung parts of the world and many citizens of this region take these opportunities, particularly during the cold winter months.

But the overwhelming majority of them chose to spend the peak summer weeks in their holiday cottages, simple places with few amenities or frills, often only a short drive from their homes. This 'getting back to nature' appears to be a major source of satisfaction and enjoyment for these affluent, sophisticated consumers.

9 I believe that in the luxury market the balance of power has changed irreversibly from industry to consumers, due to a range of factors but most notably developments in ICT. Consumers now increasingly demand experiences rather than products and services, and they want the power to create their own bespoke unique experiences where the suppliers merely help facilitate what the consumer wants. Consumers are no longer content to simply purchase the standardised products and services offered by suppliers. This trend towards the idea of experiences has massive implications for the idea of luxury in tourism, hospitality and events which the industry needs to take on board.

10 Despite economic downturns and uncertainty in the global economy, it seems likely that, in general, people will continue to become more affluent across the globe albeit from very different base levels. Therefore, over time, more and more people will have the money to afford the material trappings of a luxury or at least more luxurious lifestyle. I believe that the more this happens, the more some people, particularly those for whom being wealthy is not a new experience, will cease to be satisfied with purely material goods. This obviously links to our discussion about self-actualisation earlier in this chapter. It seems likely therefore that luxury will be defined increasingly in terms of our ability to reach our full potential as human beings whether that be a matter of skills, knowledge or values. Ir believe that this trend will also lead to a greater focus on authenticity in the luxury market. This all has major implications for industry and tourist destinations in terms of their offers.

11 I want to finish by predicting that despite all this talk of change in the concept of luxury, the behaviour of many people in the existing luxury market will remain little changed while many of those who enter the market for the first time will continue to practice what we might term 'traditional luxury practice'.

The market for large five star hotels, Michelin starred restaurants, high end all-inclusive resorts, and shopping malls selling expensive things no one needs but lots of people aspire to buy, will not disappear. There will still be people clicking their fingers and expecting a waiter to bring them a drink within seconds without even a 'thank you'. Still people who want to be pampered throughout their vacation, even if it means golf courses and swimming pools that can only be provided at the expense of water shortages for local people.

However, while such products and behaviours will continue on a large scale they will increasingly be living alongside different behaviours based on new ideas of what the term 'luxury' means.

15

Towards a new definition of luxury?

So the final question revolves around whether it is possible to devise a new definition of the meaning of luxury in tourism, hospitality and events, at least that would have some value.

I believe that, disappointingly perhaps for some readers, the answer is 'no'. No single definition could encompass such complexity in a meaningful way.

However let us say that any definition of luxury in tourism, hospitality and events would have to certainly include the following elements to be relevant for the future:

- Tourism, hospitality and events do not exist in isolation and any definition of luxury needs to take on board trends in luxury in other sectors, whether that be retailing, fashion or the car industry to give just three examples.

- Luxury is not an absolute – it is a relative concept whose meaning varies depending on the circumstances and values of different groups of people.

- The idea of luxury is not fixed, it changes over time in response to changes in the world.

- The meaning of luxury is not homogeneous and certainly will have subtle differences between countries and cultures.

- Luxury is about more than having and spending money; it is increasingly about improving your mind, learning new skills, enjoying new experiences, or doing things that make you feel good about yourself.

- Luxury is still partly about rarity, but that is no longer restricted to things which have a high price because of their rarity value. One can now enjoy some truly unique experiences which cost little money or occasionally are even free.

- Luxury is perhaps becoming less about how you are seen by others and more about how you see yourself.

- It will probably become less about short term personal gratification and more about longer term personal development.

Well, deciding where to end a book is always the most difficult part but the I believe we have arrived at that point. As always you may have lots of new questions rather than answers. But that is the reality of knowledge creation and my hope is that those questions will lead to research, which will find answers and new questions that will take our knowledge of this fascinating subject further.

Conclusions to Part 5

This is a very difficult section to write because the whole of Part 5 has been an attempt to conclude the book by identifying key conclusions and looking into the future. However, by way of final reflection I would like to make the following points.

☐ First, academics have done the world a disservice by not focusing more research effort on the area of luxury, given it is fascinating and, more importantly, it is a vitally important sector of the industry in terms of revenue and jobs.

☐ Second, there is no simple definition of good quality for it is a highly subjective concept which means different things to different people, not least based on the realities of their everyday lives.

☐ Third, the traditional idea of luxury is becoming less relevant as economic growth gives more and more people material means, but the process of gaining these benefits means they have less and less time to enjoy them

☐ Fourth, technological developments are literally revolutionising what luxury means in terms of everything from service delivery to the purchase process. And it could be argued that technology is 'levelling the playing field' of consumption in tourism, hospitality and events. A young person of limited financial means with lots of technological devices and the skill to use them could be able to enjoy experiences not available to their much more affluent parents.

☐ Fifth, the idea of luxury will continue to evolve rapidly in response to a wide range of inter-related factors, from economic development to social change, technological innovation to terrorism, the impacts of climate change to the cult of celebrity.

☐ Sixth, perhaps the concept of luxury based almost wholly on ostentatious consumption and wealth will be replaced by, or at least joined by new, ideas of luxury. Luxury based on ideas around values and ethical consumption, as well as the joy to be found in simple things and making the very best use of what is fast becoming the greatest luxury of all for humans, time!

15

Part 6: Case Studies

I have compiled the following case studies in an attempt to provide examples of some of the issues covered in the book. I have deliberately endeavoured to develop case studies from different parts of the world and from different sectors of tourism, hospitality and events.

   When reading these please bear in mind that any case study is only a snapshot in time and that things change constantly. Nevertheless, I believe that these 'real world' examples will help you understand the complexity and diversity of the meaning of luxury in tourism, hospitality and events.

In general, the case studies are based on material which is in the public domain, which should make it easier for you to follow them up and look at the organisations and phenomena in more detail for yourself.

Contents

Case study 1: César Ritz – the man whose name became a byword for luxury

Few words evoke the idea of luxury in tourism and hospitality as 'Ritz' but it all started with a man born in the 19th century in a small Swiss village, César Ritz. From humble beginnings he rose to a position where he was known as the 'king of hoteliers and hotelier to kings'. In his career he transformed the hospitality industry.

He was dismissed from his first job in the industry in Brig and he was told that ' he would never make a true hotelier'. Ritz left for Paris and gained experience in modest hotels there and eventually returned to Switzerland to work in Lucerne in a management position, where he met the great French chef, Escoffier. Because of the seasonality in the Swiss lakes he split his time between Lucerne and the French Riviera where he spent his winters. Both places were playgrounds for privileged travellers and even royalty.

In 1888, he acquired his first properties, a hotel and restaurant in the fashionable spa resort of Baden-Baden. This was followed by a the purchase of a hotel in Cannes on the French Riviera. The Ritz 'empire' took off from this point. He moved to London, took on what was in effect a management contract at the Savoy and persuaded its owner to purchase Claridges. Like today's celebrity chefs, Ritz got involved in many ventures simultaneously.

By all accounts Ritz was not an easy man to work with or work for, being strong-willed and obsessed with hygiene. One of his tasks at the Savoy was to dismiss Escoffier for alleged financial irregularities. Eventually in 1898, thanks to a financial backer, Ritz opened the Paris hotel that was to bear his name. This was added to a growing portfolio of hotels and restaurants. In 1906 he went on to open the Ritz Hotel in London.

Sadly his personal story did not end well and he died after a battle with mental illness in 1918. However, his legacy was immense and was nicely summed up in an article from 2016 in 'e-hotelier':

> 'Ritz was a snob, a perfectionist and a taskmaster, yet always ambitious and driven. He was indefatigable in his attempts to deliver perfect service within the luxury and comfort of a grand hotel setting. Many of Ritz's original insights are part of today's industry standards. For example, a hotelier's duty to a guest is to "*guide him, advise him, anticipate his wishes and, above all, remember him in order to offer what he likes when he comes back*". Another motto was "*Never say 'no' when a guest asks for something, even if it is the moon. You can always try, and anyhow there is plenty of time afterwards to explain that it was not possible*". Ritz

also probably created the most famous of hospitality's maxims, "*the customer is always right!*" (ehotelier.com/insights/2016/03/29/industry-icons-cesar-ritz)

Ritz represents that old-style formal style of hospitality that has become a benchmark against which all luxury end hospitality came to be judged. He also created that culture where guests are, at the same time, pampered, shown huge respect almost to the point of sycophancy, but also manipulated and treated almost as children

In this book I have suggested that this highly formalised, traditional style of service is now being challenged, even in luxury establishments, by more informal service styles and guests serving themselves. But Ritz still deserves recognition as the man who transformed an industry and who has influenced the idea of luxury for more than a century.

I feel a personal connection to Ritz, as from 2008 to 2011 I had the privilege of being Academic Director of César Ritz Colleges in Switzerland, a prestigious private hotel school with a campus in Ritz's home town of Brig as well as Le Bouveret and Lucerne. Although the curriculum was wholly modern the idea of exceptional personal service was undoubtedly part of the ethos of the institution.

Case study 2: Luxury cruising yesterday and today – Cunard

Cunard is a world famous name in luxury cruising with a history dating back to the mid 19th century. While the company was taken over by the Carnival Corporation in 1998, the brand still exists and retains its image as a luxury liner operator.

The origins of the brand date from the days before air travel, when the main function of ships was as a means of transport from one place to another for both passengers and mail. They played a vital part in economic development and in connecting countries with their colonies. Liners were also vital to the mass emigration that took place in the 19th century from Europe to the so-called 'New World'.

As with most liner companies of the time, the focus was on the fastest possible journey times, and competition on the lucrative Transatlantic route was sharpened by the 'Blue Riband', which was awarded to the ship achieving the quickest passage on the route. Cunard held this prestigious award several times but gradually fell behind until the early 20th century when the British government provided loans that allowed Cunard to launch the fastest ships afloat, such as the legendary *Mauretania*.

Starting in the late 19th century, a new class of privileged travellers arose for whom a 'cruise' was a leisure activity as much as or even more than a means of transport. By the early 20th century, liners sailing under many flags were plying the oceans of the world, offering those with plenty of leisure time the opportunity to see the world by ship.

From the beginning liners were very class conscious and usually had several classes from a highly luxurious first class to a very basic steerage class which will be familiar to those who have seen the movie *Titanic*.

At the top end, everything was luxurious. Large sumptuous stateroom cabins had nearby more humble accommodation for servants and there were ballrooms, swimming pools and restaurants, presided over by some of the greatest chefs of the time.

The luxury cruise reached a peak between the World Wars but in the 1930s the British government again offered loan guarantees to help Cunard build two ships that would become icons of transatlantic cruising, the *Queen Mary* and the *Queen Elizabeth*. This shows that governments saw cruise lines as important strategic assets for a maritime nation, and in both World Wars cruise ships were often pressed into service as troopships or floating hospitals, both of which were at odds with the luxury image the companies wished to portray.

What was interesting about Cunard was that its focus was always on the Transatlantic routes and North America. This was undoubtedly the most glamorous cruise market in the world, with an endless stream of celebrities travelling in each direction. Then, after World War Two, in common with other cruise companies Cunard saw a sharp decline in demand; the world was a different place and ships now faced competition from air travel. The whole cruise market went into decline for around 20 years or more.

However, in recent decades the cruise sector has experienced a major rejuvenation which has been based on a number of factors including:

- The general growth in international travel and the desire of tourists for new experiences.

- Modifying the cruise product to meet the needs of modern travellers, with two week holiday periods, rather than the endless leisure time of the early era luxury cruise passengers. This includes fly-cruises, where the passenger flies to a port of embarkation close to the region where they want to cruise, rather than spending days at sea just to get to the Mediterranean or the Caribbean. It has also involved the development of short break 'taster' cruises for those new to cruising.

- Increasing the range of itineraries and ports of call to increase consumer choice.

- Major investment in making the ships suitable for the desires of the consumer of today in terms of leisure activities and entertainment

- The rise in the main cruise markets of specialist intermediaries promoting cruises and offering discounts, even on luxury cruise products

- Launching new ships with a capacity of thousands of passengers to achieve some economies of scale, although even the largest ships will also have luxury class accommodation available.

- Deliberate attempts by some companies to make cruising more attractive to younger travellers.

- The use of themed and special interest cruises to attract new segments; when I consulted the Cunard website in October 2017 there were Transatlantic themed cruises around genealogy and fashion, for example.

Cunard has done all of these things but is still distinguished by a reputation for offering a rather more elegant and stylish, older style of luxury experience. The three ships currently in service all carry the names of queens of Great Britain which adds to the image of Cunard as a luxury end operator.

The March–December 2018 cruise calendar included more than 20 Transatlantic UK- new York cruises, around 20 Mediterranean cruises, 15 northern Europe cruises and other cruises to Canada and the Caribbean. It also included around 20 short cruises of as little as two nights' duration.

Prices of the short cruises started at £409 with Transatlantic and Mediterranean cruises of seven nights starting at a little over £1000. However, prices vary understandably, based on the cabin and the package. In October 2017 I looked on the Cunard website at an eastbound New York-Southampton cruise in early July 2018. The price of a cabin varied from £1,699 for a windowless inside cabin to £14,019 for one of the Grand Duplexes with a 360 degree all round view and a cabin area in excess of two hundred square metres, priority embarkation and disembarkation, access to the Queen's Grill Lounge, butler service and even personalised stationery!

The Cunard brand has clearly made the transition from traditional to modern luxury cruising successfully and looks set continue to be part of the cruise scene for many years to come.

Case study 3: Ritual luxury – the phenomenon of afternoon tea

In the 1840s a British aristocratic lady is credited with starting the fashion for afternoon tea, a light snack between lunch and dinner, although there is evidence of this happening as far back as the 1600s. By the late 19th century in the UK, it had developed into something of an occasion, with society ladies dressing up in expensive clothes to partake in afternoon tea as a social occasion with friends.

From the beginning it is important to recognise that afternoon teas were the embodiment of luxury and privilege. First they meant you could afford to eat four times a day at a time when many people were lucky to eat three times a day. Furthermore it meant you must have lots of spare time to be able to partake in a leisurely ritual such as afternoon tea. And of course, during the 19th century tea was a relatively expensive commodity.

As time went by afternoon tea became a grander affair with a range of savoury and sweet items including the 19th century British invention, the sandwich. It is interesting that it became popular in the UK at the height of the British empire and coincided with the practice in India of taking a light afternoon meal called 'tiffin'.

Over time men started to join in and it became fashionable to have afternoon tea outside, again a sign of luxury in that it required the host to have a sizeable garden. For decades though afternoon tea was something taken at home in a domestic situation. An etiquette arose around the ritual of afternoon tea including the kinds of food to serve, dress codes and the type of crockery to use.

In the late 19th and early 20th centuries, afternoon tea left the confines of the home and began to be offered in upscale hotels like the *Ritz* and the *Dorchester*, and in lavishly decorated teashops and tea rooms, sometimes located in high end department stores such as Fortnum and Mason. At this time it was largely confined to London, although it was also developing in the more affluent towns and cities as well as in the country houses of the aristocracy. Quickly though it was adopted by the growing middle class as they endeavoured to copy the behaviour of the upper classes.

In the early 20th century the practice of afternoon tea was exported to the British colonies, even where the climate seemed most unsuitable for such a thing. To the colonials it was a way of staying connected to the traditions of home.

By the middle of the 20th century, afternoon tea was falling out of favour and seemed in danger of dying out. It was still offered in the UK but it seemed to be the preserve of the elderly with little appeal to those under retirement age. Yet in recent years we have seen a great renaissance in the idea of afternoon tea in the UK, but more interestingly we have seen it appearing and growing around the world. Perhaps this is because tea drinking is becoming more widespread or because it appeals to new generations of luxury travellers, particularly from tea consuming countries in Asia or because the hospitality industry has realised that it can be a very lucrative market.

Now most upscale hotels in the UK and many leading department stores and tearooms offer afternoon teas at different price levels. At the time of writing, the website Afternoontea.co.uk was listing 361 places to have afternoon tea in London alone, with prices varying from £11 to £99. In other words, an afternoon tea can cost as much as lunch at a Michelin starred restaurant! The *Timeout* website talked of *'twenty-three kick-ass afternoon teas'* in London, language which suggests that the appeal of afternoon tea now extends far beyond the elderly. And afternoon tea has changed dramatically in the UK in response to changing demand, so we now can see Prosecco as part of the package, gluten-free cakes and vegetarian afternoon teas. It is even more interesting to look at where else in the world afternoon tea is now popular. A quick internet search produced some interesting results. *Fodor Travel Guides* in 2015 identified their ten best afternoon teas in the world, of which four were in the USA with one each from Thailand and Malaysia. In the same year online travel comparison site *Skyscanner* suggested that the best afternoon tea in the world was to be found at a hotel in Cape Town. And in 2017 *Teletext Holidays* in the UK suggested that hotels in Morocco, Spain and France offered some of the best afternoon teas in the world. However, it is interesting to note that most of the venues identified as the best for afternoon tea were either luxury hotels in former British Colonies or high end hotels in destinations that have been popular with luxury travellers since well before the dawn of the age of mass market tourism.

The world that created the phenomenon of afternoon tea no longer exists but this example of a luxury ritual has been reinvented for a modern age. Dress codes are more relaxed, the duration of the ritual has been shortened somewhat and different dietary requirements accommodated. It is now, though, something which almost wholly takes places outside one's home while on vacation or a day trip.

There are parallels with cruising which has also gained popularity and new consumers following a makeover that has taken account of social change. Cruise liners are now purely floating resorts rather than a means of travelling between two points. And short duration cruises have been introduced to take account of the fact that most people only have vacations of limited duration rather than the endless free time of the upper class leisured classes of previous times.

In conclusion, afternoon tea remains something of a ritual and one associated with the past, aristocracy and privelege, in one particular country. It is a view of luxury which seems to have a fascination for people, as evidenced by the interest of international tourists in the British royal family and the global popularity of shows such as *Downtown Abbey*.

Case study 4: 'You are what you wear' – dressing for luxury travel

Clothing and travel have always been linked throughout history. At first it was about dressing for comfort or even survival, whether one was on a long sea crossing, climbing a mountain, skiing or crossing a desert on an overland adventure. Those setting out to for unfamiliar places would first visit specialist outfitters who would kit them out with everything they would need, usually at considerable expense. Guides, published in small numbers, contained plentiful advice about clothing and equipment needs.

In those times virtually all travel – apart from travel for military purposes, economic migrants and refugees – could be seen as luxury travel for it was being undertaken by people with plenty of both time and money.

As the number of high end leisure travellers grew from the mid-19th century, so the demand for clothing and accessories began to grow. Louis Vuitton made their first pieces of travel luggage in the 1850s in Paris, while 'steamer trunks' grew in popularity and are once again fashionable finds in antique shops. Clothing such as pith helmets and khaki coloured clothing were adopted from military use for travel to tropical countries.

On the ships luggage weight was not an issue for the privileged traveller as they would usually have their own domestic staff or an army of porters to carry their luggage at every stage of the journey.

When air travel first began in the early 20th century, people dressed in their best attire for the journey. All early air travellers were people of wealth and they wore their best clothes to demonstrate their wealth, but perhaps also to make them feel more confident as they took part in this still relatively new and quite dangerous form of travel.

When I first flew in 1963, it was still the norm to dress in your best clothes to fly; ladies in formal outfits and gentlemen walking across a windy apron in suit and tie with their best shoes, probably new and being worn for the first time, exposed to the rain. Hotels and restaurants still often had strict dress codes particularly for men requiring jackets and ties in the public areas.

However, as mass market tourism grew and formality in societies lessened there was a dramatic change, even in the luxury market. Lighter fabrics emerged and the emphasis was on clothes that were comfortable rather than 'showy'. Many hospitality establishments relaxed and then dropped their dress codes as the tide of informal dress washed over them. Luggage allowances on aircraft were reduced so that the emphasis moved towards lighter, easier to pack clothing.

Those who meet cabin crew of more mature years often hear them nostalgically lament that you can no longer tell who will be sitting in business class or first class based on their clothing. Shorts, jeans, t-shirts and even one piece sleep suits are to be seen in all classes of travel today, alongside the few who still maintain the tradition of dressing up to fly. The emphasis is now on comfort, and flying for many is quite normal and no longer glamorous but just a chore to be endured as the price paid to get where you want to go.

Dress codes on cruise ships have also been relaxed, although most ships still have 'formal nights' when people dress in their best, and for many passengers this is a highlight of the whole cruise experience.

However, what we have seen in recent years is the development of a range of specialist accessories for travellers and high specification clothing for particular adventure activities that have become popular in recent years.

One tradition that does seem to endure in tourism is the purchasing of items of clothing as souvenirs on one's travels, whether it is the fez in Egypt, the sombrero in Mexico, the kilt in Scotland, fur hats in Russia or clogs in the Netherlands. But at the luxury end, it also means buying high end clothing in the recognised fashion centres of the world such as Milan, Paris and New York. The traveller could buy these items at home but somehow buying them in such cities gives them more prestige and authenticity.

Case study 5: Changing consumer expectations over time and the idea of luxury – the hotel bedroom

Every text about marketing and quality seems to repeat the mantra that success is about meeting and then exceeding customer expectations. To do this we need to understand these expectations and where they come from, but we also need to recognise that these expectations are constantly changing. Usually this means they get higher as travellers experience more and more products and services, and thus have more experiences to draw upon when making comparisons.

If we look specifically at the hotel bedroom, expectations have risen over time for another reason. It has often been said that the quality of the hotel bedroom needs to match or preferably exceed the quality of the guest's bedroom in their own home. And the fact is that in most countries the quality of homes has been improving in recent years in terms of everything from interior design to entertainment facilities. Thus there is pressure on hotel operators to ensure that they keep up to date with the latest developments. In the luxury sector, not surprisingly, this pressure is at its greatest, given these consumers are the most experienced travellers and are very likely to have high quality homes. Endeavouring to exceed the expectations of this most demanding segment is indeed a daunting challenge!

The simple fact is that what was a luxury yesterday, is seen as the norm today and as out-dated and sub-standard tomorrow. Furthermore, as much of what happens in the design of the hotel bedroom revolves around technological developments the pace at which this cycle occurs is getting faster all the time.

In the late 19th or early 20th century, electric light would have been seen as a luxury in a hotel room as it was a recent invention and most would have been lit by gas lamps. In the early decades of the 20th century running water was introduced widely in hotels, in terms of a sink in the bedroom with hot and cold water. A radio in the room would have been a luxury as would an interior sprung mattress on the bed. The bath and toilet would still be down the corridor in most hotels at this time. In the 1960s and 1970s, the boom in package holidays involved the introduction of rooms with 'ensuite' bathrooms, something most guests would not have had at home. The room increasingly would also have a black and white television and a trouser press as well as a telephone. Through the 1980s and 1990s we saw the introduction of colour televisions, showers as well as bathtubs, in-room movies and minibars. Some of these developments have simply represented blatant attempts by hotels to increase guest spend.

In recent years the room has been enhanced in a number of ways including:

■ Interactive multi-media entertainment systems and flat screen televisions.

■ Wi-fi access and recharging points for mobile devices.

- Hot tubs, 'Amazon rain showers' 'hydrotherapy showers' and so on in the bathroom.
- 'Pillow menus'.
- Larger beds.

All of these when first introduced were viewed as luxuries but quickly became the norm. And while these features were originally introduced in high end hotels, some of them at least have now become standard even in budget hotels.

Hoteliers have also recognised that space is seen as important by guests so the more you pay, the more space you will have in your room, and this is signalled by the use of the word 'suite' instead of 'room'.

They have also recognised the desire of high end guests for personal service through the introduction of the 'personal butler' service involving service delivered to and consumed even inside the guest bedroom. This is still generally only available in the most luxurious establishments or on the 'executive floors' which many high end hotels now have.

The trick for the industry lies in predicting what the luxury guest will expect from their hotel room in the future, and that is difficult as some technological advances which we will see are not even on the horizon today. How much further can hotel room design go?

Perhaps, most affluent consumers will reach a point where what they will look for is not more luxury in their hotel room, because nothing may be able to match what they have at home. Instead some of them may seek an experience which is in total contrast with what they have at home and may almost be the opposite of the luxury hotel room. This might mean:

- Staying in a room with no wi-fi, candles for light, open fires and so on as part of a ' back to the simple life', stress reduction vacation
- The authenticity of staying in a simple bedroom the home of an 'ordinary' person whose life is very different to their own.
- Feeling good about themselves and being a responsible tourist by staying in a room without environmentally unfriendly electric-powered air conditioning

This will not be true for all luxury travellers but it will appeal to some for certain.

But to pursue a theme seen throughout this book, the idea of what constitutes a 'luxury' hotel bedroom will remain a relative rather than an absolute concept; relative to the guest's everyday life at home and relative to other hotel rooms they have experienced. It will be a matter of guest perception rather than fact, and as no two guests are the same that will make it a most complicated matter.

Case study 6: The design of luxury hotels and resorts

Over the years we have seen a number of trends in the design of luxury hotels and resorts, reflecting trends in both tourist behaviour, hospitality fashions, and architectural thinking.

The longest established luxury hotels include the 19th century lakeside and mountainside hotels of Switzerland, the century or more old grand hotels of the great cities and the 'colonial staging post' hotels, usually in coastal locations, which again generally date back to the 19th century. Their design is about grandeur and opulence but still offering guests the latest in technology, even if at the time this was simply electric light! But otherwise everything is about tradition and continuity.

The so-called 'new world', and particularly the USA in the early 20th century took luxury hotel design to the next stage of development with city centre skyscrapers and a recognition that many high spending guests were on business rather than leisure and also wanted efficiency, modernity and convenience. In the 1950s to 1980s, with the rise of hotel chains, design took second place and large concrete boxes became the norm, even for luxury hotels, in city centres and even in coastal resorts.

Over time, as international tourism grew and new destinations emerged, new hotels often seemed to be following standard designs that had little to do with the location of the hotel or local architectural traditions. A pristine beach backed by virgin forest in an Asian country with a pronounced monsoon season would suddenly become home to a 15-storey concrete block that would not have looked out of place in downtown New York.

However, there has been another parallel phenomenon in luxury hotel design for at least 60 years, which is seen most clearly in modern destinations such as Las Vegas and Dubai, both places with few if any natural attractions for tourists as both are located in inhospitable deserts. Here the architectural style can best be described as fantasy. We have the opulent but pastiche style of the themed hotels of Las Vegas which seek to bring Venice, Paris, Egypt and New York into a corner of the Nevada desert. Meanwhile, in Dubai, we had the creation of the truly unique *Burj-el-Arab* hotel with its underwater restaurant and rooftop helipad. This hotel changed the world of luxury hotels forever, not only through its architecture but also because it claimed to be the world's first 'seven star' hotel, thus destroying forever the international convention that no hotel could have more than five stars. This simple move showed the meaninglessness of the hotel classification ideas that had existed for decades.

However, these developments were not universally popular with local communities, the media or even the customers and the architects. Criticism were heard increasingly from the 1970s and 1980s onwards including:

- The suggestion that even modern luxury hotels were becoming too standardised in terms of their architecture to the point where they were becoming rather boring and uninspiring.

- Their scale and building materials were seen too often be at odds with building traditions in the specific destination area.

- They were often sited in locations which gave the best possible views to their guests but which destroyed views for everyone else.

- They were designed in a way that created negative impacts such as: the overuse of precious water resources and the need to use electric light in function rooms located in basements with no natural light.

Slowly, these criticisms were taken seriously by the hotel industry, particularly from the 1980s when it was trying to improve its image in terms of environmental issues, as well as trying to reduce expenditure on energy and water.

Over the past two decades we have seen a number of interesting developments in luxury hotel design including :

- The rise of so-called 'designer hotels' where designers from outside the hotel industry, including people like Phillip Starck, became involved in designing hotels. This particularly influenced interior design in hotels.

- In resorts attempts were made to break up the size of units and create smaller sub-units with greater levels of privacy, such as cabanas spread around the grounds or separate buildings with a few rooms in each.

- Architects endeavoured to reflect local architectural traditions in their designs, which at its best created sympathetic buildings but at worst resulted in kitsch architecture.

- Hotel companies wanted to be seen to be seen to be environmentally friendly and tried to incorporate environmental good practice into the design of new units.

- Designers worked hard to create accommodation units that had a unique design and were unusual, or as the French would say, '*insolite*'. These could be up trees, underwater, and so on but they had to be unlike anything else that already existed.

However, the story has not always been a positive one. While the design of new properties has improved in recent years, there is still a huge stock of older units that were poorly designed and almost impossible to bring up to modern design standards. And companies investing heavily in new hotels have sometimes been tempted to over-claim in terms of their sustainability credentials. Many are marketed as 'ecolodges', particularly in Africa, Asia and South America, despite being far from truly sustainable or environmentally responsible.

Finally, we need to recognise that in terms of luxury hotel design there is always a trade-off or compromise required between guest expectations and environmental responsibility. A guest may be interested in the environment but not if it means they cannot have any air conditioning! However, there are traditional architectural practices in many parts of the world that can help alleviate these problems in a sustainable manner.

Case study 7: The luxury of authenticity and personalisation in the accommodation sector

Travellers today have more accommodation choices available to them than ever before, all over the world. However, in recent years, there has been a clear trend towards more people choosing to use accommodation owned and operated by people who have no hospitality training and would not usually see themselves as 'hospitality professionals'. Yet for many of these people, providing accommodation has become their livelihood.

It would be wrong to suggest that this phenomenon is wholly new as in the UK, for example, we have had **'bed-and-breakfast'** accommodation for several decades. A local resident who is a homeowner opens up their house to paying guests renting out, usually, a small number of rooms, depending on the size of the house. Some are established as a response when children leave home and the house is too large for the parents living alone. They advise guests on where to go based on local knowledge and are renowned for the quality of their 'full English breakfasts', which are cooked to order rather than being pre-cooked and then kept warm on the hotplates as in many modern hotels.

Airbnb has only been around since 2008 yet its impact has been enormous. As its own website says it now has welcomed over 200 million guests to some 3 million listed properties in nearly 200 countries. The idea is that an owner rents out rooms or an apartment in their home, or the entire home, as self-catering accommodation. They are often located in less touristy parts of destinations and the owners will often give guests a lift from the airport to the accommodation and/or show them around the neighbourhood personally. Some have suggested that Airbnb can also have a negative impact, when owners convert properties which have had local residents as rental tenants into more lucrative holiday accommodation, thus creating housing issues. Furthermore, luxury hotel owners in Paris have complained that they are losing business to Airbnb, which offers some luxury apartments in the smartest neighbourhoods of the city.

Homestays have become popular in some emerging destinations in recent years as local people seek to benefit from tourism, and tourists try to 'get under the skin' of the destination and get to know the 'real' place. In 2016 I spent an excellent short break staying with a family just outside Kandy in Sri Lanka. The food, the same as that eaten by the family, was delicious and meals were accompanied by the memorable experience of the young daughter practicing playing the piano in the next room

In general, satisfaction levels are high with all three forms of 'informal' accommodation and for many tourists using them is a highlight of their trip. When asked why they prefer such accommodation they tend to offer one or more of the following answers:

- The service is more 'genuine' and personalised and is not being provided by a trained person schooled to follow a standardised approach to customer interaction. They feel they can get to know their host in a house with maybe two or three other guests staying at the same time rather than hundreds in a large hotel.

- They feel they get to know more about the destination and its people than if they were separated from local people in a hotel, resort complex or villa in a holiday village.

- They believe that by staying at such accommodation they contribute more directly to the local economy.

- They perceive them to offer better value-for-money than mainstream accommodation establishments.

In other words, they feel the experience is more authentic and personalised than that offered by the formal, commercial accommodation sector, as well as being more cost-effective.

Yet such informal accommodation does face a number of criticisms including:

- The suggestion that these establishments sometimes represent unfair competition as they do not face the same government regulation as hotels, for example. This is generally true for Airbnb and even homestays, but not bed-and-breakfasts in general where there is regulation in most countries.

- These operations usually employ no one except perhaps an assistant to help with breakfast service at the bed-and-breakfast. Therefore, they do little to help create employment unlike hotels, and make little contribution to training the future hospitality workforce.

However, it is clear that they are offering something that travellers want and feel they cannot get from the formal accommodation sector. But perhaps some of the appeal is sometimes misguided or based on a 'rose-tinted' view that the hosts are just normal ordinary local people. Many owners will be wealthy homeowners who are not typical of the neighbourhood, while others may have developed the operation to the point where it is more of a formal business than an informal accommodation operation.

Nevertheless, I predict that this phenomenon, facilitated by the Internet and mobile devices, and driven by tourists' desire for what they see as authenticity and personalisation, will continue to grow unless governments constrain it.

Case study 8: Fusion luxury – fashion hotels

In many ways, the fashion industry is the sector which most people today associate with the idea of luxury, with its high-end creations costing thousands of dollars, its globally recognised brands, and its leading designers being world famous celebrities. As the most famous designers and brands sought to exploit the fame of their brands by extending their reach into other sectors such as perfumes, for example, it is not surprising that their gaze was drawn to the hotel sector. Here they could have complete buildings, used by high spending consumers, as showcases for their talent and their brands. This has created a type of 'fusion luxury' bringing together fashion and hotels.

Given that no one has yet produced a widely accepted definition for 'fashion hotels' it is impossible to give a date for the first one, but it is clearly a recent phenomenon, with a history measured in years rather than decades.

There is also potentially some overlap with two other terms, as follows:

- **Boutique hotels.** This term again, has no accepted definition but seems to imply small-scale, personalised service and individuality in contrast to the hotel chains with their large units and standardised offer. However, the term has become debased to the point where even a five hundred bed hotel can describe itself as 'boutique'

- **Designer hotels.** Again there is no clear definition of these but they tend to take the idea of design to all aspects of the hotel not just the décor and furnishings. Leading names in this movement were Claus Sendlinger and Philippe Starck. And minimalist design seems to have been the preferred approach, which is in direct contrast with the ostentatious luxuriant style seen in many so-called fashion hotels. However, there is clearly crossover with fashion hotels in some minds as a list of ten of the *coolest designer hotels* produced in businessinsider.com in 2012, for example, was actually a list of hotels carrying the brand names of fashion designers.

Fashion hotels are hotels developed and operated under the name of fashion brands, albeit often in partnership with established hotel operators. This separates them from hotels where elements of the fabric have been created by fashion designers but the hotel as a whole is not branded in a way that associates it with a well known fashion brand.

The term 'fashion hotels' is certainly well established and often used in lifestyle magazines and their websites which have become so common in recent years. Indeed a number of these have produced lists of fashion hotels. For example, in

2017, trendspotter.net published a list of *'8 luxury fashion designer hotels and suites you must visit'* which featured:

- The *Bulgari* hotel, London
- The Dior Suite at the *St Regis* hotel, New York
- The *Armani* hotel, Dubai
- *Palazzo Versace*, Gold Coast, Australia
- *Hotel Le Bellechasse* by Christian Lacroix, Paris
- *Round Hill* Hotel and Villas by Ralph Lauren, Jamaica
- Dianne Von Furstenberg's Suite and Rooms at *Claridges*, London
- *Schlosshotel Im Grunewald*, Grunewald Suite by Karl Lagerfeld, Berlin.

Earlier in 2010 and updated in 2011, the *Huffington Post* produced a list of *'The Top Ten Fashion Designer Hotels in the World'* . Interestingly, this list contained three properties that were also in the 2017 trendspotter.net list. The *Huffington Post* list is interesting as it appeared in 2010, a year before articles suggesting the first fashion hotel was due to be developed in Dubai. This just goes to show the lack of agreed definitions that leaves open the opportunity for such apparent confusion.

Both lists show that the term 'fashion hotel' can include at least three categories:

- hotels branded simply with the name of a designer or designer brand;
- hotels which are jointly branded with the names of a hotel company and a designer;
- hotels where designers' names appear in relation to particular suites or rooms.

These lists are also interesting in that they show that while most fashion hotels are based on designers from Europe or North America, they are now a worldwide phenomenon, as are the brands whose names they carry.

An interesting article published in May 2017 by *lemiani.com* and written by James Davidson provided some interesting perspectives on the idea of fashion hotels and suites. For example it pointed out that:

- The refurbished *Ritz* hotel in Paris had created a suite inspired by, and named after, Coco Chanel which costs €18,000 per night. So fashion designers' names can help market a hotel even if they have had no involvement in the design of the property.
- Karl Lagerfeld was said to be planning to launch a chain of branded hotels. Bulgari already has a mini chain with established hotels in London, Milan and Bali, restaurants in Tokyo, new hotels opening in China and Dubai in 2017 and a further opening in Moscow scheduled for 2019.
- Fashion designers, including names such as Narciso Rodriguez, are being called upon to design ultra-stylish 'uniforms' for staff in luxury hotels.

- In Antwerp there is a townhouse that includes an upscale holiday rental apartment alongside a retail fashion outlet and a restaurant.

In 2015, Dallabona discussed the fact that fashion hotels represented brand extension for the fashion brands and noted that "whilst brand extension is associated with certain benefits, it is also characterised by significant risks, in particular the one of affecting the parent brand's prestige and of 'diluting' it" (Dallabona, 2015). In that respect, being associated with a glamorous business such as hotels is probably a low risk for these brands.

She went on to suggest that "even though not everybody can afford to stay at these (fashion) hotels they also offer a series of services that are more affordable and could appeal to a broader public than the very rich. Through their bars and restaurants for example such hotels allow the people to live the brand for less" (Dallabona, 2015). This fits nicely with the idea put forward in this book about the segment that cannot afford a wholly luxurious experience but which chooses to purchase one or two luxury elements in their vacation experience, whether that be a fine dining meal or a room upgrade in the hotel.

Finally, Dallabona stated that "within the high end hotels associated with luxury fashion brands that are a function of brand extension ....co-exist elements of horizontal brand extension that sees fashion labels turning into lifestyle brands capable of providing products and services that can satisfy virtually all the needs of their customers, and elements of downscale vertical brand extension, that sees luxury brands associating their names to goods that are very different...to the high end products that made the brands renowned in the first place" (Dallabona, 2015).

This phenomenon of brand extension has already seen the creation of Gucci and Versace branded cars, for example, but perhaps soon we will see everything from fashion brand private education establishments, fashion brand private banks, or even fashion brand air charters. However, in relation to what we discussed in Chapter 11, what is interesting is that the relative power of fashion and hotel brands may be illustrated by the fact that hotels have yet to introduce significant brand extensions of their own such as opening retail outlets or getting involved in the fashion business.

Case study 9: The Michelin three star experience – Le Suquet, Lagioule, France

This is a very personal case study for me, as I and my family had the pleasure of eating at Le Suquet in June 2016.

Le Suquet was opened by legendary French chef Michel Bras in 1992, and by 1999 already had three Michelin stars which it has kept ever since. However, the restaurant is not in a major city such as Paris or Lyon. Instead it is in open countryside in the hills near Lagioule in the Aubrac area of the Aveyron, hours by car or train from any big city. This part of France is famous for its beef cattle and its wild flowers.

The choice of location was no accident for this is the region where Michel Bras was born and about which he is a passionate advocate. It is no exaggeration to say that his restaurant has put this area on the international food map. For example, an article by Natasha Gelling in the *Smithsonian* magazine in the USA, put Le Suquet first in a list of ten restaurants across the world that she said top chefs themselves said they would travel to eat at. It is responsible for many people travelling specifically to the area to sample the food of Le Suquet, which brings great economic benefits to the area.

In 2016 French gastronomy magazine, *Le Chef*, gave Michel Bras the accolade of naming him number one in their list of the hundred best chefs in the world, based on the opinions of fellow chefs. In 2009 his son Sebastien took over the kitchen but has continued the philosophy of his father, that the menu is a showcase for the best of regional produce. The restaurant has had this philosophy since its very beginning, long before the current fashion for using local ingredients started. As Sebastien says on the restaurant website, 'Aubrac has given us everything'. The website continues with much about the philosophy of the restaurant and the people behind it in a way that draws the reader in and gets them interested in the restaurant and the gastronomic experience it offers.

The Michelin inspectors in 2016 said of Le Suquet, '*Aubrac, Aubrac …Telle est l'incantation qui s'echappe de cette table magique. Suc du terroir, sève des herbes aromatiques; la patte de Michel Bras .. et du son fils Sebastien, qui est desormais seul aux fourneaux. On puise toujours au coeur du produit, et l'on fait chanter la terre comme nulle part ailleurs!*') it is impossible to do justice to this by translating it in to English; suffice it to say that the inspectors were as impressed with the Bras philosophy and how it transfers to the plate as the rest of the customers.

Now, let me relive, with great pleasure, his experience of dining at Le Suquet and in doing so illustrate some points about the nature of luxury in hospitality.

We arrived on a wet and foggy evening at the restaurant, which is in a strikingly designed modern building with panoramic views of the surrounding hills, as we discovered when we returned next day after the fog was replaced by sun!

Starting with the physical environment, everywhere was light and airy with modern minimalist design 'warmed' by homely touches which drew their inspiration from the farmhouses and *burons* of the region. Nothing jarred, the interior design was perfection, right down to stunning features such as the stream which ran through the dining room.

The service was perfect, combining friendliness with professionalism, but never becoming either too informal or aloof. It was not effusive or over-familiar but was always charming. Calm reigned in the dining room and plates came and went without us noticing, and likewise glasses were refilled as if by magic.

Once we had enjoyed pre-dinner drinks we were taken to the kitchen to meet Sebastien Bras who was willing to smile and pose for photos with as many guests as asked him, despite service being about to commence. The kitchen brigade, some 25 strong for 40 guests, were also approachable and pleased to talk to the diners, despite being busy with their duties.

Choosing the wine was easy; the sommelier asked us for our preferences and tastes and then recommended two low to medium priced wines that were both a perfect match for the food. He did not make any effort at any point to persuade us to buy expensive wines or take a digestif after our meal (although we did !). Furthermore no effort was made to get us to buy a bottle of mineral water; instead we were given fine Aubrac mountain water.

The bread provided was not a small roll from a basket but rather a huge freshly baked loaf with our family name cleverly incorporated in to the crust, a really nice touch.

As for the food itself, words cannot describe the quality of what we ate. You will have to go and try it for yourself. We will remember it forever, the combinations of flavours were exquisite, and it added to the experience somehow to know that the vegetables and herbs were from the restaurant's own garden that was clearly visible from the restaurant.

At the end of the meal we were offered complimentary coffee and amazing *petits fours* and left to relax in the comfortable lounge chairs. We eventually left some four hours after we had arrived, almost too stunned by the experience to speak!

So why was this a luxury experience in our eyes? The answer is complicated and simple at the same time. First, it was **a rare**, one-off event not something we do every day. Second, the price was high, with the lowest priced menu at some €140. Third, the food was simply out of this world – truly unique and produced with amazing artistry and passion. Fourth, the way in which every customer was truly treated as an individual – witness the bread with our name on it! Fifth, the environment was harmonious and of the highest quality and the ambiance was perfect for fine dining. Next, the service matched the quality of both the food and the restaurant beautifully, and the waiting staff were knowledgeable and very well trained. They served without impinging on our privacy as we dined. Finally, although it did not really matter to us, there was certainly a sense of exclusivity as we needed to book three months in advance to get a table as the restaurant has one sitting per service and only 40 seats.

However that is my opinion. As we noted in the text, luxury is subjective and in the eye of the beholder' and another person reading this case study might say luxury should mean we should have drunk expensive wines with the food and branded, bottled mineral water. Or they may have contended that luxury should mean expensive imported ingredients, not vegetables from the garden and local beef. Others may like to see more subservience or false 'have a nice day' type service when paying a lot for a meal or regret the lack of background music or entertainment. Finally people who regularly dine at Michelin three star restaurants may also have had a different type of reaction to ours.

But all I can say is that for my family it was a luxurious and memorable occasion!

Postscript

At the time of writing (October 2017) it has been announced that Bras has asked to "be stripped of his three Michelin stars". According to the report in *The Guardian* online, he has said "he wanted to be allowed to cook excellent food away from the frenzy of star ratings and the anxiety over Michelin's anonymous food judges .... He asked to be allowed to continue to work with a free spirit and in serenity away from the world of rankings. He said he wanted to be dropped from the guide from next year."

(www.guardian.com, 2017)

At the same time, in October 2017 two Michelin star chef Andre Chiang of Restaurant Chiang in Singapore announced he would close his restaurant in February 2018 and asked Michelin to take back his stars and take him out of the guide.

In an open letter he said "I am a perfectionist and for the past thirty years of my career I have been looking for that unrealistic 'moment of perfection', three Michelin stars, world's top 50 restaurants, until now I realised, it is perfect as it is" (reported on 10 October 2017 in www.straitstimes/lifestyle)

While isolated incidents these two cases demonstrate that the system of Michelin stars is rigorous but also puts great pressure on the chefs and means their reputation rests with a small number of expert inspectors rather than with the views of all their clientele. In an era of consumer generated media and consumer reviews this seems to be swimming against the tide.

As *The Guardian* reported, Bras said he would continue to cook excellent local produce "without wondering if my creations will appeal to Michelin's inspectors"

(www.guardian.com, 2017)

Interestingly in response to the request from Bras to be stripped of his stars, a Michelin spokesperson was reported by the *Guardian* as saying that it was noted, but went on to say the request would not lead to Le Suquet's automatic removal from the list and would have to be given due consideration. This may well be an indication of the power which Michelin feels it has in the field of gastronomy, a view for which there is plenty of supporting evidence around the world.

Case study 10: The changing nature of luxury in gastronomy – the 'pop-up restaurant' phenomenon

When people talk about luxury and hospitality they often have in mind the high-end Michelin starred restaurant presided over by a chef who has taken years to rise to this position through a number of jobs in the restaurants of other Michelin starred chefs. Traditionally such restaurants were characterised by high prices, large kitchen brigades, exquisite presentation, formal attentive service and innovative dishes perfectly executed. Any serious restaurant aspired to reach this point, it was seen as the only form of luxury cuisine.

However, in recent years, we have seen the rise of the 'pop-up restaurant' phenomenon where often non-professional food enthusiasts set up a temporary restaurant in an empty shop, a disused factory, an historic mansion or even a tiny suburban apartment. They may open for just one night or a few months and then they are gone, and they may be cheap or relatively expensive. In many cities they are clearly designed as social events as well as food experiences and are called 'supper clubs'.

This is a fascinating phenomenon in the context of luxury in relation to gastronomy, for luxury is often seen as being based on rarity value which is then reflected in high prices. It is also a phenomenon that is being seen in other sectors such as retailing, and in hospitality it is also extending to encompass pop up bars.

Yet while most traditional gastronomic restaurants are high priced their product is not actually rare. A fifty cover restaurant serving lunch and dinner five days a week all year round can welcome over 25,000 diners in a year. By contrast a pop-up restaurant in a Parisian apartment may have only four covers and offer five evening services in one week thus having a capacity of twenty diners in total maybe for the whole year. It is therefore a much rarer commodity or experience than the luxury restaurant. Does this make it more of a 'luxury' experience?

Pop-up restaurants are not new, having been seen in Cuba and the USA for several decades, but they are now a worldwide phenomenon, having become popular in the UK and Australia over the past twenty years. They thrive because their availability can be instantly communicated by social media and they seem to be part of the trend towards new hospitality businesses in the informal economy in the same way that Airbnb has grown dramatically. Yet, now even some young formally trained chefs are using pop-up restaurants as a way of getting noticed without needing to have the money to invest in a large permanent restaurant.

Most pop-up restaurants are used as a means of making money or even a livelihood. However, in Finland, 'Restaurant Day' invites ordinary citizens to put up their own food outlets for a single day, simply to celebrate the pleasures of eating and drinking. This has now spread worldwide and has taken places in countries as diverse as Austria, Brazil, Mozambique, Kazakhstan, Russia, and Thailand.

In London, the pop-up scene is very strong and some permanent restaurants are even closing and re-opening as pop-up restaurants. And chefs can organise a pop-up even within a hotel or in an existing restaurant, on evenings when the 'traditional' restaurant is closed! Perhaps the risk is that the conventional restaurateurs will jump on this bandwagon in the same way that big hotel brands did with the idea of 'boutique hotels', and in doing so totally corrupt the original ethos of the pop-up restaurant phenomenon.

Already the mainstream travel media has recognised this phenomenon; in 2015, for example, Fodor's published a list of its 'can't miss' pop-up restaurants across North America.

Alongside the rise of the pop up restaurant we have seen the emergence of another trendy form of gastronomy, so-called 'street food'. This was once cheap food that tourists were warned off for hygiene reasons. Now in cities around the world it is chic and not always cheap. This is not the mass market food of the hawker carts but rather creations inspired by street food traditions and may even be served in an indoor restaurant made to resemble the environment of a street.

We are also seeing the rise of 'food trucks' – the ultimate in pop-up and street food – where a truck parks and dispenses food and drink. At many festivals and in city centres, this can increasingly be of a high standard and premium priced.

The trends we have been discussing are all linked in my mind, and partly reflect some level of dissatisfaction with traditional upscale gastronomic restaurants amongst some consumers. They are seeking new experiences that are unique or at least rare and which perhaps have advantages over more traditional restaurants. This may be the chance to enjoy good food in an informal service environment and have social interaction with fellow diners, unlike those restaurants which can be as silent as a church as people seem to be worshipping what is on their plate. Pop-up restaurants and street food do not just appeal to those on lower incomes; indeed they seem particularly popular with those who dine out regularly and want new experiences. Such restaurants may tempt affluent diners to visit parts of cities they would not normally visit, as they are often located in less fashionable neighbourhoods.

I believe that this phenomenon may be an interesting illustration of how the meaning of luxury is changing in hospitality, as these are experiences which are certainly limited in supply and often highly fashionable, yet they have none of the trappings of traditional gastronomic restaurants and the food is usually far more important than the décor or service. They are often seen positively as authentic and 'real' in contrast to the perceived 'artificial and contrived' atmosphere of more traditional restaurants.

Case study 11: Luxury in the air – beyond traditional first class

We have already noted in this text that most airlines invest heavily in the cabins at the front of the aeroplane, both business class and, if they are long-haul operators, first class. Though the number of seats in these cabins may represent a small proportion of the total capacity of the aircraft they will contribute a considerable proportion of the revenue on any given flight.

The quality and facilities in the premium cabins on an airliner have become an important part of differentiating one carrier from another. However, the challenge is that a major multi-million dollar investment may only give an airline a competitive advantage for a matter of months, before a competitor copies or even exceeds the specification of the airline's latest cabin design.

Comparison websites abound which allow travellers to compare premium cabins in a few seconds and frequent travellers, the basis of an airline's financial success, are most likely to use such sites.

In recent years, great attention has been paid to tangible elements of premium products such as seats that convert into flat beds, food and wine, at-seat technology and entertainment systems. Even in first class cabins, until now you were still sharing a space with other people, relying on partitions for privacy. Yet in the past year or two that has changed on some long-haul routes, with airlines now offering 'suites' – airborne hotel rooms in which the traveller has complete privacy. Anyone who knows the history of air travel will recognise this phenomenon from the 'golden age of air travel' when air travel was for the few and many flights had something akin to the suite mentioned above. However, today, of course, the accommodation is high tech but is still trying to recreate the time when air travel was a 'special experience'

One of the world's finest carriers, Singapore Airlines has introduced 'Singapore Suites' in addition to a more familiar first class service, which means it has five different classes of product. Each cabin has its own sliding doors and a standalone bed which is separate from the seat. The suites and the individual cabins within them have, interestingly, been designed by a leading luxury yacht designer. As in a hotel there is a turndown service for the bed and a large table in the suite converts into a dining table. If couples are travelling together adjacent suites can be converted into what becomes a double room.

It goes without saying that everything else is exceptional in terms of the experience with meals designed by famous chefs and served on Wedgwood china. The entertainment system has over 1,000 channels and a 23 inch personal LCD with noise-cancelling headphones.

The suites are currently available on a few selected routes, and on A380-800 aircraft and where suites are available, no first class product is offered. The seat plan on the company website indicates that on flights where suites are available there are 12 of them on board.

Another leading carrier, Emirates Airlines, also offers a suite product on board A380 and B777 flights. Again, a sliding door ensures privacy and there is controllable ambient lighting and a full bed as well as a vanity table and mirror. In addition to the suite, passengers are invited to enjoy the on-board 'shower spa' and 2,500 channels of entertainment. Top brand toiletries by Bulgari and designer sleepwear are provided along with first class cuisine, this time served on Royal Doulton china. Interestingly, here the privacy of your suite is set alongside the opportunity to socialise in the A380 onboard lounge. It is as if airlines are creating a full hotel experience in the sky, in a hotel that is moving at some 800 kilometres per hour!

But this experience comes at a price. On a day in October I used the airline's own websites to find prices at random for a journey early in 2018. Singapore Airlines had a first class return in a suite from London to Singapore at a little over £7000; the equivalent business class ticket on the same flight was priced at £3,440, half the price of the suite while economy was less than ten per cent of the suite ticket price. Meanwhile, on Emirates, the first class return ticket on flight with suites from London to Dubai was priced at £4,100 compared to £2,236 for a business class ticket on the same flight.

The question now must be, where do we go from here? Have we gone as far as we can with on-board beds, suites, cabins and so on? Probably not but there must be limits. Or is the next step simply private charter flights which are discussed in a separate case study? Or will it be slower aeroplanes or even airships with luxury facilities but flying slowly so you can enjoy the whole experience at a relaxing pace? Slow air travel!

Case study 12: Luxury is not having to share – the private aircraft charter market

As we have seen in this book, airlines around the world have worked extremely hard and invested millions of dollars to attract the lucrative luxury market to their first class and business class cabins. The result has been flat beds, sumptuous meals, and limousine transfers to the airport. However, even such privileged passengers have to share the airport and the aircraft with other people – total strangers. Unless one buys every seat in the cabin, sharing is a fact of life and can cause dissatisfaction if your fellow passengers are noisy or badly behaved. And regardless of how much your ticket cost you still have to leave on a date and time fixed by the airline.

In a world where time, convenience and privacy are increasingly valued commodities, it is not surprising that there has been an upsurge in interest in chartering aircraft for exclusive personal use. This sector has been booming around the world in recent years with leisure as well as business customers. Not only can the traveller choose the date and time of travel but charters can often be operated from smaller airfields and airports which are easy and quick to use.

Charters can be arranged for all kinds of aircraft from small four seat propeller driven aircraft to large commercial airliners such as the Boeing 737 and the Airbus A320. I looked at the prices for chartering an aircraft with several operators in October 2017 and found the following typical prices:

- London to Nice in a six seater aircraft – €14,000
- Paris to Geneva in a four seater aircraft – €4,700
- Boston to New York in an eight seat aircraft – €5,500
- London to Dubai in a ten seat aircraft – €70,000
- New York to Geneva in a twelve seater aircraft – €88,000

All journeys were returns, usually based on next day return, but it must be stressed that these are published sample prices. A wide range of variables affect actual prices including length of stay, empty legs to be flown and negotiation, of course. On the same day I sought available fares for the same routes and collected the following random examples:

- London to Nice return in business class for six seats – €2,600
- Paris to Geneva return in business class for four seats – €1,800
- London to Dubai return in first class for ten seats – €45,000
- New York to Geneva return in business class for twelve seats – €79,000

However, it must be noted that this was not a scientifically conducted experiment but, if we take New York to Geneva for example, private charter can be quite competitive price-wise. The competitiveness will depend on factors such as timings, number of passengers, route and so on, but it is interesting.

Any extra cost may be compensated for, not just by convenience but also by the quality of the aircraft interiors, meals and service. Many of the larger aircraft will have a kitchen facility and cabin crew are trained to a very high standard in terms of personal service.

Given many people only need to travel from time to time, air charter is clearly a more cost effective option than buying your own aircraft, which is best left to that tiny group, the mega-rich. Leaving aside the cost of purchase, the maintenance costs of a small corporate jet can run into more than a million dollars per annum!

The rise of private air charter has also led to the development of specialist infrastructure where the emphasis is on quality and convenience. In the UK, for example, London Luton airport has developed a reputation has an outstanding facility for private air charter traffic as well as for general business aviation. The operator Signature provides high quality facilities and services including a champagne and cocktails, 'snooze room' on-site customs and immigration, VIP suite, and a wide range of services for the pilots themselves.

The tourism industry has also shown an interest in using privately chartered, luxuriously fitted out aircraft to offer 'air cruises' around the world with lead in prices well in excess of $150,000 from one operator. Interestingly their first seven cruises in 2017 and 2018 were cancelled. However, according to an article by Jeri Clausing in *Travel Weekly* in June 2017, operator Abercrombie and Kent is still planning to run at least two such cruises each year. Speaking of these cruises Geoffrey Kent from the company is quoted as saying *"we believe their smaller size (no more than 50 guests) is key ....the jet makes it possible to fly directly from one remote destination to the next, with no connections, and on our own schedule not an airline's timetable"* (www.travelweekly.com/Luxury-Travel/Insights/Can-air-cruises-be-successful).

I believe that over time, as the number of people with disposable income grows worldwide and as air travel becomes more frustrating, because of airport congestion and security checks, private charter will become more widely used by travellers.

Case study 13: Luxury rail journeys around the world

For most people train travel is simply a way of getting from one place to another and for some it is even the means of transport for their daily commute from home to work. However, there is a long history of glamorous train journeys dating back to the days when travel was the preserve of the privileged few. The legendary *Orient Express* is perhaps the most famous of these famous trains but it was by no means the only one.

In recent years we have seen a rapid growth in luxury rail experiences around the world for a variety of reasons including:

■ The desire of some tourists to see more of the scenery than is possible from an aeroplane and to feel part of the landscape they are passing through.

■ The recognition of a business opportunity by entrepreneurs.

■ The desire of some destination management organisations to exploit their railway heritage as a way of attracting new high spending markets.

■ The wish of some destination governments to gain greater revenue from their rail networks.

■ The rise of rail tour operators who have stimulated this form of leisure travel.

Many of the luxury rail journeys have their roots in history because the railways they feature either date from the era of colonialism – such as in India – or were instrumental in opening up new frontiers of settlement as in the USA and Australia.

Instead of being a means of transport alone the luxury train becomes a hotel on wheels, a moving resort complex. Cruise ships make stops at ports where guests disembark and explore, and similarly, some trains make stops where guests may take a local excursion. But in other cases passengers rarely if ever disembark from the train and the destination is experienced through a carriage window. Unlike a ship, where passengers can feel the sea breeze on their face and sunbathe on deck a luxury rail passenger may be wholly isolated from the climate for the whole trip.

In another way the train becomes like an olden day upper class party in a country mansion, albeit with a less select guest list perhaps, the kind of event so beloved of British mystery writers such as Agatha Christie, as setting for a murder. It is therefore no surprise that one of her most famous novels was set on a train – *Murder on the Orient Express*.

Until the rapid growth in international tourism from the 1970s, luxury trains looked obsolete, remnants of a past that was gone forever. However, with the rise in international tourists they were given a new lease of life and every year seems to see the introduction of yet another luxury train somewhere in the world.

The following short list will give the reader an idea of the variety of luxury rail vacations on offer today:

- The *Maharaja Express,* a train that unashamedly harks back to a previous age in India, offers itineraries of generally three to eight nights' duration. Prices for seven nights start from around £6,000.

- The *Ghan* in Australia, a journey of nearly 3,000 kilometres from Adelaide to Darwin that takes three nights and takes travellers across the heart of Australia through iconic places like Alice Springs. Single fares in a twin cabin in 2017-18 started at AU$2,119 (approximately £1,250) in the low season rising to AU$3,499 (approximately £2,000) in the peak season.

- The *Eastern and Oriental,* which runs from Singapore through Malaysia to Bangkok, has strong reminders of colonial days in its décor. A two day trip from Singapore to Bangkok in 2017-18 had prices beginning at around US$3,250 (approximately £2,500).

- The *Pride of Africa Rovos* makes the two night journey from Cape Town to Pretoria with prices starting in 2017-18 from SAR19,000 (approximately £1,000).

These trains have become famous brands in their own right and onboard services and facilities match those of a high end hotel, with a particular emphasis on gastronomic meals and socialising in the bar. Some have observation cars, with lots more glass than usual, to enhance the sightseeing opportunities for passengers.

An infrastructure of specialist operators and intermediaries has grown up to support this sector including a membership organisation for enthusiastic rail travellers called the Luxury Train Club.

However, there is another type of rail experience where the luxury is in the rarity value of the experience rather than the price and level of service and facilities. There are railways that attract enthusiasts in search of the so-called 'great rail journeys of the world'. These include the Trans-Siberian Express in Russia, the 'hill trains' of India, the train from Colombo to the 'hill country' in Sri Lanka and trips on steam trains in various counties.

Case study 14: Selling luxury – the new operators and intermediaries

To those with a traditional mind-set the very idea of 'selling luxury' would appear vulgar and inappropriate. They would believe that those who were in that market would know what was available and would just need somebody to undertake the mundane task of simply making the bookings. However, in a world where many aspire to enter the market and be seen as luxury consumers, there is a great opportunity for smart entrepreneurs to develop a successful business 'selling luxury'.

In some ways their role appears to involve helping these would-be luxury travellers define what the term 'luxury' means today, as well as meeting the desires of those for whom luxury is a reality every day of their lives, not just when choosing a vacation. These newer operators and intermediaries have embraced the rise of the Internet, mobile devices and social media and use all of them in their marketing. Let us now look at two interesting examples of such operators and intermediaries working within the UK market today.

True Luxury Travel concentrates on vacations to Africa and Asia and on the company website the founder, Henry Morley, explains the philosophy of the company as follows:

> Having spent 15 years both travelling and working throughout Africa and Asia, it is fair to say I have a deep rooted passion for exploring new counties and new cultures! When I founded True Luxury Travel I wanted to share those treasured experiences. (Henry Morley, ww.trueluxury.travel/about-us)

Their website goes on to say:

> Our team have unrivalled have unrivalled knowledge of their destinations simply because they visit them so often, which surprisingly is a rarity within our industry. Unlike so many tour operators, we are not driven by sending clients to the wrong places in order to make a sale. Instead we utilise that expert knowledge, to create tailor-made holidays with the aim of exceeding our client's expectations. (www.true.luxury.travel/about-us)

I find both extracts from the company website interesting. First, the founder is seeking to create empathy with prospective customers by talking about his own travel experiences and his desire to help consumers enjoy the same quality of experiences as he himself has had. Second, there is some criticism of other players within the industry, which is not something one often sees so clearly amongst longer established operators. A clear attempt is being made to differentiate this operator from other operators. And, of course, the company name itself is interesting, suggesting that their might be some 'fake luxury travel' around and seeking to reassure consumers that what they offer is the 'real thing'.

The website lists a number of concrete reasons for booking through them including: transparent pricing: independent guest reviews; 24 hour a day support; 'blank paper bespoke, no off the shelf itineraries, and 100% financial protection.

Secret Escapes is a high profile intermediary which runs major television advertising campaigns in the UK, suggesting it is aiming for a market wider than those who traditionally see themselves as high spending travellers. Indeed the reason why an expensive television campaign makes sense is that Secret Escapes is all about offering luxury hotels and holidays in the UK and internationally at discounted prices. It is thus targeting those with money who still want to think they can pay less, but it is also focusing on those who would love to be luxury consumers but may feel it is beyond their financial means. The company website promises hand-picked luxury hotels and holidays at up to 70% off the normal rate. These deals are open to anyone prepared to give the company their email address. The company emphasises that all hotels and spas are 'hand-picked' and that the great prices are a result of their negotiating directly with the supplier.

Their advertising tag line, 'welcome to the worst kept secret in luxury travel' gives the consumer the impression that they are being let into a world they would not normally know about, an attractive prospect for pretty well every human being; we all enjoy being let in on a secret.

The most fascinating thing about Secret Escapes is that its only *raison d'être* is the discounting of luxury, which is anathema to traditionalists who believe true luxury is defined as 'if you have to ask the price you cannot afford it' . Yet Secret Escapes takes the opposite view saying always ask the price and then when you know it come to us and well will get it for you at a much lower price.

Case study 15: The meaning of luxury and the events sector

The events sector is a very broad sector that is united only by the fact that it is concerned with the management of temporary happenings. In such a diverse sector there are many ways of looking at luxury, but let us just identify a few of them.

A wedding can be seen as a luxury event because, in many it is something people only do once in their life and for the family or families concerned the cost of a wedding may represent one of the largest outlays of money they ever make. However, there are cultural issues involved in this market and there is a huge difference in scale between a wedding say in India and one in the UK. The 'honeymoon' itself is often a luxury trip, a once-in-a-lifetime experience, that is seen as an integral part of getting married in many societies.

Many music concerts these days have started to develop the idea of offering a luxury dimension to the event through opportunities to purchase 'meet and greet' or 'VIP backstage pass' experiences. Here the luxury element comes in the form of the opportunity to meet the artist and maybe see behind the scenes of the concert. The development of such packages is based on the desire of promoters to 'upsell' and increase their revenue beyond ticket sales. They are offering fans a chance for an enhanced experience beyond that of most people attending the same concert.

In the sporting field one side of luxury has been the growth of corporate hospitality where companies buy packages from organisers or venues that include the best seats in the venue plus high end hospitality services. Companies often use these packages to reward existing customers or go after new business. It is controversial too as often these guests will not even see the event as they will be eating and drinking while true fans are unable to get a ticket because they are sold out, partly to these corporate hospitality clients.

There are also some sporting events that appear to be luxury almost by definition or their very nature. For example, in the UK there are a set of events which are often seen as luxurious because of either the sport itself or where the event occurs. This could include the Oxford and Cambridge Boat Race and Henley Regatta in the UK, or equestrian events which take place in the grounds of stately homes owned by aristocratic families.

Some events may appear to be part of a luxury lifestyle simply because of the price of tickets. Or the remoteness of the location may mean the cost of attending will be beyond the means of most spectators. In other cases tickets are difficult to obtain unless one has 'connections', introducing an element of exclusivity to the event.

If rarity and exclusivity are accepted criteria for the concept of luxury then luxury events do not need to mean expensive ticketed events; indeed attendance might be free. This applies to those tourists who have the opportunity to attend traditional community events while visiting a country, such as a traditional funeral in Sulawesi, or a religious event in Thailand. The visitor may not always be welcome but being there gives them experiences that very few others have.

So far we have focused on the consumer as a spectator, but perhaps the greatest luxury in some events is the opportunity to be a participant rather than merely a spectator. That could mean something as joining in a sing-song in a pub in Ireland or the bull-running in Pamplona. In these cases the nature of the event is less important than the fact that the traveller was able to join in something only reserved for 'local' people, thus gaining memories that few if any of their friends and neighbours have. And these memories can be shared via social media thus further raising the status of the traveller

Finally, events can also be set in a wider context of tourism and hospitality, and the meaning of luxury, including:

■ Specialist tour operators who organise high end tours which focus on specific events such as opera festivals around the world.

■ The accommodation operators who earn a significant proportion of their revenue from hosting wedding parties and major conferences.

■ Certain food and beverage experiences associated with particular events such as eating strawberries at the Wimbledon tennis tournament in London.

Case study 16: Islands of luxury in the Caribbean and the Indian Ocean

Throughout history travellers have felt there was something special about islands, something that set them apart from those countries with a physical attachment to a land mass. They were seen as romantic and exotic, places to escape from the pressures of everyday life. The fact that visiting them required a sea trip may also have added to their appeal and certainly to their feeling of being places that were 'out of the ordinary'. Late 19th and early 20th century writers and artists created images of Bali and Tahiti which have endured to the present day, even though they may never have been a true representation of reality.

In the modern era of mass international tourism it seems as if islands still exercise a major appeal for tourists whether it be the holiday islands of the Mediterranean and the Aegean or the playgrounds of Sentosa and Hainan in Asia.

However, islands also seem to figure disproportionately heavily in most surveys of destinations that are perceived to be 'luxurious'. And in such surveys it is not just any islands, but the islands of the Caribbean and the Indian Ocean that seem to dominate the resulting lists. Let us now look at both regions in a little more detail, starting with the Caribbean.

The Caribbean

From the beginning, tourists have been drawn to the Caribbean by a mixture of the stunning beaches and the perceived 'laid back' culture. In some parts of the region islands, such as the British Virgin Islands and the Cayman Islands have doubled as 'tax havens' and tourist destinations, with the former naturally lending a flavour of luxury to their appeal. At the same time celebrities have endorsed certain islands, again lending them a luxury air by so doing. This includes in the past, the UK's Princess Margaret and Mustique, and Ernest Hemingway with Cuba, to today's stars of music and the movies who both vacation and buy property on various islands. International airline boss, Sir Richard Branson even owns his own complete island in the Caribbean, Necker Island. Interestingly different countries view the Caribbean in different ways and historical and linguistic links also play a role in attitudes towards the image of different islands. For Americans, Cuba represents the glamour of the past while Bermuda and the American Virgin Islands are high end destinations, together with Puerto Rico which is actually an unincorporated US territory. The British Virgin Islands and the Cayman Islands rate highly for luxury, along with parts of other islands such as Barbados, Anguilla and St Lucia. Dutch travellers tend to visit islands in the Dutch Antilles such as Bonaire, while French travellers focus upon Martinique and St Barthélemy. Interestingly nationals of both countries like the island which both countries share, St Martin/Sint Maarten. The Caribbean islands also gained something of a luxury reputation through being the place which saw the birth of the luxury all-inclusive market, particularly through the Sandals brand.

The Indian Ocean

The Indian Ocean offers an interesting contrast. It is a much larger geographical area, some 70 million square kilometres compared to just under 3 million for the Caribbean. Tourism in the region developed later than that of the Caribbean and many of the smaller islands still have little tourism development; indeed most people would be unable to recognise their names. This chronology of development may have something to do with geography. The Caribbean is close to the USA as well as being well known to Europeans from the age of colonialism, while the Indian Ocean islands are accessible to the Asian travel markets which emerged later than those of North America. Again their development was first based on their exceptional natural beauty and their amazing beaches. There are archipelagos such as the Maldives where the islands are so tiny that each one is only large enough to sustain a single resort. This creates its own sense of luxury based on exclusivity. The government of the Seychelles has pursued a strategy of positioning itself as a luxury destination to make the most money from a sustainable level of tourism. Mauritius has exploited its position to attract upscale African tourists and property buyers as well as Europeans and Asians. Meanwhile Madagascar has achieved a reputation as the most exciting place for serious nature watchers; its 'luxury' attribute is its unique biodiversity.

Both parts of the world may share some interesting characteristics as destinations including:

- Both regions are largely dependent on foreign tour operators, cruise companies and airlines for their flow of tourists.

- Destinations in both are particularly vulnerable to devastating natural disasters that can decimate a tourism industry for months, e.g. the hurricanes seen in the Caribbean in autumn 2017 and the tsunami in the Indian Ocean in 2004.

- Most islands have a high level of dependence on tourism and relatively few alternative industries to help them diversify their economies.

- Prices will always be high because of the cost of transport for the goods and services needed by tourists, which means focusing on the luxury market may be their only real option.

There is one final twist in the Indian Ocean, where climate change threatens the very existence of the low-lying Maldives. Some are beginning to take the view that visiting these islands is a case of 'see it while you still can!' 'Luxury' in this case may simply mean the survival of the islands!

Case study 17: Can anything be seen as luxury – the case of camping?

Until recently there seemed to be relatively clear demarcation lines about what constituted luxury in tourism and hospitality. In terms of accommodation, luxury largely meant grand hotels with lots of facilities and exceptional service, usually in impressive locations. However, this whole book has been about how traditional meanings of luxury are changing as a result of a wide range of factors.

Earlier in the book we noted that luxury accommodation can also include bed-and-breakfasts, homestays and Airbnb apartments, which are by and large not run by trained hospitality professionals. We noted that this could be seen as luxury, sometimes in terms of issues such as authenticity and personalisation of the service. However, at least these newer forms of accommodation have walls and a roof in common with traditional hotels.

A clear idea that has been suggested in this book has been the desire of industry to put the label 'luxury' on all kinds of products and services because they know that this word helps sell anything.

One activity that – until recently at least – had never been described as luxurious was camping but all that has now changed apparently. A Google search of the term 'luxury camping' one afternoon in October 2017 produced no fewer than 17 million results in less than a second! A quick scan of the first few pages of results indicated that the idea of 'luxury camping' was well established – at least in the minds of industry marketers – in places as diverse as Australia and France, Brazil and Iceland. And it seems as if consumers are buying in to this idea that camping can have a luxury dimension if the number of 'luxury camping' products on the market is any indication.

The Google search also revealed a new word being used to suggest a more luxurious form of camping, *glamping*, a combination of the words 'glamour' and 'camping'. This fascinates me has I have never had any experience of camping that could have been described as glamorous!

The Internet has plenty of definitions of *glamping* including the following:

'a form of camping involving accommodation and facilities more luxurious than those associated with traditional camping.' (https:/en.Oxforddictionaries.com/definition/glamping)

'the activity of camping with some of the comforts of home' (www.dictionary.com/browse/glamping)

Another definition suggested it was not something ' *done by usual outdoor types who climb mountains ….Glamping is camping feminine style'* (www.urbandiction-nary.com/define.php?term=glamping)

Leaving aside the last of these definitions which is overtly sexist, the picture seems quite clear. So what does glamping look like in practice? It takes many forms but could include:

- Alternatives to traditional tents such as 'yurts', tipis, or 'geodisic pods' that are rather more substantial than a traditional tent as well as treehouses and mobile shepherds huts
- Tents which have carpets, sofas and even en-suite facilities within the tent unit itself
- Meals prepared by professional chefs delivered directly to the tent
- Solar powered lights and USB outlets for recharging electronic devices
- King size bed with high spec mattress
- Wood burning stove

In the African safari market, glamping has taken off due to the desire of people to go on safaris, but with as many home comforts as possible. The growth of glamping in this market also partly reflects the lack of capacity in the more traditional forms of accommodation in the wildlife reserves. There are luxury hotels at very high prices certainly, but usually not much else available for those on a more constrained budget who still want to take a safari. And, of course, the argument is that camping gets you closer to nature than sleeping in a normal hotel or lodge would. Safari glamping comes at a high price because of its exclusivity value and because of the logistical challenges, but some of the tented camps certainly sound luxurious with private plunge pools, spa treatments and even four poster beds.

Furthermore attempts are made to differentiate tented camps by key themes whether that be a 'green' eco vibe or a 1920s age of elegance theme, an era when tented safari camps were fashionable amongst the rich. Yet again, after a suitable time lapse, history starts to repeat itself after a fashion.

So what does the rise of glamping tell us about how the meaning of luxury is changing. I believe it reinforces a point made elsewhere in the book, namely that luxury is a relative term rather than an absolute. On that basis any aspect of the tourism and hospitality offer can have a luxury dimension if it simply offers significantly more quality and facilities than the norm.

In the specific case of camping I would like to suggest that the growing popularity of glamping in general is also due to other factors, such as the interest of the urban middle classes in rediscovering nature and the desire for what is perceived to be a slow paced 'simple life' in contrast to the stresses of daily life in the city.

Case study 18: The luxury of time - are gap years the new Grand Tour?

As we noted in Chapter 2, the 'Grand Tour' was the name given to a rite of passage for the privileged upper class, particularly in the UK, in the 18th and 19th centuries. These people travelled around the 'classical' sites of Europe, particularly in Italy and Greece, visiting centres of artistic heritage and archaeological sites. Their travels could last months, if not several years, and the 'souvenirs' they brought back from their trips consisted of artistic treasures which now represent the most valued exhibits in countless museums and stately or aristocratic homes.

Apart from wealth, the thing which everyone needed to take the 'Grand tour' was plenty of leisure time, so it was the preserve in its early days of what were termed the 'idle rich' – those with inherited wealth who did not work for a living.

A rather diluted form of the 'Grand Tour' developed amongst the urban middle classes during the 19th century, and then as the aristocracy declined and modern industrial society developed these long self-indulgent sojourns declined. A similar trend was seen in terms of the decline in round-the-world cruises and other travel which took months or even years, rather than days and weeks.

However, in a number of developed and recently developed countries a new version of the 'Grand Tour' began to emerge from the 1960s – the 'gap year'. This involved young people taking a year off either between school and university or between university and their first job. This market was stimulated by a rapid growth in young people entering higher education who were looking for a marker to show they were moving from one phase of life to another. It became a rite of passage, a last period of freedom before dcades of responsibilities and hard work.

It is no coincidence that this occurred during the 1960s and 1970s, an era of great social change when the younger generation began to be given more freedom. They were experimenting with drugs, different religions and music from around the world which increased their desire to travel. It was also the era in which travel was becoming democratised with falling prices. The world was opening up and travel was escapism without the shadow of terrorism. Countries such as Iraq and Afghanistan, that today are seen as dangerous, were then safe to visit. Popular gap year routes quickly developed, often involving Europeans travelling east through Asia, Australians and New Zealanders travelling west through Asia to Europe and North Americans spending months travelling in both Europe and Asia.

These routes became highly popular with travellers often using the same hotels, restaurants and beaches as they almost all carried the same guide books such as *Lonely Planet* and *Rough Guides,* which both fuelled and reflected the rise of gap year travel.

In the late 19th centuries the sons of rich British families often visited Paris to complete their passage to adulthood by indulging in hedonistic activities that would have been frowned upon at home. The modern gap year is similar to this in that it has its places where young men – and now young women too – can go to behave in ways that might be illegal or frowned upon in their own countries, involving casual sex, heavy drinking, drugs and so on. Certain places have achieved cult status with gap year travellers whether it is the New Moon parties on the beaches of Goa in India or the hostess bars of Thailand. Young tourists get a vicarious, voyeuristic pleasure from observing as well as perhaps being participants in these activities. In many ways, for northern Europeans at least, this is not so different to what they do on their ordinary vacations, such as a visit to the red light district in Amsterdam on a weekend break to a hedonistic week on a 'party island' in the Mediterranean.

In the harsh modern world of youth unemployment there may be implicit pressure on some young people to forgo a gap year in favour of getting on the career ladder, but gap years remain highly popular. And now we see more and more young people from emerging tourism markets entering the gap year market.

One major difference between the Grand Tour and the gap year markets today relates to how they remember and record their experiences. The Grand Tour was characterised by buying souvenirs, often on an epic scale, keeping diaries and painting watercolours of the places they visited. Today's travellers, taking advantage of technological advances, tend to buy few material possessions as they are usually travelling light. Instead they use their mobile devices to take copious photos which they share with the world via social media.

The gap year market also differs from the Grand Tour in levels of spending, with generally low spending per day, with the aim of living cheaply so as to extend the amount of time that the traveller can be 'on the road'.

Currently, there are two particularly interesting trends taking place in the gap year market:

- Many gap year travellers are spending all or part of their 'year' volunteering, doing unpaid voluntary work, either for altruistic reasons or because they have been told this will impress future employers. There are now companies who act almost like tour operators offering such experiences, often at high prices! There has been criticism of many of the projects gap year travellers have worked on, saying they were of little value and were more about massaging the ego of the traveller and giving them stories to tell back home.

- A growing number of older people are taking gap years either between jobs or more often at the end of their careers between work and retirement. There seems a desire to mark the passage between these stages in life by making a major trip which might include a round-the-world cruise or overland travel.

This is a major trend which may be adversely affected if the predictions come true of those who suggest that future generations will need to work until they are older and older because of the challenges in meeting state pension payments faced by governments around the world.

Whatever form the gap year takes it is based on the idea of time as a luxury commodity, and the modern version is often taken by those who are not rich but who can make a limited budget last a long time by visiting poor countries, and who may be working along the way when they need money. Or they may be relying on parental subsidies transmitted to them as they travel around the globe

Case study 19: The luxury of time – the 'slow travel' movement

In a number of places in this book I have suggested that free time is becoming a luxury commodity for many people in a modern world, where the pace of life appears to be increasing and people claim they are busier than ever. Therefore, it is interesting to see the beginnings of a 'slow travel' concept following on from the 'slow food' movement which has gained ground in many countries in recent years.

So what is slow travel? Here are two definitions:

Slow travel is not so much a particular mode of transportation, as it is a mind-set. Rather than attempting to squeeze as many sights or cities as possible into each trip, the slow traveller takes the time to explore each destination thoroughly and to experience the local culture.

(Independent Traveler/www.smartertravel.com/2017/06/19/art-slow-travel)

Slow travel is a mindset that rejects traditional ideas of tourism and encourages you to soak in your environments and keep yourself open to new experiences

(www.theartofslowtravel.com/what-is-slow-travel)

It certainly seems to have grown in popularity, as a Google search of the term in September 2017 produced no fewer than just under 30 million results! Everywhere there are people and organisations defining the terms and exploring what it might mean for tourism.

Hilary Gardener, quoted on the hiddeneurope.co.uk website talks of a 'manifesto for slow travel, and suggests that:

Slow travel is about making conscious choices…it is about deceleration not speed. The journey becomes a moment to relax rather than a stressful interlude imposed between home and destination. Slow travel re-engineers time, transforming it into a commodity of abundance rather than scarcity.

(www.hiddeneurope.co.uk/a-manifesto-for-slow-travel).

An organisation based in Barcelona makes an interesting distinction between two types of slow travellers, "there are those who try to slow down as much as possible the journey they take and there are those who focus more on the destination they're visiting" (www.barcelonaslowtravel.com/slow-travel). They clearly see these as two discrete groups and do not suggest any links between them. They then go on to suggest five good reasons to adopt slow travel as follows:

- relax, re-charge your batteries and improve your health

- empower (the) local economy wherever you travel

- leave a positive footprint and contribute to preserving the environment

- become part of local life

- get unique memories and even often life changing experiences

(www.barcelonaslowtravel.com/slow-travel)

These few random quotes suggest that slow travel is quite a complex idea. First, it seems to be about benefits for both the traveller and the destination. Second, it appears to be about more than just time, and seems to embrace ideas from responsible tourism and value authenticity. It seems to be a movement rooted in the northern hemisphere amongst those countries which have been major generators of outbound tourism longest.

At its simplest it can be applied to any type of vacation even a weekend city break; it is about how time is spent in the destination, perhaps, than about the amount of time spent in the destination. But I recognise that the nature of the journey to the destination does seem central to some views of slow travel, so it may certainly have implications for the transport sector. Perhaps this is easier to put into practice in relation to domestic and short-haul rather than long-haul travel. You can substitute train for air from Amsterdam to Paris, and bicycles can replace the car on a short domestic trip. For its annual vacation in rural France, a German family can hire a horse-drawn mobile home or a river cruiser. However, the only realistic way for 99% of Europeans to take a trip to Asia is by air unless they are 'time-rich' and can afford the time and money to travel overland or taking part of a world cruise.

Perhaps, ultimately, slow travel is more about encouraging people to vacation nearer to their homes, which would clearly be beneficial in terms of the environment, but would be a major problem for destinations that rely heavily on long-haul travellers.

Case study 20: Second homes – the ultimate luxury?

In a world where many people struggle to find a place to live and many are homeless, it seems ironic that the world is experiencing strong growth in the ownership of second homes, a luxury that no one actually needs but many aspire to possess.

I would contend that the link between tourism and second homes is obviously a strong one, as most people choose to buy one in a place previously visited on vacation. However, there are some interesting points to be made about second home ownership in the context of luxury in tourism and hospitality.

The first point is that we can perhaps produce a typology of second homes that might be interesting. This diagram shows that both the supply and demand sides of second homes are complex and highly diverse. Not all are at a luxury price level either.

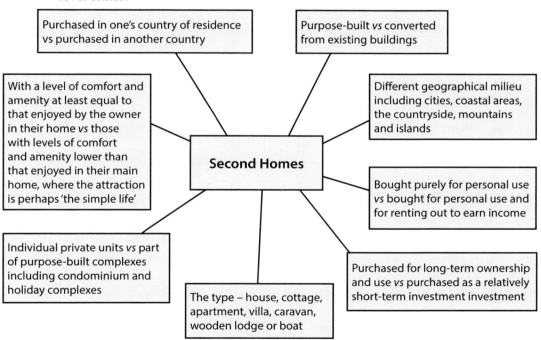

Purchased in one's country of residence vs purchased in another country

Purpose-built *vs* converted from existing buildings

With a level of comfort and amenity at least equal to that enjoyed by the owner in their home *vs* those with levels of comfort and amenity lower than that enjoyed in their main home, where the attraction is perhaps 'the simple life'

Different geographical milieu including cities, coastal areas, the countryside, mountains and islands

Second Homes

Bought purely for personal use *vs* bought for personal use and for renting out to earn income

Individual private units *vs* part of purpose-built complexes including condominium and holiday complexes

Purchased for long-term ownership and use *vs* purchased as a relatively short-term investment investment

The type – house, cottage, apartment, villa, caravan, wooden lodge or boat

Table 1 shows levels of second home ownership amongst selected European countries. We can see that high ownership of second homes is not a function of levels of income alone. Greece has six times the level of second home ownership of Germany but an average income of less than half. This may be partly explained by the fact that many second homes in Mediterranean countries have been in existence for some time and are inherited by families; they often represent rural or coastal properties no longer required for permanent residence.

Table 1: Second home ownership in Europe. Source: RE/MAX Europa 2015

Country	Average monthly salary in Euro 2015	Percentage of population owning a second home
Greece	1064	32.8
Spain	1634	20.4
Czech Republic	795	19.2
Austria	2304	15.4
Italy	2022	15.2
Sweden	2617	11.8
France	2417	8.2
UK	2596	7.0
Germany	2609	5.4

Table 2 shows both the number of percentage of second homes found in the 'old' regions of France – 'old' as France has just redrawn and renamed its regions.

What this data shows is that second homes are a function of the level of tourism, the perceived attractiveness of the area and the cost of property, for instance. France is also interesting in that much of the demand comes from international buyers who tend to prefer rural locations while most French-owned second homes tend to be in coastal locations

Table 2: Second homes by region in France 2015. Source: French-Property.Com, INSEE, 2015

Region	Number of second homes	Percentage of total dwellings
Alsace	18.823	2.4
Aquitaine	169,425	11.6
Ile-de-France	149,775	3.0
Languedoc-Roussillon	249,134	20.9
Limousin	43,297	12.5
Nord-Pas-de-Calais	51,254	3.1
Provence-Alpes-Cotes D'Azur	377,015	17.3

Table 3 identifies the counties in the USA which have the highest number of second homes. Interestingly, apart from the top county, Maricopa, located in the warm 'winter sun belt' of Arizona, the other nine counties are largely or wholly coastal, and all but one are in the southern, warmest, half of the country, which have a long tradition of attracting northern 'snowbirds' who visit during the long northern winters.

Table 3: Counties in the USA with most second homes. Source:eyeonhousing.org/NAHB 2016

County	Number of second homes
Maricopa, Arizona	118,282
Palm Beach, Florida	98,627
Lee, Florida	93,152
Broward, Florida	92,907
Miami-Dade, Florida	88,940
Riverside, California	76,700
Pinellas, Florida	65,867
Barnstable, Massachusetts	62,317
Collier, Florida	61,905
Los Angeles, California	59,742

The majority of second homes featured in Tables 1, 2 and 3 will be domestically owned, but in terms of the luxury market what is perhaps most interesting is the international market. In recent years we have seen a trend in people from major outbound tourism markets buying property in other countries. If we look at the UK market this has tended to be dominated by purchases in Spain and France. But now the net is being cast far more widely, encouraged by tv shows and magazines such as *A Place in the Sun* and now includes the Eastern Europe, USA, Australia, India, Thailand, Malaysia, India, and Brazil. All of this has not happened without controversy, and major debates rage about how sustainable second home ownership is and even if it is morally acceptable. Let us look at some sides of this discussion

The Spanish government in the 1990s and early 2000s promoted the idea of 'residential tourism' and encouraged people to buy property in Spain as second or retirement homes. But when the economic downturn came prices crashed and coastal Spain was left with virtual 'ghost towns' – large-scale developments for which the market had evaporated.

The major attraction of foreign second home buyers in France is the abundance of inexpensive rural property which appears not to be wanted by the present generation of French people, who seem to prefer town or city living. Affluent foreigners buy up quaint rundown old properties and renovate them. The scale of this in some parts of France is huge, although often it exists alongside communities of foreigners who have moved to France permanently, often having been second home owners there for a while. Houses of second home owners are empty most of the year and bring no income to the area but one has to ask: would these houses otherwise be derelict, due to a lack of domestic market desire to live in the countryside?

In the UK where property prices are very high there is a particular problem with second homes. The most beautiful coastal areas and villages tend to be in more isolated, economically poorer parts of the country such as Cornwall. Second home ownership pushes the price of housing far beyond the reach of those born in the area, who often have to move out of their place of birth to afford somewhere to live. This understandably leads to resentment and attempts to restrict second home developments, such as was seen recently in the community of St ives.

As tourists are now able to travel easily around the world, owning a second home is no longer just an aspiration for the super rich. If one chooses a country with a low cost of living, second home ownership can come within the reach of mainstream middle class families. Even in some European countries a small holiday home can be purchased for less than a year's salary for a middle class professional in the UK, and mortgages are available to help spread the cost, and bring it down to a few hundred Euro per month.

However, there is no doubt that having more homes than you actually need, when many have none certainly seems like a luxury.

Case study 21: The luxury experience that can cost you your life – climbing Mount Everest

It was not until 1953 that Mount Everest was climbed for the first time; by the end of 2016 no fewer than 4,469 people had stood on the summit, some having done so on a number of occasions. Each season now between 600 and 700 people reach the top of the peak and on a single day more than 100 people can reach the highest point in the world. On such days photographs of Everest show something akin to a human traffic jam as people trudge wearily to the top to complete this unique experience.

For many years the only people who attempted to climb Everest were experienced mountaineers. However, in recent years we have seen the growth of commercial organisations who can help wealthy 'adventure tourists' to reach the summit, for a price. School-children and retired people are now regularly reaching the top of the peak.

Climbing Mount Everest qualifies as a luxury experience for three main reasons, as follows:

- Mount Everest is unique, because it is the highest point on Earth. Luxury is about exclusivity and rarity value and no-one can deny that Mount Everest represents both.

- Depending on whether one uses a local or foreign operator the average cost of summiting Everest is between $35,000 and $65,000.

- The average time taken to complete an ascent and come back down is around two months, so it is only available to those who can spare so much time.

However, what has begun to look like an industry rather than an individual challenge is not without its critics. The two main criticisms faced by commercial operators include the following:

- The overall environmental impact of mountaineering on Mount Everest, which include the carbon footprint of each tourist on their journey to the mountain range, the quantity of litter left behind by the climbing expeditions and the major sanitation issues caused by having so many people in such a remote location.

- The relatively low pay and poor working conditions of the Nepalese sherpas, the experienced local guides who are largely responsible for helping so many tourists to reach the summit. There have been some improvements recently in their situation but they still tend to have poorer equipment that the tourists and are expected to often risk their lives when a client gets into difficulties because of the client's lack of experience or inadequate fitness levels.

There have also been well publicised cases of mountaineers walking past injured or dying fellow climbers, either because of the risk to themselves of stopping to help, or maybe because of their focus on reaching the summit given that they will often have one only opportunity to do this before they need to descend.

By spring 2017 the total death toll on Mount Everest stood at just under 300; in the 50 years between 1922 and 1972, some 28 people died on the mountain. However, 32 died in two terrible avalanches in 2014 and 2015, while in 2012 and 2013, 20 died excluding avalanches.

An interesting recent development has been linking the ascent of Mount Everest to charity so the participant has to raise the money for their trip and also raise money for a chosen charity.

A quick search of the Internet in October 2017 found advertisements for at least eleven private companies offering Mount Everest summit experiences. Not surprisingly they focused on health and safety on their websites but also drew attention to other benefits of booking with them, such as wi-fi access at Base Camp.

For those unable to afford the time or money to make a summit bid on Mount Everest we have seen a massive growth in recent years of trekking trips to the Base Camp of Mount Everest. So participants walk to base camp, look at the mountain, experience life there, and then leave the area. These treks follow a pretty standard format with a duration of around two to three weeks and a cost normally between $1,000 and $2,000, although it can be much higher, for a journey of some sixty kilometres in total. This includes simple accommodation and meals and a domestic flight from Kathmandu to Lukla. There are obviously far more trekkers than mountain climbers and as a result their impacts are considerable, not least in terms of the carbon footprint of their flight from Kathmandu to Lukla.

The appeal of making it to the summit and the anticipation of the experience and the status it may bring for the traveller clearly motivate many people to risk their lives for the ultimate luxury of standing on top of the world.

 # References and Further Reading

You will find below a selection of recommendations for further reading as well as the sources of material quoted in this book. You will have noticed fewer references in the main body of the book than is normal for an academic text. This was a conscious decision based on three reasons which are set out in the Preface. I wanted to take a broad overview of the subject with a fresh eye and hence used very few academic texts or journal papers in writing the book.

However, if this book is to serve one of its aims, namely to stimulate further research in this field, I feel I should provide signposts to further reading that could generate new research ideas. That is why a selection of some of the most important works in the area are provided by way of recommendations for further reading. I have tried to focus on work published in the last few years, given how rapidly things change in tourism, hospitality and events.

This is still a field which holds enormous potential for future research as there are still so many major gaps in the literature in relation to luxury in tourism, hospitality and events. Chapter 13 discusses some of these opportunities while also offering a critical perspective on current research in this field.

Books and journal papers

Akli Achabou, M. and Dekhili, S. (2013) Luxury and sustainable development: is there a match? *Journal of Business Research.* **66**(0), 1896-1903

Atwal, G. and Bryson, D. (eds) (2014). *Luxury Brands in Emerging Markets.* Palgrave MacMillan. London

Atwal, G. and Williams, A.J. (2009) Luxury brand management – the experience is everything. *Journal of Brand Management.* **16**(5-6), 338-346

Bakker, M. (2005) Luxury and tailor-made holidays. *Travel and Tourism Analyst.* Mintel. **20**, 1-4.

Barren, P. and Greenwood, A.P. (2006) Issues determining the development of cruise itineraries: a focus on luxury market. *Tourism in Marine Environments.* **3**(2), 89-99

Barsky, J. (2009). *Luxury hotels and recession: a review from around the world*. Marketing (formerly Marketing and Law). Paper 2.

Berry, C.J. (1994). *The Idea of Luxury: a conceptual and historical investigation*. Cambridge University Press, Cambridge

Beverland, M. (2006). The 'real thing': brand authenticity in the luxury wine trade. *Journal of Business Research*. **59**(2), 251-258

Brenner, L. and Aguilar, A.G. (2002) Luxury tourism and regional economic development in Mexico. *The Professional Geographer*, **54**(4) 500-520

Buckley, R. and Mossiaz, A.C. (2016). Decision-making by specialist luxury travel agents. *Tourism Management*. **55**, 133-138

Buigit, S., Braendle, U. and Sarjelwani, D. (2017) Terrorism and travel advisory effects in international travel. *Asia Pacific Journal of Tourism Research*. **22**(10), 991-1004

Chattalas, M. and Paurav, S. (2015). Impact of value perceptions on luxury purchase intentions: a developed market comparison. *Luxury Research*, **1**(1), 40-57

Chen, A. and Peng, N. (2014) Examining Chinese consumers' luxury hotel staying behaviour. *International Journal of Hospitality Management*, **39**, 53-56

Ciornea, R., Pop, M.D., and Bacila, M.H. (2012). Segmenting the luxury market based on the type of the luxury consumed: empirical study of young female luxury consumers. *International Journal of Economic Practices and Theories*. **2**(3), 143-152

Conrady, R. and Buck, M. (eds), (2011) *Trends and Issues in Global Tourism*, Springer, Cham.

Crick, A.P. and Spencer, A. (2011) Hospitality quality: new directions and new challenges. *International Journal of Contemporary Hospitality Management*. **23**(4), 463-478

Csaba, F.F. (2008) *Redefining luxury: a review essay*. Creative Encounters working Paper 15. Copenhagen Business School/Imagine.

Cser, K. and Ohuchi, A. (2008). World practices of hotel classification systems. *Asia Pacific Journal of Tourism Research*. **13**(4), 379-398

D'Arpizia, C., Levato, F., Zito, D. and de Montgolfier, F. (2015). *Luxury goods worldwide market study, Fall – winter 2015*. Bain and Company.

Davies, I.A., Lee, Z. and Ahonkhai, I. (2005). Do consumers care about ethical luxury? *Journal of Business Ethics*. **106**(1), 37-51

De Barnier, V., Rodina, I. and Valette-Florence, P. (2006). Which luxury perceptions affect most consumer purchase behaviour? A cross-cultural exploratory study of France, the United Kingdom and Russia. *Proceedings des Congrès Paris-Venice des tendances marketing*. Paris, pp 8-17

Dewey, D.N. (2009). *Back to the future of luxury*. Presentation to the Luxury Marketing Council and the Franco-American Chamber of Commerce. Houston, Texas.

Dubois, B., Czellar, S. and Laurent, G. (2005) Consumer segments based on attitudes towards luxury; empirical evidence from twenty countries, *Marketing Letters*, **16**(2), 115-128

Dubois, B. and Duquesne, P. (1993) The market for luxury goods: income vs culture. *European Journal of Marketing*, **27**(1), 35-44

Erdogan, E., Icho-Lattimore, C., and Memarzadeh, F. (2012) Air the anger: investigating online complaints at luxury hotels. *Journal of Hospitality and Tourism Technology*. **3**(2), 96-106

Fine, B. and Menictas, C. (2015). Market segmentation using the true meaning of attitudes and values. *Research World*, **52**, 42-44

Fionda, A.M. and Moore, C.M. (2009). The nature of the luxury fashion brand. *Journal of Brand Management*. **16**(5-6), 347-363

Fortune (2007) Luxury goes mass market, *Fortune Magazine*.

Frank, R.H. (1999). *Luxury Forever: Why money fails to satisfy in an era of excess*. The Free Press, New York.

Furnham, A. (2004). *Management and Myths: Challenging business fads, fallacies and fashions*. Palgrave Mac Millan. London

Gastaldi, F. (2012). 'Internet, social media, and luxury strategy' in Hoffmann, J and Coste-Manière, J, (eds), *Luxury Strategy in Action*, Palgrave MacMillan. London.

Ghosh, A. and Varshney, S. (2013). Luxury goods consumption: a conceptual framework based on a literature review. *South Asia Journal of Management Studies*. **20**(2), 146-59

Grafton-Milne, J. (1916) Greek and Roman tourists in Egypt. *The Journal of Egyptian Archaeology*. **3**(2/3), 76-80

Gurzki, H. and Wolsetschlager, D.M. (2017). Mapping the luxury research landscape: a bibliometric citation analysis. *Journal of Business Research*. **77**, 147-166

Hai, D.I., Jung T. and Gibson, A. (2014). 'Dublin AR: implementing augmented reality in tourism', in Xiang, Z. and Tassyadiah, I. (eds). *Information and Communication Technologies in Tourism*. Springer, Cham.

Horwath, H.T.L. (2011). The future of luxury travel – a global trends report. ILTM. Junho. https://www.iltm.net/ files/the-future-of-luxury-travel-report-pdf

Hudson, S. (2010). Wooing zoomers: marketing to the mature travellers. *Marketing Intelligence and Planning*. **28**(4), 444-461

Hwang, J. and Hyun, S.S. (2017). First class airline travellers' perceptions of luxury goods and its effect on the loyalty function. *Current Issues in Tourism*. **20**(5), 497-520

Hyun, S.S. and Han, H. (2013) Luxury cruise travellers; other customer perceptions. *Journal of Travel Research*. **54**(1), 107-121

ILTM (2010) 'Global trends in luxury travel: a white paper'. ILTM Leaders Forum, Cannes. December 2010

Inglis, F. (2000). *The Delicious History of the Holiday*. Routledge. London and New York

Israeli, A., Mohsin, A. and Kumar, B. (2011) Hospitality crisis management practices: the case of Indian luxury hotels. *International Journal of Hospitality Management*. **30**(2), 367-374

Kapferer, J.-N. (2012). Abundant rarity: the key to luxury growth. *Business Horizons*, **55**(5), 453-462

Kapferer, J.-N. (2014) The future of luxury: challenges and opportunities. *Journal of Brand Management*, **21**(9), 716-726

Kapferer, J.-N. and Bastien, V. (2009) The specificity of luxury management: turning marketing upside down. *Journal of Brand Management*. **16**(5-6), 311-322

Kapferer, J.-N. and Michaut, A. (2015) Luxury and sustainability: a common future? The match depends on how consumers define luxury. *Luxury Research*, **1**(1), 3-17

Kiessling, G., Balekjian, C. and Oehmichen, A. (2009) What credit crunch? More luxury for your money. Europe's rising stars and established markets. *Journal of Retail and Leisure Property*, **8**(1), 3-23

Kim, H.B. and Kim,W.G. (2005) The relationship between brand equity and firms' performance in luxury hotel and chain restaurants. *Tourism Management*, **26**(14), 549-560

Lee, J.H. and Hwang, J. (2011). Luxury marketing: the influence of psychological and demographic characteristics on attitudes towards luxury restaurants. *International Journal of Hospitality Management*, **30**(3), 658-669

McCartan, S. and Kvilums, C. (2013) 'Next generation unltra-luxury cruise ship: a passive design eco-luxury cruise ship for the Mediterranean'. Presentation at the Design and operations of passenger ships conference, Royal Institution of Naval Architects. London

Mc Kelvie, J. (2007). Luxury Travel. *Travel and Tourism Analyst*. **12**, 1-42

Mc Neil, P. and Riello, G. (2016) *Luxury: A Rich History*. Oxford University Press, Oxford, UK

Mandel, N., Petrova, P.K. and Cialdini, R.B. (2006). Images of success and the preference for luxury brands. *Journal of Consumer Psychology*, **16** (1), 57-69

Mareuil, C. (2006). New trends in luxury tourism. *Espaces, Tourisme and Loisirs*. **241**, 12-20

Mohsin, A. and Lockyer, T. (2010) Customer perceptions of service quality in luxury hotels in New Delhi, India: an exploratory study. *International Journal of Contemporary Hospitality Management*, **22**(2), 160-173

Mok, C., Sparks, B. and Kadampully, J. (2013). *Service Quality Management in Hospitality, Tourism, and Leisure*. Routledge. New York

Nickel, P.M. (2015). Haute philanthropy and luxury. *Luxury*, **2**(2), 11-31

Nueno, J.L. and Quelch, J.A. (1998). The mass marketing of luxury. *Business Horizons*, **41** (6), 61-68

Okonkwo, U. (2009). The luxury brand strategy challenge. *Journal of Brand Management*, **16**(5-6), 287-289

Park, K.S. and Reisinger, Y. (2009). Cultural differences in shopping for luxury goods: Western, Asian and Hispanic tourists. *Journal of Travel and Tourism Marketing*, **26**(8), 762-777

Park, K.S., Reisinger, Y. and Noh, E.-H. (2009) Luxury shopping in tourism. *International Journal of Tourism Research*. **12**(2), 164-178

Phau, I. and Prendergast, G .(2001) Consuming luxury brands: the relevance of the 'rarity principle'. *Journal of Brand Management*, **8**(2), 122-137

Pine, J.B. and Gilmore, J.B. (1999). *The Experience Economy: Work is theatre and every business a stage*. Harvard Business School Press

Popescu, I.-V. and Olteanu, V. (2014). Luxury tourism: characteristics and trends of the behaviour of purchase. *SEA Practical Application of Science*, **12**(2), 319-324

Pratt, M.L. (2007). *Imperial Eyes: Travel writing and transculturation*. Routledge. London

Prayag, G. and Hosany, S. (2014). When East meets West: understanding the motivations and perceptions of young tourists from the United Arab Emirates. *Tourism Management*, **40**, 35-45

Presbury, R., Fitzgerald, A. and Chapman, R. (2005) Impediments to improvements in service quality in luxury hotels. *Managing Service Quality*, **15**(4), 357-373

Richards, G. and Wilson, J. (2006). Developing creativity in tourist experiences: a solution to the serial reproduction of culture. *Tourism Management*, **27**(6), 1209-1223

Roberts, F. (2015) *Global luxury travel trends report*. Produced for 2015 ILTM conference. Euromonitor

Rovai, S. (2016). Chinese outbound shopping tourism: a market driven approach for the luxury and fashion industry. *Symphonia Emerging Issues in Management*. **1**, 56-63

Sandbrook, C. (2009). Local economic impacts of different forms of nature-based tourism. *Conservation Letters*, **3**(1), 21-28

Scheyvens, R. (2011). The challenge of sustainable tourism development in the Maldives: understanding the social and political dimensions of sustainability. *Asia Pacific Viewpoint*, **52**, 148-164

Sharman, R. (2007). *Class Acts: Service and inequality in luxury hotels*. University of California Press. Berkeley and Los Angeles

Sharpley, R. (1994) *Tourism, Tourists and Societies*, 2nd edn. Elm Publications. Huntingdon, UK

Smith-Maguire, J. (2015). 'Authenticity is the new luxury: marketing myths and the reproduction of consumer culture'. Paper presented at the American Sociological Association Annual Conference, Chicago, August 2015

Surlemont, B. and Johnson, C. (2005). The role of guides in artistic industries: the special case of the 'star system' in the haute-cuisine sector. *Managing Service Quality*, **15**(6), 577-590

Thurlow, C. and Jaworski, A. (2012). Elite mobilities: the semiotic landscapes of luxury and privilege. *Social Semiotics*, **22**(4), 487-516

Tourism Economics (2016). *Shaping the future of luxury travel: Future traveller tribes 2030*. Amadeus

Tynan, C., McKechnie, S. and Chhuon, C. (2010). Co-creating value for luxury brands. *Journals of Business Research,* **63**(11), 1156-1163

Tyrell, B. (1987). The leisure paradox. *Museums Journal.* **87**(4), 207-209.

Urry, J. (2002) *The Tourist Gaze. 2nd edition.* Sage, London

Verissimo, M. and Loureiro, S.M.L. (2013). Experience marketing and the luxury travel industry. *Tourism Management Studies,* Special issue, **1**, 296-302

Votalato, G. (2007). *Transport Design: A travel history.* Reaktion Books. London

Wiedmann, K.P., Hennings, N. and Siebels, A. (2009). A value-based segmentation of luxury consumption behaviour. *Psychology and Marketing.* **26**, 625-655

Worner, J. (2015). 'Luxury beyond luxury: understanding the nature and processes of customer value in ultra-luxury travel'. Doctoral thesis: Stellenbosch University. Stellenbosch.

Yang, FX and Lau, WMC (2015). Luxury hotel loyalty: a comparison of Chinese gen X and Y tourists to Macau. *International Journal of Contemporary Hospitality Management,* **27**(7), 1685-1706

Yang, W. and Mattila, A.S. (2014) Do affluent customers care when luxury brands go mass? The role of product type and status seeking on luxury brand attitudes. *International Journal of Contemporary Hospitality Management,* **26**(4), 526-543

Yang, W., Zhang, L. and Mattila, A.S. (2015). How do consumers react to hotel price promotions? The moderating role of consumers' need for status. *Cornell Hospitality Quarterly,* **57**(1), 82-92.

Yeoman, I. (2010) The changing behaviours of luxury consumption. *Journal of Revenue and Pricing Management.* **10**(1), 47-50

Yeoman, I. and McMahon-Beattie, U. (2006) Luxury markets and premium pricing. *Journal of Revenue and Pricing Management,* **4**, 319-328

Yeoman, I. and McMahon-Beattie, U. (2014). Exclusivity: the future of luxury. *Journal of Revenue and Pricing Management.* **13**(1), 12-22

Yeoman, I. and McMahon-Beattie, U. (2016). The future of food tourism. *Journal of Tourism Futures,* **2**(1), 96-98

Zhu, D., Xu, H. and Jiang, L. (2016) Behind buying: the Chinese gaze on European commodities. *Asia-Pacific Journal of Tourism Research,* **21**(3) 293

Online sources

www.oxforddictionaries.com, accessed 24 August 2016

www.merriam-webster.com, accessed 25 August 2016

theeverygirl.com/the-new-meaning-of-luxury, accessed 26 August 2016

www.fivestaralliance.com/articles/what-is-your-definition-luxury-part-1, accessed 25 August 2016

www.aluxurytravelblog.com/2013/03/26/so-what-is-luxury-travel, accessed 25 August 2016

www.luxurytravel.about.com/odhotelandresorts/tp/Luxury-Hotels, accessed 25 August 2016

cruiseweb.com/blog/2013/02/defining-luxury-cruising, accessed 25 August 2016

http://zai.ch/blog/the-meaning-of-luxury, accessed 25 August 2016

https://paleofuture.gizmodo.com/what-international-air-travel-was-like-in-the-1930s-1471258414, accessed 30 August 2016

www.travelmarketreport.com/articles/luxury-Brad-Depot-things-are-looking-good-for-2015, accessed 18 September 2016

www.brickworkindia.com/luxury-travel-sector-wooing-the-chinese-and-indian-traveller-2014, accessed 3 November 2016

www.travelandleisure.com/articles/2014-international-luxury-travel-market-trends-and-festival-highlights, accessed 4 November 2016

www.travelweekly.com/travelnews/travel-agent-issues-2013, accessed 4 December 2016

www.eturbonews.com/9512/examing-global-luxury-travel-market-during-the-recession-2009, accessed 6 February 2017

www.traveldailymedia.com/236822, Indian luxury travel market grows by 12.8%, accessed 15 April 2017

www.augment.com/blog/augmented-reality-in-tourism, accessed 9 May 2017

www.travelweekly.com/Luxury-Travel/Insights/Can-air-cruises-be-successful, accessed 30 July 2017

www.signatureflight.com/locations/LTN/t1, accessed 25 September 2017

www.singaporeair.com/en_UK/gb/flying-withus/cabins/suites/, accessed 6 October 2017

www.emirates.com/uk/english/experience/cabin-features/first-class.aspx, accessed 10 October 2017

www.theguardian.com/world/2017/sep/20/sebastien-bras-french-chef-three-michelin-stars-le-suquet-laguiole, accessed 13 October 2017

www.straitstimes.com/lifestyle/food/two-michelin-starred-restaurant-andre-to-close-feb-14-chef-wants-to-return-the-stars, accessed 14 October 2017

www.hiddeneurope.co.uk/a-manifesto-for-slow-travel, accessed 15 October 2017

www.theartofslowtravel.com/what-is-slow-travel, accessed 16 October 2017

www.slowmovement.com/slow_travel.php, accessed 17 October 2017

www.barcelonaslowtravel.com/slow-travel, accessed 18 October 2017

Index